October, 1994

To Colin —

Please Enjoy the Book —
We all have Memories!
Your mother-in-law
had to Travel to Vietnam
for this gift. Again
Enjoy!

Best
David U. Christen
Author

Note — Whenever I get
depressed I read page
"138 to 154" & realize life
is "O.K. - Today".

VICTOR SIX

VICTOR SIX

*The Saga of America's Youngest, Most
Decorated Officer in Vietnam*

by

David Christian and
William Hoffer

McGraw-Hill Publishing Company

New York   St. Louis   San Francisco   Bogotá   Hamburg   Madrid
Milan   Mexico   Paris   São Paulo   Tokyo   Montreal   Toronto

1 2 3 4 5 6 7 8 9 DOC DOC 9 5 4 3 2 1 0

ISBN 0-07-010856-0

Library of Congress Cataloging-in-Publication Data

Christian, David, 1948–
    Victor 6 : the saga of America's youngest, most decorated officer in Vietnam/
David Christian and William Hoffer.
        p. cm.
    ISBN 0-07-010856-0
    1. Christian, David, 1948. 2. Vietnamese Conflict, 1961–1975—
Veterans—United States—Biography. 3. United States. Army—
Biography. 4. Veterans—Education—United States. 5. Veterans—
Employment—United States. 6. Veterans—Medical care—United
States. I. Hoffer, William. II. Title.
DS559.73.U6C47 1990
959.704'3'0922—dc20
    [B]   90-30260
                                                              CIP

This book is dedicated to:

My mother, Dorothy, a soldier under General Douglas MacArthur in the South Pacific—thank you for my strength.

and

My wife, Peggy, a soldier in the social war through the 60s, 70s, 80s, and up to the present—thanks for fighting at my side.

—Dave Christian

Acknowledgments

Numerous persons have contributed unselfishly to the production of this book. Some must be singled out for special mention.

Thanks to my children: Coleen Ann, David A., Maureen, and K.C., and to all the members of my extended family, especially my in-laws, Marge and Ed Todd, my disabled veteran brothers Daniel and Douglas, and my three sisters, Dorothea, MaryAnne, and Gloria. Thanks to the Christian family of Northport and Tuscaloosa, Alabama.

Thanks to Marllyn Mona Hoffer for her total effort; she shared every moment of the composition and organization of the book. Thanks to our agents, the late Michael Powers, Betsy Nolan, and Mel Berger, and our editor, Dan Weaver. Thanks to Dan Deitz for his technical advice. Thanks to Sandra Capella, my longtime secretary and aide-de-camp. Thanks to Ann Craig, editing supervisor, for her assistance in striving for perfection.

Thanks to a very special group of people who fought alongside one another in a strange war: Company F of the Fifty-Second Infantry (the "Lurps") and all of the First Infantry Division; the Recon Platoon ("Christian's Butchers"); and the Eleventh Armored Cavalry Regiment.

Very special thanks to George Day, John McCain, John Dramisi, John Fritz, and their POW/MIA brothers.

Thanks to my many friends from Camp Zama, Japan, especially Joe Wecker, Chris, Jay Fretis, Bernie, and the many wonderful nurses. Thanks to Red Cross worker Connie Beck, who administered doses of hope and encouragement during the dark days at Valley Forge General Hospital. Thanks to the staff and patients of the Philadelphia Naval Hospital. Thanks to former Mayor Frank Rizzo, who took time out from running the city of Philadelphia to visit a pile of bandages with my name tag on it.

Thanks to Bob Hope, Ann Margaret, Chris Noel, and the Golddiggers for the memories.

Thanks to the Veterans Fraternity and the Alumni Association of Villanova University, especially Father Riley and Bob Capone, and to the University of Alabama for helping veterans matriculate into society. Thanks to Douglas Clifford and Bunker Hill (Massachusetts) Community College. Thanks to the Tarheels of the University of North Carolina for allowing the ROTC to provide a rebuttal to Jane Fonda.

Thanks to the members of the Legion of Valor, especially Charles Rush and Leon Rennebaum.

Thanks to my veteran friends back in the States: Mark Hutchinson; all the friends of "Bill W."; unsung hero Bob Muller, Mary Stout, and all the Vietnam Veterans of America, especially Chapter 210 in Pennsylvania and Chapter 1 in Vermont; Rich "Airborne" Montgomery; Joe Loboda; James Lamont, aka "Joe Banyas"; and Tony "the Veteran's Veteran" Diamond. Thanks to Mike Milne and the Veterans of the Vietnam War. Thanks to Rusty Lindley and Ron Kovic for rolling into my office to lend their support.

Thanks to Ileen, Irwin, and Steven Hochberg, and all the gang at H.B.S.A. Thanks to Tom Burch in Virginia. Thanks to Sam Rappaport for demonstrating that tough guys have big hearts. Thanks to Tom Herbert and his Vietnam newspaper in Connecticut. Thanks to Jackie and M.J. Christian, my father, for introducing me to Bill and Doctor Bob. Thanks to a group of guys, including Werner Fricker and Frank Kelly, who believed, when no one else would. Thanks to Art Lohan, who was more than a boss. Thanks to Pat DiPilla and the many friends who, if their names appeared here, would lose their jobs; you know who you are. Recognition and thanks to the fighting Cubbage family.

Thanks to Bill Snyder and Tony Felipe for their financial support; to Jim and Helene Breen for having the guts to stand up for their beliefs; and to Dennis Crowley for cleaning and dressing my wounds while I was a patient at the Philadelphia Naval Hospital. Thanks to Bill Scanlon, a man with class and conviction. Thanks to John Dwyer from Ohio for being a veteran when it wasn't cool. Thanks to friend and fellow warrior Denny Place. Thanks to Reds Snyder and his family. Thanks to Colonel Chuck "No Nonsense" Allen. Thanks to Dan Fraley and Dennis Fink, veterans of private wars. Thanks to former U.S. Marine Captain Ron Castile, who left a leg in South Vietnam but brought a mighty big heart back home. Thanks to Peter Janazinski and Art Skypeck for their inspiration. Thanks to Steven Bell, a correspondent who stood by the Vietnam veterans in the war and at home.

Thanks to Leon Scull, Joe Welsh, and the other fine people of the U.S. Veterans Employment Service. Thanks to Len Gilmore and Dean Phillips for their leadership on the issue of veterans' preference in employment.

Thanks to Texas Assemblyman Larry Don Shaw for his early support of Agent Orange legislation, and to Frank McCarthy, who spearheaded the national fight and had the guts to confront his boss, President Jimmy Carter. Thanks to Wayne Wilson and Stockton State College in New Jersey for pushing Agent Orange programs into law.

Thanks to Coors Beer (under Warren Hutchinson and Peter Joannides) for its support of Vietnam veterans. Thanks to Dr Pepper and "Foots" Woodrow Clements for welcoming veterans home to Dallas.

Thanks to Joe Buscher, Charles Fisher, and Stan Swain for manning the trenches when the you-know-what hit the fan.

Thanks to Kim Lohan for designing such a wonderful jacket cover.

Thanks to Harry and Mary Fawkes for prescribing the cold shower. Thanks to the union members who put their jobs on the line, especially Ironworkers Local 410, Jack Coyne of Carpenters Local 1462, and Tom Miller, president of the Pennsylvania Building and Construction Trades Council. Thanks to the AFL-CIO's Lane Kirkland for supporting me for the Veterans Administration cabinet position. Thanks to the Brotherhood of Railroad and Airline Clerks Union; we will always miss Fred Kroll, the man who taught me when to hold 'em, when to fold 'em.

Thanks to three of the toughest guys I know: Pasquale T. Deon, Charles Simone, M.D., and Joseph Jingoli, Jr., for facing the Vietnamese Communists and the Khmer Rouge.

I would like to recognize my birthplace of Gainesville, Florida, my relatives and childhood summers in the Baltimore, Maryland, area; and my distant relatives in Dallas, Texas, and Sacramento, California.

Thank God for giving me the strength and ability to "go for it."

This is a true story.

The characters are authentic, the events real. Quotations have been recreated as accurately as long-term memory allows and, where possible, have been documented by two or more witnesses.

PART

ONE

All wars are planned by old men in council
rooms apart,
Who plan for greater armament and map the
battle chart.
But where their sightless eyes stare out
beyond life's vanished joys
I've noticed nearly all the dead were hardly
more than boys.

—Grantland Rice,
Two Sides of War

1

It took seventeen hours for baby-faced Second Lieutenant David Alan Christian to move his special detachment into position for the attack on the enemy's regiment-sized base camp. Careful planning was critical for this predawn raid in November 1967. Eighteen men were going in after hundreds of the enemy, in an area where they were out of radio contact with their base. If something went wrong, they would be unable to call for support, or rescue.

In the dim starlight, a wisp of reddish mustache, so faint that it could have been penciled in, was barely visible over Christian's tightened lips. Facial hair was something he toyed with from time to time, letting it grow, evaluating its effect on his appearance, shaving it, then recultivating. He stood a wiry but tough five feet, ten inches tall. Some of the troops he commanded were larger, some smaller, but size did not matter, for Christian was convinced that he could pound the bejabbers out of any of them, if necessary. So were they.

The young lieutenant was a veteran of street wars. Fatherless and just into his teens, he had taken off from his home in Levittown, Pennsylvania, and made it on his own in New York for four months by working a succession of menial jobs in Brooklyn, the Bronx, Queens, and all up and down Sunrise Highway on Long Island. By the time he returned home, he believed he could meet any challenge. In the few years since, he had applied the tough techniques of street life to the realities of a more normal society. Now he was ready to apply the same methodology to the art of war.

The men trusted the young lieutenant to bring them out safely. He had already demonstrated a special aptitude for leadership in war, an uncanny ability to combine effective amounts of craziness and caution. It did not matter that he was still a teenager, for none of his men knew the secret of his age.

Shortly before sunrise, everything was ready. One five-man team had a machine gun trained on the front gate. Another team was positioned to race through the rear of the base camp, spraying automatic fire on sleeping enemy soldiers. A third had quarter-pound blocks of TNT ready with short, four-second fuses and blasting caps to blow up the motor pool. Plans called for the raiding party to be in—and out—before the enemy had its pants on.

The sticky job was to neutralize the Command Post, identifiable by the constant trail of enemy officers who moved about it. Some of the men believed this to be the kamikaze part of the entire operation; whoever attempted it would first have to get past the sentries and then move about 100 meters into the camp, alone. Part of Christian's unorthodox command technique was to walk the point, something that other officers rarely did, and he nominated himself for the most hazardous portion of the assault; he alone would take out the Command Post.

Dressed in an enemy uniform, Christian moved down the trail leading to the main gate of the camp. With barely a glance, the sentinel allowed him inside and pulled the barrier of concertina wire back into place. Idly, Christian tossed the sentry a cigarette, making sure his aim was short. As the sentry bent over and groped on the ground for his prize, Christian slipped past him and headed toward the Command Post tent.

He approached with stealth, his heart pounding. Slowly he lifted the flap of the tent and lowered his rifle to fire on the high-ranking officers lounging inside, thus signaling the beginning of the battle.

Suddenly he felt arms grab him from behind. He turned to see the cigarette-fumbling sentry, his eyes full of questions. Standing around the sentry were a dozen or more enemy troops.

Christian screamed a defiant rebel yell and charged toward the edge of the ring, but angry arms grabbed for him. He fell to the ground and felt a stick pierce his upper lip. He struggled fiercely, but numbers were against him, and the rest of his men were still outside the concertina wire.

The first rays of dawn were showing on the horizon when he muttered the truth to himself: "You're a prisoner of war."

Enemy troops stripped him naked, handcuffed him, chained him to the back of a jeep, and paraded their new war trophy. They drove slowly through the camp, forcing Christian to run. Whenever he fell, he had to drag himself to his feet without the use of his hands. Tormentors stood at the side of the rutted trail and threw buckets of water on him.

After a time, the enemy took its prisoner up a set of wooden steps to a second-floor interrogation room. Christian sat, naked and shivering, on a wooden chair in front of a small desk. From the other side of the desk, an officer asked, in perfect English, "Would you like a cigarette?"

"Yes," Christian replied weakly.

The officer produced a pack of Marlboros. He lit one and offered it across the table. With his hands still cuffed behind him, Christian leaned forward and opened his mouth. In one quick movement, the officer rotated the cigarette and thrust the burning end between his captive's lips.

Christian yelped and spat out the fire. He leaped across the table and butted the officer with his head. The man crashed to the floor and Christian was able to deliver a couple of kicks before others pulled him away. The enraged enemy soldiers dragged their prisoner to the door and roughly threw him down the outside stairway. With no way to break his fall, Christian bounced heavily to the hard ground.

For two and a half days the enemy allowed him no food and little sleep. During interrogation sessions a soldier would occasionally grab a tuft of hair on Christian's head, or under his arm, or even in his groin, and rip it out. Between sessions soldiers took him outside, still naked, and threw more buckets of water on him.

On the first day Christian fought back, mentally, by repeating a litany to himself: "It's all bullshit. They can't kill me." But by the end of the second day he had changed his mind. "Maybe they can kill me."

On the third morning, a U.S. Marine Corps captain strode into the interrogation room and ordered Christian released.

Hours later, dressed and fed, but still shivering with cold and—perhaps worse—humility, Christian rode in the back of a pickup truck, returning to his class at the JFK Special Warfare Center at Fort Bragg, North Carolina. He vowed: "If and when you get to Vietnam, David Christian, you will fight to the death. You will never allow yourself to be captured, because if this is what they do to you in a game, what would they really do to you?"

Christian's father, M.J., was a good ol' boy from Alabama, a tall, handsome, dusty blond who loved his booze and agonized over his given name, Marion Jackson. "Call me M.J. or Chris or don't call me at all," he liked to say. One day when Dave was seven, M.J. left the house, supposedly to get the lawn mower fixed. But he took his last paycheck from the Rohm and Haas chemical plant with him, and he never returned.

Young Dave thought: No Dad, no booze, no problems. But, of course, the problems were just beginning.

Dorothy Christian assumed the task of keeping the family together. A WAC veteran who had served on General Douglas MacArthur's administrative staff in the Philippines, New Guinea, and Australia, Dot brought a military precision and determination to her role as sole provider. Dave always thought of her as the bravest soldier he had ever known. Stretched out full, she still stood an inch shy of five feet, but she possessed the stocky build as well as the fortitude of a bulldog. Long before liberation was fashionable, she worked as a cab driver, trod picket lines, and fought for womens' jobs.

Despite suffering from chronic back trouble, Dot Christian taught herself how to handle repairs on her humble home and, at Christmas time, told her children: "Don't get me anything stupid. All I want is tools." Her proudest possession was a power saw. On Christmas Day, Dot invariably recounted to her children the story of how she had met M.J. during the war, in the Philippines, when she was a soldier and he was a typewriter repairman.

As Dave, the second eldest son, grew toward his teens, he assumed the paternal leadership role, using a natural talent for glibness to fend off interfering social workers who wanted to split up the family.

But he was always a party animal, and a scrapper. Family friends often looked askance at young Dave, telling his mother that he had M.J.'s rebellious, 80-proof blood in his veins and quietly predicting that he would "go bad."

He proved them wrong. After his mother remarried a steelworker named Tony Nau, Dave migrated to New York. He was only thirteen years old. After a four-month stint on the streets, he went back home and settled in to hard work. Throughout his years at Woodrow Wilson High School, he worked a 7 P.M. to 3 A.M. shift at Optical Scanning Corporation, which specialized in printing academic tests that were encoded to prevent cheating.

There was no money for college. After his high school graduation in 1966, encouraged by his mother and enticed by the GI Bill, he enlisted in the army, following a family tradition that dated back to the Civil War, when his great-grandfather fought for the Confederacy. His plan, however, was not to fight. He was confident that he was too smart to wind up in South Vietnam.

In those years almost every young, able-bodied American man had a grand strategy for staying out of the remote, unfathomable combat taking place halfway across the world. Christian's working plan was to delay his duty assignment by taking every available course, sequestering himself in one military school or another, until the war ground to a halt. With this plan in mind, he wrote a letter to the Congressional Armed Services Committee, asking for the unique opportunity to attend Officers' Candidate School despite his youth and his lack of college. After administering a battery of tests and interviewing him extensively, the army brass decided to accommodate the young man.

Although he often felt culturally inferior to his fellow students at OCS, Christian excelled, and, on August 1, 1967, Dot Christian and her youngest son Daniel journeyed to Fort Benning, Georgia, to pin gold bars on David's shoulder. She beamed a grin at him and allowed, "I'd like to burst." At the age of eighteen, her son was the youngest officer in the entire U.S. Army.

Christian moved on to airborne school, and then to the JFK Special Warfare Center. He was a "candy-striper," with a single horizontal slash decorating his Special Forces green beret, and his job, as far as the army was concerned, was to earn the coveted diagonal flash, the lightning-bolt insignia that would mark him as a highly trained specialist.

At Fort Bragg, he linked up with his older brother Doug, a specialist, fourth class (Sp 4c, popularly called a spec 4) who was already a veteran of service in South Vietnam and who was hoping to return. In the meantime, Doug bought a car. As an enlisted man, he needed help with the financing, so his younger brother, the officer, cosigned the loan.

During that winter of 1967–1968, Dot Christian's health began to fail. The brothers made frequent, sometimes unauthorized visits home to Pennsylvania, driving in Doug's car. On the night of January 21, 1968, when their eldest sister Dorothea was at her junior prom, their mother, suffering from pneumonia, collapsed and fell down the stairs in her home. Dave's two half-sisters Mary Anne and Gloria, aged three and four, found her at the bottom of the steps, unconscious and dying. Not knowing what else to do, they placed rosary beads around her body.

Dot Christian's sons, without official permission, once more drove from North Carolina to Pennsylvania, to attend the funeral. Upon their return to Fort Bragg, Doug was disciplined, under the provisions of Article 15 of the Uniform Code of Military Justice, for being AWOL.

An officious lieutenant colonel dealt with the younger brother, lecturing him solemnly about his accumulation of unexcused absences. He warned, "You're gonna have to go through the course again if you want your flash."

Christian listened halfheartedly, distracted by the ache in his belly that had attacked the moment he learned of his mother's death. His ears heard the lieutenant colonel's next words, but it took him a few moments to comprehend them.

"You're getting things out of priority," the lieutenant colonel declared in a softened, fatherly tone. "People are going to die. You have to get used to that. The army is your family now."

Christian wanted to cry, but he simply laughed in the lieutenant colonel's face. Then he walked away from the meeting, repeating the litany that had helped him get through his three days of "capture" and torture: "It's all bullshit."

Without his mother—his best friend—and without his flash, Christian lost his desire for any more military courses, but he tried desperate measures to avoid a shooting war, even making an unauthorized visit to the Pentagon. There, he hunted up a personnel officer and demonstrated his fluency in German. "Great," the officer commented, "maybe you'll run into some krauts in Vietnam."

2

War Zone D, South Vietnam
June 1968

On a sweltering afternoon, Christian found himself leading a frustrated five-man patrol through the damnable double-canopy jungle that covered most of War Zone D, situated just north of Saigon, the capital city of the Republic of South Vietnam. He was here—he was told—"to win the hearts and minds" of the South Vietnamese people.

After the men had blown the better part of the day wading across vermin-ridden rice paddies and stumbling through underbrush, tempers were short. They should have reached their objective hours ago. By now, they should be enjoying the relative comforts of the base camp.

Christian paused along the jungle trail and removed his floppy hat, revealing a shaved head. In his mind the nearly nude scalp made him look older, tougher, and he sloughed off the knowledge that others equated the hairstyle with brassiness and unwarranted cockiness. He wiped the arm of his fatigue blouse across his brow, thankful that he had, weeks ago, abandoned the traditional steel helmet for the floppy hat. Aside from being cumbersome and ringing through your ears like a gong when you happened to encounter a tree, the helmet boiled your brains in the South Vietnamese sun. What's more, a floppy hat fit in with the cowboy image that the young officer relished.

Although he had been at this war business for only a few weeks, Christian had eighteen solid months of training behind him, and he fancied himself a quick study. Already he expected superior performance from himself and his men.

This patrol was part of a special detachment of troops assigned to the army's First Infantry Division, aka the "Bloody Red One," headquartered at Lai Khe base camp, and on call to fly in by chopper to wherever they were needed in War Zones C and D. Lai Khe was a huge rubber plantation that the U.S. Army leased from its French landowner, with the provision that it would pay compensation for any rubber trees damaged by bullets or explosives. One of this unit's jobs was to conduct long-range reconnaissance patrols, a task known by its acronym, LRRP. These men had come to call themselves "Lurps," and Christian liked that. He believed that nicknames were good for morale.

On this day, the Lurps were not living up to their reputation as a crack reconnaissance unit. There was supposed to be an enemy base camp sequestered somewhere amid this maze of jungle trails, but it was nowhere to be found, and Christian could only conclude that G-2 (Intelligence) had screwed up the map coordinates. He knew that the camp existed—he had seen the evidence in aerial photos—and he vowed that he was damn sure going to find it.

He led his men in an ever-widening circle, their grumbles of frustration increasing with each moment.

They were hiking across a rice paddy when the sound of a few rounds of enemy fire cracked the midday silence. Almost simultaneously, bullets pinged into the dirt at their feet. The five men jumped for cover, instinctively leaping away from the direction of the fire and into the knee-high water of the soggy rice paddy. Kneeling in warm, viscous mud, they returned fire, blazing away, with their M-16s on automatic, at the shadow of an elusive enemy. At this response, their tormentors raced for the safety of the jungle.

Christian caught a quick glimpse. The snipers appeared to be a pair of young Vietcong (VC) guerrillas, probably not a day older than sixteen, clad in black pajamas. No doubt they were armed with Russian-made guns.

All of the U.S. and ARVN (Army of the Republic of South Vietnam) troops hated the VC. They would rather fight the North Vietnamese army regulars—the NVA—any day. The latter were true soldiers, fairly well trained, decently disciplined, a brave and honorable foe. But the VC were

South Vietnamese revolutionaries, pesky gnats who employed sting-and-run tactics. It was beyond their capability to win any kind of major battle, let alone a war.

In the streets of Brooklyn, where Christian had learned the fine points of fighting during his four-month hiatus from the family, there was an unwritten code of honor. One of its principles was that after the battle—win, lose, or draw—you maintained a certain respect for your opponent. But how could you respect an enemy that refused to stand and slug it out?

Guerrilla tactics seemed to Christian not the acts of honorable soldiers, but of gutless terrorists. In the field, the VC booby-trapped the trails with homemade mines filled with trash metal and broken glass. They set strategically placed pungi sticks—sharp bamboo spikes, their tips dipped into infection-causing human feces—where they would be stepped on by unwary U.S. soldiers.

Their infiltration activity was even more diabolic. VC operatives were indistinguishable from the civilian South Vietnamese workers employed at U.S. base camps, and they were often successful in their attempts to gather intelligence concerning the locations of ammo dumps, helipads, and other strategic targets. They surreptitiously monitored the activities of the Americans and reported directly to NVA intelligence officers, who placed the pieces into the proper mosaic.

Only recently VC infiltrators had scored a major victory. At the division's Lai Khe base camp, supposedly safe in the rear echelon, they had placed an electrically detonated explosive beneath the pool table in the Officer's Club, and they were smart enough to set the timer to go off in the midst of Happy Hour, as the brass were shooting pool and guzzling discount drinks. The blast killed several high-ranking U.S. officers and mutilated others.

Such attacks were effective, and galling. How could you fight a war when you could not distinguish friend from foe? To Christian, it somehow seemed wrong.

The VC never, *never* stood up to you in a fair fight. The U.S. Army called it "unconventional warfare"; Christian thought that was an understatement. This afternoon, as he stared out from the gunk of the rice paddy into the green and black maze of the jungle cover, he wondered where the honor is in squeezing off a few potshots, dunking your targets into contaminated water, and then running like hell.

Satisfied that the enemy was gone, the men of the patrol dragged themselves from the rice paddy. They buddied up, stripped off their shirts, and squirted army-issue insect repellent onto the elongated, slimy black leeches that clung to their backs. The parasites recoiled at the first contact of the caustic liquid—so strong that it doubled as paint remover—and gave up their hold. Men plucked them off one another, leaving trails of crimson on the skin.

Christian hunched down and extracted a four- by eight-inch plastic case from inside his fatigue blouse, opened it, and removed an army map. He smoothed it out and double-checked their location, employing the day's code names for the check points. "We started at Michelob and worked our way from Budweiser to Schlitz. They gotta be here, at Schlitz." But the enemy wasn't at Schlitz, and Christian made an educated guess. "They must be at Miller," he grunted.

Staff Sergeant Woodruff replied in a southern drawl, "S-u-u-r-h, we'll go wherever you say." A smile broke beneath his thick moustache. Woodruff's introduction to the young officer had been inauspicious. One of Christian's first adventures was to examine a new, unfamiliar M-16, wondering as he did so why the army trained you at home on the old M-1 and M-14 and then threw an entirely new weapon at you once you got to war. Christian had plucked at the wrong clasp, liberated a spring, and watched the innards fly about the room. The incident had brought scorn from Woodruff, but he was subsequently impressed with the man's ability to learn quickly. He taught Christian how to clean an M-16 and, in turn, Christian taught him about survival in a hostile environment. For example, this young lieutenant was the best map reader Woodruff had ever encountered.

What Woodruff did not know was that Christian was about to teach him and the others a new technique of jungle fighting. Christian had been with the unit for a month, and had allowed himself to absorb the considerable knowledge of its skilled men. Now he was ready to synthesize their basic abilities with his own concepts of how a war should be fought: take the best training the army can provide, study the work of the men out in the field, and then apply a few carefully chosen tactics of the street fighter.

The men moved off across the paddy dikes and onto a jungle path. They trudged silently for several minutes, their eyes focused on the trail ahead of them. Most Americans avoided these trails, VC and NVA footways, creations of the enemy; but the Lurps trampled the paths for the same reason that others avoided them, because the paths signaled that the enemy was near. They *wanted* to find the enemy.

Suddenly another round of potshots assailed the patrol from the rear. Again the men dropped for cover, this time amid a jungle underbrush of wait-a-minute vines that grew up into the trees. The nickname came from their ability to stop a man in his tracks; he would call out "Wait a minute!" as he extricated himself.

Again they raked the enemy with fire. Again the two young VC ran off.

The day dragged on into the unmerciful heat of the mid-afternoon sun. The patrol retraced its steps several times, searching in vain for the objective.

Finally Christian announced a "smoke-'em-if-you-got-'em" break. He lit a Marlboro and glanced around to make sure there was no red ant mound nearby; these ¼-inch-long insects would attack without mercy, tear pieces of flesh from the body, and send a man screaming to his comrades for help. Satisfied that the ground was clear, Christian once again puzzled over his map.

Without warning a single bullet crashed into the trunk of the tree next to him, level with his nose. Around him, every man hit the deck and prepared to return fire. But their trigger fingers froze when they saw that their commander was still on his feet in front of them.

This is wrong, Christian thought. There's gotta be some rules here, guys. I'm tired of this bullshit.

Woodruff's astonished eyes saw his commander throw his M-16 down in disgust and race headlong toward the direction of the attacking fire, shrieking a blood-curdling rebel war cry, "Yee-haw, ya!" punctuated with a challenge: "Fight like men! Fight like men!"

The two young VC appeared to be shocked into paralysis. They crouched down in a defensive position, trying to hide, apparently not noticing that their attacker was unarmed. This crazy American, whoever he was, covered 100 or so meters very quickly, and his mouth emitted high-pitched screeches that grew steadily in volume as he closed the distance. As the apparition neared their position, the VC jumped from the bush and tried to flee.

"You little bastards!" Christian bellowed at their retreating backs. "I've had it with you!"

Flying through the air like a linebacker, Christian tackled them both, knocked them to the ground, and reached for a grasp on their scruffy necks.

"You motherfuckers!" he roared. He held the collar of a black pajama shirt in each hand and shook the boys violently, with frustrated fury. Their heads bobbed helplessly on their shoulders as their ears tried to comprehend their attacker's words: "Fight like men! Damn it, if you're gonna fight, fight like men!" He threw them to the ground. The two teenagers lay dazed and whimpering, waiting wide-eyed for certain death.

The jungle grew silent, save for the sound of three heaving chests.

Moments passed before the two young men realized that the American was making no move to kill them. They shared a panicky glance, scrambled to their feet, and were gone.

Still watching from a distance, Woodruff saw Christian pick up the enemy's discarded Russian-made AK-47 rifles and an ammo pouch—not much of a haul, but salable souvenirs nonetheless—and saunter back. Woodruff rose to meet him and stood wordlessly, his mouth open in amazement. He was, if anything, even more shocked than the two VC guerrillas.

Christian said in a matter-of-fact tone, "Let's get back to work, okay? We'll try Coors."

3

Lai Khe Base Camp, South Vietnam
June 27, 1968

In OCS, the instructors had drilled one particular fact into their students: in South Vietnam, in battle, the average life expectancy of an infantry second lieutenant was about sixty seconds. By that measurement, Christian was already living on weeks of bonus time.

A LRRP patrol was among the most dangerous of all assignments faced by U.S. troops in South Vietnam. The job was to act as the eyes and ears of the entire division, seeing and hearing war. The men would climb aboard a chopper, drop into hostile territory, verify intelligence reports, pinpoint the enemy's location, and return with a full report detailing numbers of personnel, types of weapons and equipment, and the apparent mission of the enemy. In theory, the role was not to fight but to pave the way for major assaults by the division. In reality, the patrols often encountered enemy units face-to-face, leaving them no choice but to stand their ground and slug it out.

The patrols were small, usually consisting of only five men, and the missions were always conducted in an area thick with VC or NVA. The men of this special unit were all paratroopers, all volunteers. They were the only men in the first Infantry Division—a ground outfit—to receive jump pay ($55 per month for enlisted men, $110 for officers) in addition to the $55 per month hazardous duty bonus paid to all U.S. troops stationed in South Vietnam.

Christian was executive officer of this unit, assuming the position until the regular CO, a captain, recovered from battle wounds and finished an extended thirty-day leave. In a matter of weeks he had proved himself to be a cunning jungle fighter who found, to his surprise, that he enjoyed the hunt. Woodruff and the other enlisted men thought of Christian as a civilian-soldier with a better grasp of reality than many career officers.

For their part, the career officers did not care much for the new "shave-head." Division scuttlebutt held that Christian was either incredibly savvy or incredibly lucky. Ninety percent of search-and-destroy missions in this war were fruitless, resulting in no enemy contact. But those who went out on the hunt with Christian reported that he seemed to possess an unaccountable talent for sniffing out the presence of the enemy. At times, he appeared eerily prescient.

As a result, these men who called themselves Lurps were becoming the talk of the division. The unit brought back intelligence reports that enabled the regular troops to fight with efficiency, and logged enemy kills in the process; for the first time in reasonable memory, the First Division was actually making inroads against entrenched NVA units here in War Zones C and D.

War, like football, is supposed to be a team effort, but it is subject to considerable intrasquad contention. To the ranking officers, sequestered in the relative safety of headquarters, Christian was a natural target of jealousy. It was a mystery to them how a fuzzy-chinned second lieutenant could account for numerous enemy kills and keep himself alive in the process. He was a *wham-bam, thank you, ma'm* upstart who had set the division on its ear. Some of the brass—at first privately and then more openly— expressed the opinion that Christian was neither savvy nor lucky; some said he was just plain "full of shit."

For his part, Christian doubted the abilities of many of the field-grade officers, and he had developed a theory to support his conclusion. Many years had passed between the Korean War and this war, or conflict, or police action, or whatever you wanted to call it. Those years had been relatively peaceful ones in the world, and while this was a blessed eventuality for civilians, it took the sharp edge off the military. Many of the ranking officers had never really seen war. They had studied it in textbooks and played at it in countless war game exercises, but they had no real feel for it. Yet they were in power. Christian had decided to listen carefully to what they said, save the wheat, throw out the chaff, and proceed to fight the war in his own style.

The tension came to a head one day when a Christian-led Lurp patrol radioed in what was becoming an almost routine message. They had hit an enemy outpost and killed three NVA soldiers. A skeptical radio officer at headquarters responded, "Oh, sure."

Angered, Christian decided to show the rear echelon officers the real faces of war. He ordered his men to carry the bodies of the three NVA troops to the pickup zone where they would rendezvous with choppers for the ride back to base camp. As the helicopters zeroed in on the smoke of the marking grenades, Christian asked his men to pick up two of the dead. He hoisted the third body onto his own shoulders.

The chopper pickup was quick, as always, in order to whisk the craft away from an area of vulnerability. Only after they were airborne did the pilot, turning to survey his load, realize that he was carrying dead—not wounded—enemy. This was against regulations, and he demanded, "Throw them off my aircraft."

"I've been ordered to bring these bodies back for intelligence purposes," Christian lied.

The copilot glanced at one of the faces, its eyes frozen and lifeless. "That guy looks eerie," he said. "Can't you cover his eyes?"

"Sure." Christian tugged the edge of the man's blood-soaked shirt up over his face.

Back at the base camp, the patrol loaded the bodies onto the rear of a deuce and a half, the army's workhorse two and a half-ton truck. "I don't want to get anyone else in trouble," Christian remarked. "But I have to put an end to the REMFs' bullshit." REMFs was the fighting man's acronym for "Rear Echelon Motherfuckers."

"We're coming with you, sir," Sergeant Woodruff replied. "If there is going to be trouble, we're all in this together."

When the deuce and a half arrived at the Division Tactical Operations Center, Christian ordered the driver out of the truck. He took the wheel and backed the vehicle to the brink of the stairway leading down to the two-story bunker that housed the nerve center of division operations. He scribbled out a quick note—"Next time you won't question my body count"—crammed it into the mouth of one of the dead soldiers, and rolled all three bodies down the steps. Then he scrambled into the truck and drove headlong back to the Lurps' encampment.

The sight of three dead enemy troops tumbling into their underground haven incensed the brass, almost to a man. The exception was a wizened full-bird colonel, who saw in the defiant action the attributes of a unique kind of officer. He issued sharp orders to a grim-faced major and, as the man ran off on his mission, opened a dossier entitled CHRISTIAN, David A. 05345884, 2nd Lieutenant, Infantry.

The colonel found much there to interest him. Here was a young, unpolished ruffian who could travel one of two distinct paths in life and in South Vietnam. He could create interminable havoc, or he could make something positive out of the division's major negative, a Recon platoon dubbed the "shit-burners."

Perhaps he would do both.

By the time the deuce and a half arrived back at the unit's camp, the company's first sergeant was waiting with a message. "You've got to go back to Division," he reported. "The brass are calling and they want your ass, sir."

"Screw them, Sarge!" Christian yelled. "Tell them you gave me the message and I told you I was going to get drunk. I'm opening the company bar early this evening. Just tell them I'm at the bar with my men, celebrating the killing of those three gooks."

Within a few minutes, the Lurps were busy at the nightly task of inebriating Puppy Fag, their adopted stray dog. He was short-haired and ugly, reminiscent of an undernourished pig, but he was a loyal drinking companion. Puppy Fag liked a shot of whiskey added to his cup of beer. After he lapped it up, he would wobble around the perimeter of the area, raising his leg. Most male dogs utilized urine to mark their territory, but Puppy Fag seemed to treat it as an aphrodisiac to lure another male dog. Whenever one approached, he greeted him by edging up to him backward, presenting himself.

Before the sport had gone very far this night, a tall, lean, crisply dressed major strode into the company's ramshackle bar—just another tent, really—and sought out Lieutenant Christian.

"Can I help you, sir?" Christian asked, glancing up from his beer and shot. His face bore an impertinent smirk. Behind him the men broke into laughter, but the major silenced it with a fist that pounded on the wooden surface of the makeshift bar.

"Outside!" he roared. "Outside, *Second* Lieutenant Christian!"

The Lurps could hear the conversation clearly from inside the tent. They heard the major scream: "You bald-headed, pompous peacock, we don't take to second Lieutenants who shave their heads and drink their beer with rye! In my opinion, you're an asshole, Lieutenant Christian."

Inside the bar, Sergeant Woodruff felt a laugh billowing in his throat. The major's crewcut was nearly as short as Christian's. Who cared what anyone drank? And as far as the "asshole" appellation, was that not an obvious case of the pot calling the kettle black? He heard Christian retort, "Major, I must admit, you are entitled to your opinion of me. However, I am beginning to form an opinion of you."

The major's rage multiplied. He ordered, "Get into the jeep, you insubordinate bastard. You have a lot of explaining to do at headquarters."

The major drove, bouncing at breakneck speed through every rut in the dirt roadway, past groves of rubber trees and plantation palms, saying no more until he screeched the vehicle to a halt in front of a mobile home. An incongruous, manicured flower garden graced the entrance of the trailer.

Gruffly, the major ordered the lieutenant inside. The structure had been converted into a small conference area and a bar. A handful of officers sat around their drinks. Christian forced a polite smile. He realized that all of these men outranked the major who had escorted him here. On this totem pole, the major was low man, nothing but a gofer. As he heard the major slam the trailer door shut behind him, Christian removed his floppy hat, revealing his shaven head.

An undercurrent of mumbles flowed about the narrow room, but no one spoke directly to him, so the young lieutenant strode up to the bar—the Formica sinktop of the mobile home's kitchenette—and asked the bartender, a lieutenant colonel, for a shot of Canadian Club and a beer.

"No!" roared the furious voice of the major, standing behind him. "You will drink a highball or a beer, but officers do not drink both together. Nor, I should add, do officers shave their heads."

With a sigh Christian asked, "How about a cold beer?"

"All our beers are cold," the major retorted.

Christian grabbed the can of beer offered by the lieutenant colonel and turned around to survey the enemy. The center of attention appeared to be a round, patio-style table, and the rotund, stern-faced figure who held court here was a colonel—a full colonel—with silver eagles pinned to his fatigue collar.

"Lieutenant, please sit down," the colonel invited.

As he sat, Christian noted that the man also wore the G-2 insignia.

"Lieutenant Christian," the colonel noted, not unkindly, "you seem to have a way of making your presence known."

Chuckles emanated from behind Christian's back, and he was aware that all other conversation had ceased.

The colonel's posture stiffened. He lectured: "Today's incident with the bodies was absolutely wrong."

Moments of uneasy silence ensued. The colonel and the lieutenant commenced a staring contest. The only sound in the room was the incessant hum of the air conditioner.

It was the colonel who finally spoke, acknowledging, "You proved your point." His face broke into a broad grin and he extended his hand across the table. Christian clasped it and found himself shaking the paw of a friendly bear. The colonel glanced pointedly at the major and roared, "Bring Lieutenant Christian a shot and a beer, please!"

As he drank, the colonel's tongue loosened, and he reminisced: he had been a second lieutenant once himself, and he also fancied himself as a bit of a cowboy. He understood the temptation to fight against the unfathomable wisdom of the brass. And he admitted that the brass could sometimes benefit from turmoil, but he cautioned Christian not to overdo it. He declared that the lieutenant would be in a "shit load" of trouble for what he did today if it were not for the fact that his men were providing better intelligence information—and killing more enemy—than any comparable unit in the rest of the division.

Christian attempted diplomacy with his new drinking pal. He demurred, "Sir, the only reason our enemy contact is so high is because your intelligence is so good. . . ."

". . . Look, Christian, I don't need bullshit," the colonel interrupted. "Every once in a while in war I run across someone who has a sixth sense for combat. You have it and we're going to use it, so cut the crap. Some of the officers here," he waved his arms wildly, "would like to see you brought down a notch or two. But we are going to stop resisting your talents." He lowered his voice to an inebriated whisper and declared that more of the Lurps would be recruited to work with special Central Intelligence Agency teams, the elite, secret soldiers in this war. "We're counting on you to give us your best men," he said.

Christian was somewhat nonplussed by this news. Over the past few weeks the CIA had skimmed the cream from his unit and now, just as it was coming into its own as a smooth fighting machine, it was to be raided again.

The colonel reminded him that his command was only temporary, that his captain was due to return soon from his R&R. Now his voice grew even fainter, so that Christian had to lean close, over his beer and shot, to hear the solemn lecture.

According to the colonel, the enemy had pushed into what it hoped would be the final phase of this war. This year had started with the Tet offensive, and it was an indication of things to come. Ho Chi Minh, the president or dictator—or whatever you wanted to call him—of North Vietnam, believed that his troops were poised to achieve victory. They planned an accelerated rate of terrorist attacks against civilians while increasing their political moves among the farmers. Furthermore, they were determined to discourage the American forces with human wave attacks against American base camps. To do this, the enemy was hustling troops and supplies into all areas along the South Vietnam–Cambodia border.

Yes, the colonel allowed, Christian would be forced to relinquish his position of command when his captain returned. But before that happened, he had ambitious plans for the young second lieutenant.

4

War Zone C, South Vietnam
June 28–29, 1968

It was 0635 on a sultry, quiet morning in South Vietnam, less than ten hours after the Intelligence colonel promised Christian special action. A squad of hand-picked Lurps lolled about outside a tent, catching a few extra winks as, inside, Christian and Sergeant Woodruff took their seats at a briefing table. Woodruff wondered Why were we awakened an hour ago and told to saddle up? What's going on?

On the table was a large map that encompassed all of South Vietnam, Cambodia, and Laos. A spec 7 began the briefing: "It is suspected that a battalion-plus troop movement, the NVA 271st, is within the vicinity of the South Vietnamese base camp at An Loch." Battalion-plus referred to a regular fighting battalion augmented by an extra company—close to 1,000 enemy troops.

Intelligence reports indicated that the enemy planned to execute a major surprise assault on An Loch this very night. The NVA would be in an offensive-minded mood, ready to celebrate a great rout. Instead, said the spec 7, the ARVNs hoped to catch their cousins by surprise, attacking them first at an ambush point on the northern end of War Zone C, before they reached An Loch.

"We want to stop the enemy mainly with our allies, the ARVN forces," the spec 7 declared. "This is the main reason we are sending you guys in

small numbers. If we send in a team of Special Forces or reinforce the area
with a battalion of military trainers, we'll have an intelligence leak. Your
mission will be to serve as liaison with the military and the South Vietnamese
political leaders. Also, we are going to send in a crack platoon of South
Vietnamese Rangers. We hope that you and the ARVN Rangers can pinpoint
the enemy movement prior to the actual attack.

"You will be flown into a Vietnamese night defense perimeter (NDP),
where you will be briefed further. You can grab some C rations at the
Operations bunker there. You won't leave that bunker until 1530, at which
time you will meet your Vietnamese counterparts. At present it is our
understanding that a Vietnamese sergeant major will be leading the patrol
for our allies. However, Lieutenant Christian, you will remain in command
of the U.S. forces."

At 1630 the allied unit would move out from the NDP and make its
way east. Waiting behind would be a much larger force of ARVN troops.
The vanguard unit would melt into the jungle, position itself directly in the
path of the unsuspecting enemy as the enemy moved forward for his own
attack, and await the night. The moment the NVA appeared, Christian was
to call in artillery and/or air strikes. Once the American support groups had
softened up the enemy, the main force of ARVN troops would move in to
mop up.

"We need to hit tonight, and we need this to be a South Vietnamese
victory," the spec 7 stressed. "Your job is to locate the enemy but avoid
contact. We want the ARVNs to do the real work." Now he lowered his
voice and declared solemnly, "Gentlemen, you may never realize the importance of tonight's mission. But it will ripple back to Washington."

It was a clear and acceptable strategy to Christian and Woodruff. They
would supply the eyes; American artillery units and strategic air wings
would provide the real muscle; then the brass would give the credit to the
South Vietnamese army. Neither the lieutenant nor the sergeant had any
quarrel with such obviously political decisions, which were the proper realm
of their superiors. What did it matter who got the credit, so long as the
enemy was annihilated?

The spec 7 concluded, "If you have no questions, you can grab some
coffee."

They spent the day in nervous waiting. Sequestered in order to guard
against intelligence leaks, the squad killed time in the Vietnamese NDP
Operations bunker by listening to Chubby Checker records and playing
poker. Christian was down $200 to Buck Sergeant Ernest P. Davis, a tall,
rippling-muscled black soldier from Florida, when he was called out into

the bright afternoon sun. "See you on payday," he promised Davis. The first of the month was only three days away.

Outside, he was introduced to a young ARVN private.

"Where's the sergeant major?" Christian asked.

An American captain explained. The Vietnamese sergeant major originally assigned to the mission had been felled by a malaria attack. His replacement, another sergeant major, spoke no English, so this private had been assigned as interpreter.

Fifteen minutes later, in the late afternoon sunlight, the allied unit moved out into a jungle that swallowed them up quickly. The main force would stay well behind and await the call to battle.

Christian was anxious to keep moving, for they had a lot of ground to cover before darkness. He grew irritated by what he considered to be too-frequent rest breaks called by the Vietnamese sergeant major, but he muttered to himself, "Keep your mouth shut; this is supposed to be an ARVN mission." However, when the ARVN commander ordered a third break within the space of two hours, Christian huddled with the private/interpreter. "Tell him we need to keep moving," Christian suggested. "We have to reach the ambush point within the next hour."

The private delivered the message. Nevertheless, they had resumed their march for only ten minutes before the sergeant major decreed yet another break. Now, Christian's irritation turned into solid anger. He suspected that, for whatever reason, the South Vietnamese commander was not anxious to accomplish the mission. He approached the ARVN private, standing next to his sergeant major, and asked, "What's going on? Why the hell are we stopping again?"

"Sergeant major wants to stop, so we stop," the private explained logically. "I just interpreter. I not boss."

"Well, tell your boss that I want to talk to him. Tell him we must move out to accomplish our mission."

Christian watched as the private translated. When the conversation ended, the sergeant major turned to look directly at him. He flashed a faraway smile, then fell suddenly, face forward, onto the ground.

"What's wrong? What happened?" Christian yelled, sinking to his feet to offer assistance. He grabbed the man's shirt and rolled him over. The ARVN commander smiled up at him, twirled his eyes, and appeared to pass out.

Christian let the man's head fall roughly to the ground, and he growled in disgust, "He's drunk. The motherfucker is drunk! How are we going to complete our mission with this asshole in charge?" It was a rhetorical question, and Christian did not wait for an answer. "You!" he barked, jabbing a finger toward the interpreter. "You, my friendly private, are in charge of the Vietnamese Rangers. Tell the sergeant major that he is fired and get these men up and move them out."

Christian stomped away to regroup his men. Behind him he heard a spate of excited Asian chatter, which he ignored until he was stopped in his tracks by the crack of a single gunshot. Turning, he saw the ARVN interpreter lying dead on the ground in a puddle of his own blood. The smiling sergeant major stood over him, a smoking pistol in his hand.

"You drunken motherfucker!" Christian shouted. Ignoring the pistol, he leaped toward the man in rage.

The sergeant major dodged out of the way easily, held up his hands in defense, and said in crisp English, "No, sir."

Christian stopped short, trying to understand. "Why, you rotten bastard, you speak English?"

"Yes, sir." The sergeant major glanced at the dead private and proclaimed, "He no good. He Charlie. He number ten no good." On the Asian scale of values, number one was the best, number ten was the worst. "Here, I show you," the ARVN commander continued. He dropped to his knees and searched through the dead man's pockets. Discovering a cigarette lighter, he stood and exhibited it to Christian. "Here, see." On the side of the lighter was the inscription: *271 NVA*. The sergeant major's face beamed with vindication. He declared, "See, I told you. He Charlie Cong."

Christian was totally confused. Who were the good guys and who were the bad guys in this war? He mumbled questions: "Why did you fake being drunk? Why did you pretend not to know English?"

"Because Intelligence say that new private is traitor. He Charlie! I pretend to be drunk to see what kind of orders he give. He fired me, and told the men mission over. He told the men we go home now. He hurt mission, so I kill him. Now we have good mission."

"Holy shit!" Christian exclaimed. He shuffled back toward his men, shaking his head in consternation. Behind him he heard the sergeant major practice his English, echoing, "Holy shit! Holy shit!"

Christian gathered the American soldiers about him and declared, "We have a mission to complete. I don't know who is who, but I can tell you this: if anyone gets in my way, I'll kill him. Sergeant Woodruff, let's move out."

The American lieutenant took control now, and the South Vietnamese sergeant major acquiesced. Pausing for no more breaks, the team drove forward, moving into place within the hour, taking up ambush positions in clumps of scrub brush along the edge of a field that broke out into an expanse of neglected rice paddies, overgrown with scattered clumps of ten-foot high elephant grass and thickening vines. If the enemy was moving toward An Loch, as suspected, it would have to cross here, where it would be vulnerable.

The ambushers established a perimeter of small lookout posts, each manned by one American and three or four ARVNs. Working rapidly but silently, each group armed an array of Claymores in front of its position. The U.S.-built Claymore mine was a simple, black, horseshoe-shaped plastic box, about twelve by eighteen inches, standing on tiny tripod legs. It contained a supply of C-4 explosive that propelled roughly 10,000 shotgun pellets out from the open end of the horseshoe when the "clacker," the hand-held detonator, was pressed.

Once the Claymores were armed and wired back to their clackers, the ambush was ready. The men sat back to wait.

Monsoon rains began, first as a slight patter, then as an unrelenting drumbeat. The troops unrolled the long sleeves of their fatigue jackets and unfurled plastic rain ponchos over their heads. Still, they were chilled almost immediately. This South Vietnamese weather was an anomaly—steaming hot during the day, viciously cold in the night rain.

Two hours passed. The rain pelted down with increasing force. The mud deepened. Christian tried to communicate via hand signals with the three Vietnamese Rangers who shared his outpost and felt frustrated, as if he were fighting a war alongside deaf mutes.

Finally he left his post at the northernmost point of the ambush line and worked his way through the darkness, moving stealthily from group to group, delivering the same message to each of his men. "This looks like a false alarm tonight," he whispered. "But try to stay ready anyway. If we see the enemy, I'll signal."

"What's the signal?" Woodruff asked.

"I'll blow a Claymore on them if they get close enough," Christian replied. "But I don't think they will. Matter of fact, I think we'll. . . ."

The whispered conversation was interrupted by the tugging hand of a Vietnamese Ranger, grabbing at Christian's pants. The man pointed a finger out toward the darkness.

Christian looked, but could see nothing, and he shrugged off the man's gesture impatiently.

Alarm registered in the increased pressure of the ARVN's grip on Christian's trousers. Emphatically he pointed again.

Once more Christian stared through the heavy rain, trying to focus his eyes. This time, on the horizon, he saw the dim outline of a gloomy shape. Then another. Then more. There were men out there, headed this way. Christian gave the thumbs up sign to Woodruff, and scurried back to his own post, where three ARVN Rangers waited. "VC, VC," he whispered, pointing.

The enemy force approached catlike, advancing through the night rain, working its way toward the dawn attack. Silhouettes multiplied by the minute until Christian muttered to himself, "Whoa, shit! It looks like the whole North Vietnamese army." He felt his pulse rate quicken.

It was difficult to calculate accurately, but he estimated that there were at least 200 enemy soldiers approaching, compared to his combined force of about twenty South Vietnamese and six Americans, counting himself. At these odds it would be smart to stick to the original script and avoid contact, allowing artillery and air strikes to take care of the superior force. But this was now impossible. As it happened, the NVA troops were advancing directly toward the blanket of scrub brush screening the ambush line, and there was no choice but to alter the battle plan. Christian was glad he had his St. Joseph's prayer on him.

He grabbed his radio and whispered a message back to the NDP, so far away: "We have enemy forty meters to our front and it looks like we will be forced to make contact. Give me an artillery marking round."

He switched off his radio and glanced at the Rangers at his side, motioning for them to hand him the clackers that would detonate the Claymores. The Rangers shrugged and played dumb. It was characteristic of what Christian had seen in ARVN troops before. They reasoned: maybe if we don't bother them, they won't bother us. The ARVNs seemed willing to take the gamble, but Christian was not. He slipped the safety latch off his M-16 and leveled the barrel between the eyes of one of the ARVN troops. "Everyone is waiting for my signal," he murmured, "so I might as well start by shooting you guys."

Just then an artillery shell exploded about 1,000 meters to the northeast. The enemy soldiers stopped in their tracks, unsure of what was happening, how they had been spotted, which direction was safe. Quickly, one of the Rangers handed over the clackers. Praying "Work, please!" Christian pressed the buttons.

Ka-boom! The Claymores in front of their position exploded, showering the enemy with thousands of shotgun pellets. All along the line other Claymores went up, decimating the enemy's point men. Automatic rifle fire followed, along with "Willie Peters," white phosphorous grenades that sent fiery streamers through the night.

With mines, rifle fire, and Willie Peters in front of them and artillery to the rear, the NVA troops were like slabs of meat in a sandwich. A few ran, scattering in various directions, but most of them dropped prone, taking refuge in the elephant grass and the filthy water of the rice paddies. They began to fire back at their unseen attackers.

"Give me illumination," Christian said into the radio. "Come over 200 meters east of my position and drop 800. Fire illumination. We have an army of the enemy trapped in an open field. The enemy has hit the ground and is returning fire."

The next moments were filled with the crack of bullets and the glare of muzzle flashes. Then, with another *Ka-boom!*, the illumination rounds hit. Bright flares dangled in the sky over the enemy troops, setting them up as easy targets if they exposed themselves in the field of fire. The allied force, firing from cover, picked away at anyone who moved.

"Fire for effect a volley of butterfly and a volley of H.E. (high explosive artillery)," Christian shouted into the radio. "Right where you put the illumination. You are right over the top of the bastards."

Only a few moments had passed, but it was time enough for the enemy to lick its wounds and assess the situation. It had taken quick, tough losses, but it was obvious from the low level of rifle fire that the ambushers were only a small force. Christian could hear authoritative shouts, and he knew that the NVA commanders were mustering their survivors. He reasoned that they were preparing to do what he would do: storm the ambush posts. They would take additional casualties, but action was preferable to remaining out in the open, pinned. Offense is better than defense.

"Damn, where's the artillery?" Christian asked over the radio.

"Shot out," came the reply. "We already. . . ." The transmission was drowned out as a barrage of butterfly rounds found its target. The rounds detonated high over the enemy force, releasing hundreds of smaller, grenadelike bombs that flitted toward the ground and exploded about fifteen feet in the air. A few more of the NVA troops jumped up to run away, but they were torn apart by M-16 fire as soon as they exposed themselves. Then came the more standard H.E., which sent hot metal ripping through the air. Then more butterfly rounds.

"Repeat fire mission!" Christian radioed. "Your artillery is logging quite a few kills tonight."

During the next momentary lull in artillery fire, the bulk of the enemy troops broke and fled the ambush, racing for the safety of the jungle at the far side of the field. At that moment Christian knew the battle was his, and he felt a tingling sensation encompass him. He stood up, ripped off M-16 rounds, and taunted, "Come on, you mothers. You wanna fight? Come on and fight, you candy-ass Commies!"

Those NVA soldiers who remained in the field of fire still outnumbered his own troops, but Christian knew that they were wounded, terrified, disoriented—ripe for the kill. He dropped to his knees, grabbed the radio, and called for an end to the artillery. "I'm going off the air for a few minutes," he explained. "We're going to charge what's left of the enemy." He muttered, thinking out loud, "Damn, I wish we had bayonets."

"What?" asked a radio voice.

Christian ignored the question. He dropped the radio, stood, and shouted out, "Sergeant major, get your Rangers up. Woodruff, get our men up. Let's move out and see who and what we can capture."

The allied unit slogged through the mud, out toward the open field, weapons blazing away at scattered resistance. "Whoop it up!" Christian yelled out. "I want you to sound like a bunch of Indians hunting for scalps."

All about him the Lurps broke into screams and howls. The ARVNs yelled, "*Cho Hoi! Di Di Mao!*" Surrender! Do it fast! They kept up a steady stream of fire.

At the sight of the approaching unit of men screaming like banshees, more of the NVA troops broke and ran. Several of these were cut down by rifle fire.

The mopping up operation went quickly. After a brief time, silence and the heavy patter of rain retook the night.

Sergeant Woodruff and the Vietnamese sergeant major reported to Christian that there were thirty dead NVA bodies in the field. They had also captured considerable enemy equipment and weapons. The casualty total on their own side was zero.

"Great," Christian said. "Give me the radio. We're going to report this, then move to another area and set up another ambush 'til daybreak, in case they come back. If we stay here, we're liable to buy the farm from enemy rockets and mortars."

Only then did Christian remember the original orders. He was not supposed to make contact with the enemy and thereby steal the glory from the South Vietnamese army. It didn't matter, he concluded. Both the American and the South Vietnamese high commands would take this victory gladly.

Indeed they did, with more enthusiasm than Christian could envision. When he jumped out of a chopper and stumbled back into the base camp the following morning, he was greeted by a captain from G-2 who proclaimed, "Great mission! Three hundred kills!"

"Sir," Christian tried to explain, "we only killed thirty."

"Whatever," the captain replied with a shrug. "Numbers don't matter. We accomplished our mission and I think there is going to be a great treat for you as a result."

"What do you mean?"

"We're going to be guests of honor tonight. Well, I should rephrase that—you are going to be the guest of honor tonight."

"Where?"

"At dinner, with the vice president of South Vietnam, Nguyen Cao-Ky."

5

Saigon, South Vietnam
June 29, 1968

Christian reluctantly surrendered his M-16 at the door of the presidential palace. He suddenly felt naked.

Accompanied by the Intelligence captain, he stepped through an ornate, gilded portal and into a palatial hall. The backdrop was Renaissance architecture, the foreground, French-imported appointments, and the players were dignitaries of two nations, exuding a general ambiance of self-regard, power, and money. A monstrous doorway in the rear of the hall opened onto lush gardens, where most of the guests had assembled.

In addition to top brass of both the American and South Vietnamese armies, the captain explained, tonight's guests were members of the Supreme Court of South Vietnam. The list was rounded out by several cabinet officials.

Such wine was heady to the teenage lieutenant. "Who're the military brass?" Christian wanted to know. "Our military."

"Well," the captain replied, "there are a couple of colonels and generals, but I can never figure out who's from the army and who's from the CIA." The captain excused himself to make conversation with an old friend, a South Vietnamese provincial chief.

Left alone for a moment, Christian's excited eyes studied the scene. He wanted to share every detail in a letter to his bride Peggy, and he knew that he was here tonight as the titular representative of all the men of his unit; they too would want to hear everything. The male guests were attired either in full military dress or tailored, pressed business suits, and the women wore expensive evening gowns and oozed jewelry. Christian felt very much out of place, clad in jungle fatigues.

His eye settled upon a group of late-arriving guests, and he was struck by an unforeseen absurdity. The new arrivals were South Vietnamese, obviously individuals with power and authority, for high-ranking U.S. military officers greeted them with deference—almost reverence. Most American troops looked down on the South Vietnamese, but tonight, in this courtyard full of cocktails and hors d'oeuvres, the tables were turned. This was South Vietnamese turf. For that matter, Christian realized with a silent, rueful chuckle, the entire country was. At the moment, he felt alien and unclean.

"Relax," he commanded himself. "Try to be yourself."

He strode over toward a tableful of hors d'oeuvres, grabbed a stuffed shrimp, and wondered if he was capable of making small talk in this milieu.

"So, you are the hero from last night's mission?" The question came from an impeccably attired, middle-aged South Vietnamese man.

"Yes, I guess you can say that," Christian mumbled through a mouthful of shrimp.

The brief conversation was interrupted by a white-jacketed waiter bearing a tray of Asian delicacies with names that Christian found unpronounceable. His new acquaintance dug in eagerly, but Christian found himself reluctant to partake. He wished that he had a bottle of Cajun hot sauce with him to disguise the taste of whatever it was that they wanted him to eat.

Additional trays of drinks floated past his field of vision, and he decided to concentrate on this facet of the party. French wine and martinis housed in tall-stemmed crystal glasses shot by before he could react, but he managed to halt a waiter carrying a tray of stubby tumblers filled with iced drinks. He grabbed one of these, commented bravely, "This is going to be a great night!" and tossed it down in a single gulp. "Scotch," he mused, wiping his mouth on the sleeve of his fatigue blouse. He preferred Canadian Club, but decided he could enjoy Scotch for a change.

He gazed idly about the courtyard, and his eyes locked upon the quizzical stares of two South Vietnamese gentlemen, even more nattily attired than most of the guests, who responded to his sudden attention by scurrying toward him in mincing steps. Aw shit, he thought. Why am I getting stuck with these two? He suddenly missed Peggy more than ever. What was she doing tonight, back home, so far away? Then he remembered, it wasn't even night in Penndel, Pennsylvania.

"Pardon me, lieutenant," one of the approaching men said in a lilting falsetto tone, "but you don't seem to know anybody. We saw you looking around for possible company."

Christian smiled politely, but asked himself, "Why do I attract all the weirdos?"

"Where were you educated? Stateside, or overseas?" one of the gentlemen asked. Without waiting for an answer, he noted that he, himself, held a degree from Harvard, and his friend was an Oxford man. Then he paused, and his friend joined the question, both of them asking, "You?"

"Oh, I was educated at Woodrow Wilson," Christian stammered. He did not add the words "High School."

The two men shared a conspiratorial smile, and one of them commented, "Very fine school of international affairs."

Christian was interrupted by a sudden commotion, as everyone turned toward the courtyard entrance.

The crowd parted like the waters of the Red Sea to make way for a stunningly beautiful South Vietnamese woman, dressed in a silken, lavender-hued sheath that revealed every nuance of her body. She was followed by her mate—a *dude*, Christian thought—a small but formidably stiff character, dashingly decked out in a tailored, black-silk air force dress uniform. An ascot of shimmering lavender—matching his wife's dress—added a splash of color.

A swashbuckler, Christian thought. He felt a kinship. Then he became self-conscious, realizing, I don't even know how to spell his name.

Nguyen Cao-Ky strode slowly through the crowd, allowing everyone to watch, acknowledging friends and associates with a nod here and a wave there, but maintaining an authoritative silence. His title of vice president was nominal; amid the ebb and flow of South Vietnamese politics he was, at the moment, the man in charge. When he turned abruptly and led the way toward the dining room, the assembled dignitaries queued anxiously to follow.

The Intelligence captain suddenly appeared at Christian's side and said, "I'll tell you where to sit." As they walked inside the mansion, the captain briefed, "Ky will give a speech in Vietnamese and English, acknowledging you and the joint allied mission. You just smile and nod your head in grateful humility. Understand?"

Christian answered with a grin, "Yes, but it's going to be difficult being humble."

The captain led the honored lieutenant to the very center of an immense table fashioned of mirror-polished teakwood. Vice President Ky sat a few seats off to his right and Mrs. Ky was equidistant on his left. Glancing up, Christian was dismayed to see the two foppish South Vietnamese men directly across from him. The Harvard man smiled and flashed a wink. Christian returned the smile, but not the wink.

Dinner proceeded uneventfully, even though he found the unfamiliar chopsticks difficult to wield, until an officious waiter plopped down the main course. Christian's plate contained a boiled chicken head, sitting atop a mound of rice. Confused, he looked about and saw others digging in, helping themselves to dishes of various meats, poultry, and fish delicacies, which they ladled onto their plates of rice and garnished with abundant helpings of spices. Why was he the only one with a chicken head?

"You're the guest of honor," the captain whispered in his ear. "It's their way of honoring you."

"What?"

"The chicken head. It's supposed to be the best part."

"Ugh," Christian moaned. He glanced up to find himself again exchanging smiles with the too-friendly Orientals seated across from him. Quickly he returned his eyes to the chicken head. "Lucky me," he muttered.

The vice president seized this moment to begin his speech, and Christian seized the same moment—when all eyes were on Ky—to slip the abominable chicken head into a pocket of his jungle fatigues.

6

Lai Khe Base Camp, South Vietnam
June 29, 1968

Very late that night, Christian shared a celebratory beer with the men of Sergeant Woodruff's squad, telling them every detail of the incredible dinner and displaying with pride the liberated chicken head. But he found himself upstaged by the visit of a couple of former Lurps, now recruited as CIA operatives. One of the men showed off a gold Rolex watch and boasted, "We get paid $2,400 a month, tax free."

Christian, a boy from Levittown, was interested in big money like this, and wondered how he could get himself dealt into the game. Reasoning that he was "big shit" now that he had dined with the vice president, he believed it would be a simple matter to talk his way into larger and more important missions. The CIA wanted more of his men? How about taking their executive officer? He copied down the name and private telephone number of the CIA contact in the U.S. embassy in Saigon.

That same night Staff Sergeant Garcia took out a five-man patrol to see if the allied ambush had managed to stop the NVA activity in the area near An Loch. On the outskirts of a village they stumbled into an ambush. Ernest Davis took a bullet in the head and was killed instantly.

Back at the base camp, Christian was monitoring the radio as he continued his conversation with the CIA men. Suddenly he heard Garcia's voice screaming into the night: "They're gonna overrun us! We're gonna be killed! We need artillery fast!"

Christian ran for the concrete bunker that housed the Tactical Operations Center and took over the radio, trying to act as liaison between Garcia in the field and the South Vietnamese artillery officer back here at camp. Garcia was so panicked that he forgot to provide map coordinates. They couldn't fire artillery until they knew where to fire it. Christian took a deep breath and let the air out slowly. Then he depressed the radio call button and said in a quiet voice, "Calm down, Garcia, this is Chris. Damn it, we need to help you, but we can only help you if you help us."

"Sir," Garcia cried, "we're gonna be killed. They already got Davis and we need artillery, bad. I'm gonna kill those motherfuckin' artillery guys if they don't get it out here quick."

Christian gulped at the news of Davis's death, but he pushed sadness out of his mind. Grieve later. Save these other boys now. "Give me the coordinates," he ordered Garcia, "okay?"

The sergeant calmed down as he heard the note of control in Christian's voice. He repeated the artillery coordinates. Only minutes later, the resulting barrage saved the remainder of the squad.

Christian learned a lesson from the experience. In battle, never let your emotions run away with you. The only way to get help is to make sure that the base camp hears your coordinates clearly. A panicked radio voice indicates that you are no longer in control. It makes the people in the rear assume that you are doomed, and might cause them to panic as well.

7

Lai Khe Base Camp, South Vietnam
July 1968

In mid-July, Christian's commanding officer returned from his R&R. Shortly after that, he called his young lieutenant in for a personal conference. He had heard about the $200 poker debt Christian had racked up. Christian countered that he had sent a check to Davis's widow. The captain ripped into him, proclaiming that it was inappropriate for an officer to gamble and drink with his men. But he had another bone to pick. On his desk was a letter forwarded halfway across the world from a finance company in North Carolina. The army had shipped Christian's older brother Doug to Germany, and he had decided to ignore the payments on his car. The CO decreed that Christian, as cosigner, had to meet the payments.

"Doug's in the army, too. He can pay it just as well as I can," Christian contended.

"No, you're an officer. You have to pay."

The CO made Christian fill out an allotment form instructing the army to send $80 of his monthly pay directly to the finance company.

Christian was ordered to make his first payment immediately. This payment, combined with the money he had sent to Davis's widow and what he sent home routinely to Peggy, left him with a severe cash flow problem. He knew it was time to act.

"I'm going to stand down for a few days," he told Sergeant Woodruff one morning. "Cover for me."

He sequestered two side arms beneath the blouse of his combat fatigues: a .357 magnum and a nine-millimeter pistol, the latter a 1930's vintage Spanish Armada collector's piece that he had taken off the body of a dead enemy soldier. He talked his way past an MP at the perimeter of Lai Khe and hiked along the roadway outside for a brief distance until he was able to hitch a ride in a battered civilian jeep, sharing the journey with two Korean men who were ferrying an ancient refrigerator. They bounced along the rutted road for more than two hours before Christian hopped off at an American-run air terminal on the outskirts of Saigon.

8

Saigon, South Vietnam
July 1968

Christian located a military telephone and dialed the secret number of the CIA.

"I want to talk to the general," he whispered into the phone.

"Who are you? How did you get this number?" replied an anxious voice.

"I want to talk to the general," Christian repeated.

He heard evidence of confusion on the other end of the line, until a gruff voice asked, "What?"

"I want to work for the CIA," Christian announced.

There was a moment of silence as the unknown presence on the line considered the available facts: the caller had the special number; he knew it was a CIA phone; he even knew about the general! "Where are you?" he asked. "We'll send someone to pick you up."

Within half an hour a black limousine had lurched to a stop at the appointed rendezvous station. Christian clambered inside, wondering how the CIA hoped to maintain a low profile in a Third World capital when it insisted on setting up clandestine meetings via limo.

A mute, unsmiling driver took him to a two-story French villa, decorated in marble and polished wood. He was led across thick Oriental carpets and into a meeting room dominated by an elongated mahogany conference table. A handful of men wearing the uniforms of field grade officers—navy admirals and army colonels—sat at the table, awaiting him. Junior grade officers stood to the sides. Christian took the seat he was offered, and waited.

The man who called himself the general, seated at the head of the table, waved a hand and asked with dispatch, "Well, what is it you would like to do?"

"I'm Lieutenant David Christian, with the First Division," the young officer began. "You're recruiting some of my guys, and I'd like to work for you, too."

The general dismissed the introduction, as if to indicate that he already knew the identity of the interloper. He repeated his question, "What do you want to do?"

Christian had formulated a brash plan, a two-level plot. He intended to propose a military operation so grandiose and fanciful that the CIA, although it could not possibly approve, would accept him into its bosom as an officer possessed of the necessary bravado. "I'll tell you what," he responded. "You let me pick my own troops, and I'll kill Ho Chi Minh."

Smiles flashed about the perimeter of the room. The junior officers shook their heads in amazement at the nerve of this whacko lieutenant. But Christian noted that none of the brass was laughing.

After a moment of stoic silence, the general muttered softly, "You won't get back."

"I'll get back," Christian prophesied. He explained further. He would handpick a small unit of men—some of the Lurps, his brother Doug, and Michael Peters, a childhood friend. Both Doug and Michael had already served hitches in South Vietnam and were fluent in the language. What's more, Doug's special skills as a chemical warfare expert might come in handy. Christian did not mention the possible side benefit of having Doug close at hand, where he could thrash a few car payments out of his hide.

The men around the table remained quiet, so Christian continued to detail his improbable scenario. The select group of commandos would undergo a severe regimen of training, and they would submit themselves to plastic surgery to slant their eyes. They would ingest drugs and use topical ointments to alter skin pigmentation, turning their flesh yellow. Disguised as the enemy, they would airdrop at night into North Vietnam, near Hanoi.

Christian noted that once a week Ho Chi Minh came out onto the steps of his palace to greet his people, and he saw nods of agreement ripple around the table. During one of these public appearances, the lieutenant announced, he and his men would assassinate the North Vietnamese leader.

"It could end the war," Christian proclaimed. "Right now, we're fighting a stupid war. We fight for a piece of land. Men die to gain a hill. And what do we do after we win the hill? We pull back."

There were more nods, encouraging Christian's mouth to rush forward: "That's not the way you win anything. You don't win a boxing match or a football game on defense. Let's do something on offense."

The stillness of the room broadcast an unbelievable message. Christian was overwhelmed by the realization that these men were actually considering his plan. *"They're nuttier than I am,"* he thought.

Finally an "admiral" spoke up, offering a strange preamble. "Lieutenant," he began, "we are not military officers. At least, the majority of the people in this room are not military officers. For that reason, you must say nothing about this place, or us."

"Yes," Christian acknowledged.

Then the "admiral" said, "We like your idea. Go back to your unit and do your job. We'll get back to you."

9

Lui Khe Base Camp, South Vietnam
July 1968

Christian met once again with the colonel from G-2 who had promised to put his flair for combat to special use, but his mind was back in Saigon at his recent meeting. With his senses aflutter, wondering how long it would take the CIA to whisk him off to glory, he found it difficult to concentrate, until he remembered that the "admiral" had ordered him to get on with his job for the present.

The colonel pierced through Christian's daydreams and announced that it was time for the young officer to move to a new assignment. Because of the prowess he had demonstrated, he was now going to receive a singular honor for a fledgling officer. He was to get his "6," the radio designation for the commander of a combat unit. It was to be a very special element, used to conduct highly sensitive operations. Security would be paramount, because public knowledge of some of the unit's actions would cause a firestorm of protest back home.

After Christian whipped his new boys into shape, the colonel hinted, "We might drop your teams into the enemy's backyard." Much of the work would be similar to LRRP patrols. "But your men must be as skilled as Special Forces. We will need you to confirm troop movements, types of weapons, and supplies," the colonel said. "Then we will have the air force or the navy come in and blow their asses to kingdom come. Understand?"

"Understand, sir."

The colonel spoke slowly, softly: "We may even put you into Cambodia. Understand?"

"Understand, sir."

Just to be sure, the colonel spelled out the implications. In the beginning of his crusade to take over the southern half of Vietnam, Ho Chi Minh had simply planned to send waves of North Vietnamese troops directly southward across the 17th Parallel, the demarcation line between the two halves of Vietnam. They would conduct an unstoppable sweep through the countryside, ending ultimately in Saigon. But after his armies were systematically beaten back by the combined resistance of U.S. troops and their South Vietnamese allies, he had devised an alternate, subtler strategy, cashing in on the American regard for the niceties of international politics.

The United States was not in conflict with Laos or Cambodia, and Ho Chi Minh reasoned, more or less correctly, that Americans would not choose to carry the fight onto neutral soil. Laos posed no problem to him, for its Communists cooperated freely. Cambodia, under the rule of Prince Sihanouk, was in bed with everybody, and therefore weak. The NVA simply appropriated a healthy slice of the eastern section of Cambodia. Sihanouk did not have the muscle to resist. For the most part, Cambodian citizens abdicated the territory in fear of the invaders.

Thus was established the Ho Chi Minh trail, a politically untouchable pipeline through Laos and Cambodia. Through this pipeline troops and supplies poured into the south from the north, traversing the rivers and slogging through the triple-canopy jungle—where aerial surveillance was difficult—uncontested until they reached the border. The trail was a test of physical stamina to the North Vietnamese troops, who spent months laboring toward the fight. But the American soldier considered its existence a test of spiritual endurance. He *knew* where the enemy was, but the machinations of politics would not allow him to carry the fight even a few feet across the border into Cambodia, where the enemy massed.

Now, at the highest levels, decision-makers were pondering whether they could continue to allow Ho Chi Minh to get away with his plan. The colonel announced quietly that selected groups of skilled commandos were preparing to conduct a clandestine war in the forbidden territory of Cambodia. Christian was to lead one of the units that would violate the border if and when the word came down from above.

. There was good news and bad news.

The good news was that Christian was to enjoy a bit of R&R, and then he would be promoted to first lieutenant.

The bad news was that his new outfit, which he was supposed to fashion into an efficient—and very special—fighting machine, was the problem platoon of an entire battalion, a group of misfits who had already gone through a number of would-be commanders. Officially it was designated the Reconnaissance platoon for the First Battalion of the Twenty-sixth Infantry Division. Its radio code was Victor. But its men had earned another nickname for themselves.

"They're the 'shit-burners,' " the colonel declared.

10

Nui Ba Cam, Night Defense Perimeter, South Vietnam
August 1968

Concerned that quasi-permanent outhouses might foul the South Vietnamese countryside, U.S. Army engineers constructed even more primitive temporary facilities. They cut multiple holes into elongated plywood planks and installed toilet seats atop them. But instead of digging pits underneath, they slashed 50-gallon drums in half and positioned them beneath the seats as a target zone. Although this procedure saved the integrity of the environment, it created a chore so distasteful and humiliating that it was generally assigned as a punishment detail to the most incorrigible troops. Some time earlier, at the First Battalion's Night Defense Perimeter near the mountain Nui ba Cam, north of Bien Hoa, the task of dousing waste-filled drums with kerosene and burning the contents had befallen the Recon platoon.

As they worked at their distasteful chore one hot afternoon, someone suggested that there was a more efficient way to ignite the mass of human waste. "Stand back!" he cried out. When the others saw him waving a Willie Peter in the air, they scattered in gleeful panic. The innovator activated the white phosphorous grenade, dropped it into a barrel of feces, and joined in the general retreat.

The noise of the explosion rebounded throughout the camp. Others came running, their rifles ready to repulse the attack. But instead of the enemy, they found the men of Recon, grinning sheepishly as bits of incinerated excreta floated down upon one and all. It was the last time Recon was assigned to the detail, but they were henceforth known throughout the battalion as the "shit-burners."

Late one August afternoon, the men of Recon lounged about near their hootches, killing time before chow. They were a tough-looking, tattooed bunch, their shirts unbuttoned and their trouser legs rolled up, instead of bloused properly into their boots. Almost to a man, they swigged warm beer and puffed on acrid cigarettes. They daubed one another with repellent in an unavailing attempt to keep the mosquitoes at bay. The antiseptic aroma of the spray intermingled with their own perspiration to form a revolting mélange.

Off-color jokes and racial slurs filled their conversation, the latter delivered with a sense of affection. In a war that left no time for formal introductions, phrases such as "Move your Polock ass!" "Over *there*, you dumb Dago!" and even "Nigger!" were employed not as insults but as shorthand communication. "Dumb shit" was the generic form of address, applied without regard to color or creed.

In addition to pulling duty for the most distasteful base camp duties, Recon's job was clearly defined. It was the scout unit for the First of the Twenty-sixth, as well as for the Eleventh Armored Cavalry Division, under the command of Colonel George S. Patton, Jr., the son of Old Blood and Guts himself. But it had compiled an unimpressive combat record. Whenever Recon had gone out on patrol under its previous commanders, it had applied the practiced techniques of accomplished noisemakers, advertising its approach well in advance. The enemy seemed to appreciate this and graciously moved out of the way. No contact was made; no one got hurt.

Such behavior was about to change.

Christian gathered the men of Recon about him for his maiden speech. "Look, guys," he announced without preamble, "I'm taking over your outfit and I hate to tell you this, but I'm a prick. I'm airborne and I trained with the Special Forces at Fort Bragg. I've been running LRRPs missions and now we're gonna do what that unit was doing, and more. My job is to kill the other son of a bitch before he kills me, and that's your job also. We're gonna kill more enemy than any other unit in the division. And you know what? We're gonna have fun while we do it."

Well, he's got enthusiasm, thought Dennis Going.

Christian noticed that at least one man was paying attention, and he approached, asking, "Who are you?"

"My name is Going."

"Dong?"

"No, Going."

"Everybody should have a nickname," Christian declared. "You're Dong. Where you from?"

"Idaho."

"Good. You do what I tell you, Dong, and your ass will get back to Idaho, okay?"

"Yes, sir."

The others fidgeted noisily and shuffled their feet in the crimson dust. They traded glances that were knowing and conspiratorial. They had already ruined the budding careers of a number of young officers; this one should not pose a problem.

"I'm here to fight the enemy," Christian continued, trying to maintain a steely stance, searching for the words that would counter the insolent stares of the shit-burners. "I don't give a shit about communism," he declared. "I'm here to take my ass home and your ass home. You fight with me and we'll blow off their asses. You fight against me and I'll blow off your asses."

This brought no comment, so Christian added a pronouncement about his antidrug attitude. "I'll fight with you guys," he said. "I'll drink with you guys. I'll do everything with you, but I won't smoke with you."

A few eyebrows were raised, not at the obvious reference to a disapproval of the use of marijuana, but at the indication that the lieutenant *would* drink with them. Even over here, officers kept themselves aloof from the grunts. Whoever heard of a lieutenant drinking with his men?

Christian's eye settled on a tall, skinny but muscular, red-headed Italian-American, standing off to one side, who mumbled a wisecrack. The words "substitute teacher" and "King Kong" burned into the young lieutenant's ears and drew snickers from several men. The new CO realized intuitively that if he was going to be effective with this group of shit-burners, he would first have to squash this fellow.

At an even six feet tall, the insolent soldier stood a couple of inches above Christian. He was shirtless in the 100-degree sunlight, revealing a chest full of wiry red hair and a pair of tattoos, one on either shoulder, that reflected somewhat conflicting philosophies of life. "It's a groove," announced the message on his right shoulder. "All 4 one," proclaimed the other.

In his first twenty-one years, Max Marinelli had never been to a funeral, never seen a dead body. By now, after nearly three months "in country," he had seen—and smelled—enough death to last a lifetime. He had learned that one way to avoid the death that stalked this land was to act and talk like what was popularly called a "fuck-up." He was a relative newcomer to the shit-burners, but had quickly become a leader in Recon's general revolt against authority.

Christian regarded Marinelli's audacious stare for a moment, allowing the others to sense the meaning of the impending confrontation.

Marinelli smirked and glanced around, as if to say, "Here's the new HMFIC ("Head Motherfucker In Charge") and we'll eat him up, just like all the others." But his gaze returned to the lieutenant as Christian strode over purposefully and stood in front of him, staring up.

Two determined sets of eyes challenged one another unblinkingly, until Christian, not lowering his gaze, pulled his souvenir bayonet from his ammo belt. With a quick, unannounced thrust, he hurled the honed blade into the ground, less than an inch from the toe of Marinelli's boot.

"Hey!" Marinelli shouted. He jumped backed a step, despite his intention to stand firm. "What's the matter with you?"

Christian retrieved the bayonet, balanced its weight in his palm, and again rammed it into the dust between Marinelli's feet. "Think you're bad?" he taunted. He threw the bayonet a third time. "Think you're bad?"

"You're nuts, man, you're nuts," Marinelli declared, backing off further.

"Wanna fight?" Christian challenged.

"No man, you're nuts. I don't want to fight you." Marinelli kicked at the ground and shuffled his feet. "You're fuckin' nuts," he repeated.

The staring contest resumed beneath the hot Asian sun. Both men could sense, all about, the presence of the spectators, silently taking sides. Finally, saying nothing more, Marinelli dropped his gaze.

The next day, Marinelli went off on a scheduled five-day R&R. Christian knew he would have to deal with the man later. In the meantime, he had men to train.

The teenage commander prepared for his first mission with Recon like a college student cramming for finals. He studied intelligence reports carefully, seeking to determine the area where they were *least* likely to encounter the enemy. What he envisioned was a simple training mission, providing the opportunity to introduce the men to fighting techniques that were generally taught only to officers and specialists: how to read a map, how to call in artillery, mortar barrages, and air support, how to fire LAWs (Light Anti-tank Weapons), how to handle an explosive charge, and how to utilize captured enemy weapons.

About a day's march to the northeast was an isolated South Vietnamese village designated as "friendly"—although that distinction was always dubious—and Christian's attention centered upon it. The village had not been visited by Americans for some time. He could pretend that Recon's mission was to check it for any signs of enemy activity. Maps and intelligence photos covered his cot as he studied far into the night, memorizing the minutiae of the geography, paying particular attention to the locations of known enemy trails.

11

War Zone C, South Vietnam
August 1968

As Recon prepared to step out on its very first patrol under the new command, Christian ordered Sam Janney to carry the PR-25 radio, known informally as the "Prick-25." Janney regarded the heavy burden and replied insolently, "I don't really want to."

Previous commanders would have raged at this minor mutiny, but Christian said calmly, "Carry it for the first few 'clicks' [Kilometers] and then we'll give it to someone else, okay?"

Surprised at the combination of authority and deference in the licutenant's voice, Janney shrugged and responded, "Okay."

"Got a cigarette?" Christian asked.

Janney handed one over, wondering why he was suddenly cooperating with this man so much. Suddenly he confronted the lieutenant with a suspicion, asking, "How old are you, sir?"

Christian regarded the dark-haired, juvenile-faced soldier carefully. He saw intelligence in Janney's eyes, coupled with an irreverence for authority; the man was a possible obstacle. "Old enough," he responded, adding a bald-faced lie, "twenty-three." In truth he was now, at nineteen, the youngest first lieutenant in the U.S. Army, but he had no intention of admitting that to Janney or to any of the other shit-burners.

Recon headed from the base camp toward the bottom of the mountain, where a rice paddy guarded access to the northeastern stretches of the jungle. Here, Christian found himself challenged again, this time by Sergeant Jesse Lascano, the ranking NCO of the platoon, the man supposed to act as his commander's right arm.

An American Indian married to the daughter of his tribal chief, a star wrestler, a soccer player, and a career soldier, 33-year-old Lascano was the kind of gruff, unschooled hulk who learns that he can achieve a measure of power in the form of sergeant stripes if he just stays in the army long enough. He was about Christian's height, but stockier. The scar of a deep gash from some ancient encounter decorated one burly arm.

As the NCO in charge of Recon, Lascano was one of the few without a true shit-burner's mentality. He was anxious to build a good fighting record, partly due to a desire to bring honor to his Indian nation, and partly because his tribe had promised him a cash bonus for every medal he won in combat. He had vowed not to leave South Vietnam until he won at least a Purple Heart.

Lascano prided himself on the fact that his combat experience was greater than that of all the fuzzy-faced officers sent to handle Recon, and he threw down the gauntlet at the first opportunity. Just as Christian was ready to deploy the men in the configuration he wanted them to assume whenever they crossed a rice paddy, Lascano yelled out orders of his own, drowning out his CO's words. Grins on the shit-burners' faces announced that they were onto the power play.

"Come here, Jesse," Christian barked.

The Indian complied, glaring pointedly.

"I understand that you've got more combat experience than me," Christian acknowledged. "And I understand that you're good."

Lascano grinned, sensing that an audience was listening.

"But I'm better!" Christian railed, his words wiping the smirk off the sergeant's face. "If you ever, *ever*, tell me what to do in front of the men, I'll blow your fuckin' head off. Understand?"

"Yes, sir," Lascano mumbled. He took up his post at Christian's side, docile as a chastised puppy.

At the far end of the rice paddy, as the patrol stepped into the jungle, Christian began to lecture: "We will *not* travel through the jungle the way other American troops do." Most American units, dressed to the nines for combat, avoided the enemy's interlaced web of trails, fearful of booby traps, and plunged into the jungle instead, hacking away with machetes, advertising their approach by bashing their steel helmets into obstacles, and frequently becoming enmeshed in a hopeless tangle of wait-a-minute vines. Christian had learned more effective tactics on LRRPs' missions. "Who moves through the jungle more quietly and efficiently, the Americans or the Vietnamese?" he asked.

"Charlie," someone replied.

"Right. And why? Because he uses the trails. He can walk those trails safely because he knows how to recognize and avoid a booby trap. *You* will all learn how to spot a booby trap, and we will move into the jungle along the enemy's own trails. It's faster and quieter, and besides," he added with a grin, "that's where we're more likely to make contact."

They reached the quiet, hidden waters of the Dong Ny River and Christian said, "Smoke 'em if you got 'em." The men sat on the river bank, lit cigarettes, and prepared to relax, when their lieutenant struck up a conversation. Dong had to admit that Christian was right when he proclaimed, "You guys are a bunch of goof-offs." And he pricked up his ears when Christian suggested, "Let's train a little bit, okay?"

Christian posed an eerie and unanswerable question. He asked: "Suppose I get killed, right now. Can you survive without me?"

The men grew nervously silent, exhibiting a training phenomenon common to U.S. troops. Basic training—especially the frantic kind supplied at times like these, when the army was desperate for fresh bodies—often turned out troops capable only of following their leader. Aside from the fact that the leader could always be killed (after the radio operator, the unit commander was the enemy's prime target), too many of the leaders were incompetent themselves. "It's your life," Christian pointed out. "You'd better learn how to save it."

He pulled out a map and asked if anyone could show him where they were. The men gazed at it blankly. "You have to know where you are at all times," he declared. He proclaimed that awareness of geography was critical to any war, this one in particular. What were the strengths of the American troops? Certainly not numbers. The strengths were support, in the form of choppers, artillery fire, tactical bombing strikes, and awesome B-52 raids blasting away at the jungle. But to bring those advantages to bear upon the enemy, you had to know where you—and the enemy—were. Radio the wrong coordinates back to base camp and you might find your own artillery raining down on you.

A helicopter gunship armed with twenty-millimeter cannons can strafe every square inch of a football field in sixty seconds. "Wouldn't you rather guide it to the enemy than to your own position?" he asked rhetorically. It takes courage to tell the artillery boys to drop their range another twenty-five meters when you are only fifty meters away from the target, and that courage is born of the confidence that you know *exactly* where you are at all times.

And what if you simply get lost? If you can't read a map, you might head toward danger instead of safety.

"Look around," Christian advised. "Orient yourself. See what you can find here that you can also find on the map."

On the map, he located the river alongside them. Then he pointed to the surrounding hills, rising to different elevations, and he showed the men how to interpret the contour lines on the army map. "We have the best maps in the world," he said. "We've got to make use of them."

He gestured toward Janney and the Prick-25. "What if Janney gets killed?" he asked.

Janney's eyes grew wide.

"What if both Janney and I get killed? Anyone else know how to operate the radio?"

"Me," said pudgy, freckle-faced Rusty Baker.

"Okay, what if Baker, Janney, and I all get killed?"

This question was met with silence.

"The radio is your lifeline," Christian said. "Everyone *will* know how to use it."

He turned Janney and Baker into teachers. One by one the men gathered around and learned how to operate the Prick-25. Then Christian showed them a few tricks that even Janney and Baker did not know, such as how to take the trip wire from a Claymore and run it up into the trees, to extend the length of the radio antenna. He taught them about skip waves—how to bounce a radio signal off low-lying clouds and expand the communications range.

Recon was deep into the jungle when the silence of the late afternoon was interrupted by a muffled, high-pitched, rhythmic *beep-beep-beep* sound. "What the hell is that?" Christian asked.

Jim Lowe grinned and shut off the alarm on the prize wristwatch he had bought in Japan. "Five o'clock," he announced. "It's martini time, sir." Without further preamble, he poured a mixture of gin and vermouth from his canteen and offered Christian his choice of olives or onions from two separate tins. "We've got to have libation, sir," he explained. "Without libation, how can we fight this miserable, goddamn war?"

Christian regarded the slightly built private with consternation. The word "libation" was new to him, but he determined to hide this lapse in sophistication from his men. He guessed that it must be a synonym for martini.

Thin as a wire, fiercely independent, Lowe was a shit-burner all the way, but at the age of twenty-three, he was a bit older and slightly more world-wizened than most. He had avoided the draft for a few years by staying in college at Colorado State University and qualifying for a 2-S Selective Service rating. A taste of ROTC training was enough to convince him that he would hate the military. "I don't like taking orders," he explained simply.

But he jeopardized his student deferment when he dropped out of college to follow a young woman back to her home in Alaska. There, a U.S. marshal showed up at his door one day and asked, "You're James Kent Lowe?"

"Yes."

"You're not in school anymore?"

"No," Lowe admitted.

"You have three choices. Basic training at Fort Lewis. Go to Canada. Or try to elude us—if you get caught it's five years in jail." Lowe was on a morning flight to Fort Lewis.

Once in South Vietnam, it was his indefatigable habit to challenge the military's every nitpicking rule and regulation, and thus he was relegated to the shit-burners. "I can't believe the people they have in charge here," he had complained to his friend Max Marinelli. "They don't know how to read a map and they're leading men into battle." Lowe referred to Recon's previous commander as Sergeant Ignorance Personified.

Lowe would tell anyone who cared to listen that he was in South Vietnam for one reason: "I am over here to *survive*, put in my time, and get my ass out."

His was a typical Recon story. None of these men really wanted to be here, Christian included. But Lowe was the one who had most actively resisted the call to arms.

Now, his behavior raised a serious issue. Historically, alcohol is the number one tension release for all soldiers in all wars. Vietnam was no exception, yet it was popularizing a second form of anesthesia. Christian made clear his intolerance of drug use, but he knew that his men needed some means of escape from reality. He decided to allow Lowe to continue to bring "libation" into the field, so long as he partook of it only *after* they were sure that any and all combat engagements were over. "But, for God's sake, don't set the alarm on your watch," he said. Lowe agreed to the compromise.

In an attempt to forestall drug problems, Christian announced that if Lowe was going to indulge, every member of Recon should have the opportunity to enjoy libation in the field, and he quietly suggested that on future missions, everyone tote along a can or two of beer. That way, whenever they finished killing the enemy, they could libate on the spot.

The compromise was acceptable to Lowe, who explained, "We don't mean to throw a hell of a party out here. We just need to take the edge off things a bit." He again offered Christian a martini as a peace overture. "But you gotta give me back the olive," he said. "My aunt and uncle send me the olives from California. You can't get them over here."

Christian accepted.

All of this was counter to army regulations, but the men were beginning to realize that Christian was not the type of officer who always played by the rules.

In fact, he proved this conclusively early in the evening when they reached their objective, the "friendly" South Vietnamese village. He marched Recon past decrepit hootches fashioned of straw, mud, and crude lumber, and straight into the local bar, where he ordered *bom-de-bom* (three-three), the concoction that passed for beer in this godforsaken country. The bartender said he did not have any on hand, but he substituted a supply of Chinese beer.

Lascano found a dead mouse floating in his bottle.

"You gotta drink it, Jesse," Pete Andrews taunted, and the others took up the chant. The Indian, not a heavy drinker under ordinary circumstances, gritted his teeth, closed his eyes, and downed the rancid brew.

Then Christian joined the men for an impromptu swim in the Dong Ny River, allowing a South Vietnamese boy to guard their weapons. Cavorting in a game of "grab-ass," in which the objective was to dunk whomever was "it," they inadvertently overturned a small fishing boat and doused its papa-san. The old man rose from the water, spitting, sputtering, and cursing the Americans in an incomprehensible tongue. Christian tried to apologize and the men offered to help turn the boat right-side up, but the infuriated papa-san would have none of it.

Recon camped that night just outside the village. In the morning, after heating their coffee with C-4 plastic explosives, the men marched off to spend the day patrolling the surrounding countryside, searching for signs of VC or NVA activity. At one point midway through the morning, Lascano, sent off by himself to check out a side trail, radioed back to Christian, "I'm lost."

"Jesse, I think you're just one hill over from me," Christian whispered into his radio. "I need to know where you are so I can give you a compass heading."

"I'll fire a shot."

"You can't fire a shot," Christian warned. "Number one, I won't be able to tell which direction a shot comes from. Number two, you think I'm going to be the only one who hears that shot?" He suggested, "Jesse, make a noise like an animal. I'll be able to shoot an azimuth to the sound and direct you in."

A few minutes later Recon heard, rolling across the mountains: "Hee haw, hee haw. . . ."

As the rest of the men dissolved into laughter, Christian whispered angrily into his radio, "Jesse, you fucking idiot. There are no wild jackasses in the mountains!"

They linked up with Lascano and moved on, Christian's mind reeling. There were so many things he had to teach these men about combat. For one thing, he had to force them to unlearn much of their basic training. His personal philosophy in the face of an attack was at odds with conventional tactical theory, not to mention natural human reactions. When attacked, he lectured Recon, make a quick assessment of the situation and then, no matter what the odds, run like hell *toward* the enemy's strongest point. "It startles the opponent," he contended. "It catches the enemy off balance and scares the shit out of him."

He gave them a hypothetical scenario: Say you are caught in an ambush, a coordinated attack that has you pinned down, perhaps even trapped in a crossfire. If the enemy had the luxury of time, the ambush will be well planned, so that you find yourself in a lethal line of fire—known as the "kill zone"—with no possibility of escape. The natural human tendency is to find whatever cover you can, lay as low as possible, and pray for help. And because it is the natural thing to do, that is what the enemy will expect you to do.

"But think about it," Christian said. "If you stay there, you will die. So if you are going to die, you might as well go out in a blaze of glory. Charge the bastards!" You might still die, and if so, what's the difference? But you might also throw the enemy into disarray. It was important to think about such things now, calmly and rationally, he said, rather than waiting until it was too late. Should the situation occur, you simply will not have time for debate.

A corollary issue was noise. Traditionally, American soldiers are quiet fighters, and Christian sought to change that. "The problem," he told his men, "is that you don't know if the guy next to you is alive or dead. I want you to make noise, and lots of it. It's not natural, when someone is shooting at you, to jump up, scream, and start blazing away, but that's what I want you to do. I want you to whoop, holler, and scream like crazed banshees. If you don't manage to shoot the enemy, you might as well scare him to death."

It was Pete Andrews who spoke up. The buck sergeant was five feet six inches tall and weighed barely 120 pounds, but he possessed the purest killer instinct of any of the Recon troops, and he was clearly intrigued with this radical concept of war. Go on offense. Run straight at the buggers. Yell your guts out. He asked, "Sir, did they teach you these things in Special Forces school?"

"Nah," Christian replied with a grin. "I picked up all this from watching John Wayne movies."

Andrews glanced nervously at the others, and then broke into a smile. This new commander, he reasoned, was either totally bananas or a savvy bastard indeed—perhaps both.

Now Christian instructed the men to rehearse. They raced along jungle trails screaming, "Yaaaah!" "Heee-wooo!" "Ooooh yeah!" Andrews shouted, "Come on, you motherfuckers!"

Weapons training was critical. Like all American troops, Recon cursed the M-16 for its tendency to jam. It is an impotent feeling to face the enemy, pull the trigger, and hear nothing. But this was a problem with a solution, Christian announced. He told a story on himself, about how he had destroyed an M-16 the first time he had touched it. Since that time he had trained himself to become an expert, and he had learned an important secret.

The M-16 clip housed twenty bullets that could be fired out in a single, quick burst. But the designers had ignored or miscalculated the effects of that burst on the weapon itself. Twenty bullets were simply too many for the gun to handle at one time. If you filled the clip to capacity, those last two bullets often put a final strain on the spring, jamming the gun. The solution was to load the clip with only eighteen bullets. You lost two bullets from each clip, but you saved the rifle and, quite possibly, your life. And if you are using a banana clip with a thirty-round capacity, load only twenty-four bullets.

The shit-burners were amazed. This was life and death they were talking about. Dong wondered why no one else had ever explained the M-16 to them so simply.

Recon returned to the "friendly" village on the third day of its mission and encountered a Catholic priest, a South Vietnamese native, who professed great excitement at their arrival. He claimed that they were the first "round eyes" he had seen since the French had pulled out. He offered to sell the hungry Americans C rations—boneless chicken packed in water— for $33 a can. "That's one hell of a lot of money," Christian responded, "and this is our own army food."

The priest grinned serenely and offered no explanation as to his source.

Christian angrily moved his troops out, and used the opportunity to launch into yet another lecture, imparting information gleaned from his Special Forces training and his time with his previous unit. "You won't grow fat in the jungle, but you don't have to starve," he said. He showed them tart but tasty wild limes, growing profusely next to the Dong Ny River. He killed, cleaned, and cooked an ugly lizard, the kind that the men called "aggilators," which often spooked them by slithering suddenly from trees along the water's edge. There is nutrition in "aggilator" blood, he lectured. You have to boil it first, but then you can drink it.

Rabbit is the best of the wild meats, he said. You can rip the fur from a rabbit carcass with your teeth, making it easy to cook. A rabbit leaves few bones to dispose of, few signals of your presence. But never ignore such ever-present nutrition as frogs and tadpoles. Learn to catch them with your hands. If you can find tadpoles with half-decent tails on them, you cut off the tails, cook them in the bottom of a pan, shred them, and use them as a garnish on your dehydrated C rations.

The secret to all of this is spice. A good jungle fighter, Christian decreed, loves his cache of spices. Louisiana hot sauce is the best, able to turn any repugnant cuisine into a Cajun banquet.

Then there was a native salt supplement known as *Nookmom*. Its production was a local industry, and Christian explained how it was made. Vietnamese workers laid out fish by-products—heads, tails, and viscera—on a concrete slab, surrounded by a small moat. Another slab of concrete was laid on top, creating a sunoven to bake or more accurately, rot the contents. As rancid juices seeped out from between the concrete slabs, the Vietnamese harvested them and packaged them in jars. This was *Nookmom*. If you were out of Louisiana hot sauce and you could get past the smell, *Nookmom* was palatable.

As several of the shit-burners turned green faces aside, Christian proclaimed, "I love it."

In the jungle, water is life. Your body needs a couple of gallons a day just to survive. "It's as important as a rifle," Christian said. But it had to be good water or it could kill you as dead as the enemy could. Running water generally tasted good. Stagnant water, including that of the ubiquitous rice paddies, was generally bad. The army supplied iodine tablets for purification but, combined with the metallic or plastic quality the canteens gave the water, they made the water nearly intolerable. Christian suggested adding a squeeze of fresh lime.

He cautioned his men against the threat of ptomaine poisoning, and shared with them a technique that he had learned as a boy of fourteen when he had landed a brief job on a decrepit clam boat, the *Althea*, that prowled the Jersey coast. The *Althea*'s water container was a fifty-gallon drum, full of rust. The sailors taught Christian how to drink through clenched teeth, filtering the rust and spitting it out. The same technique, Christian said, could filter out fly larvae, worms, and other threats that lurked in the Vietnamese water supply.

That afternoon, as Recon patrolled a quiet trail, Dong suddenly saw Christian hold up a hand to signal silence. His eyes or his ears had detected something out here where he had expected no action. With gestures he moved Recon off the trail and into the jungle. Dong's eyes searched ahead, where the trail branched off at a small intersection, but he could see nothing.

Moments passed, and the men grew restless. But then, just as they seemed ready to break discipline with a barrage of wisecracks, a small enemy patrol moved into view, stopped at the juncture of the trails, and checked the a map.

Ernie May counted five of them, and he saw something else that bothered him. He whispered into Christian's ear, "Two of them are women. We can't shoot women."

"What are we supposed to do," Christian whispered back, "say 'ladies' first' and let them go before we kill the others? They're carrying rifles."

Recon watched for a moment, hoping that the patrol would move directly toward them, but when it became obvious that the enemy was ready to move off in another direction, Christian gave the order. Recon opened fire and the enemy scattered quickly.

Without hesitation Christian jumped up in pursuit, his M-16 blazing away, his mouth first issuing a blood-chilling rebel yell and then screaming, "You wanna fight? Fight like soldiers! Number ten. Number *ten!*"

He chased the five enemy troops up the trail for a distance of about two football fields, gunning down two of them in the back. When he was satisfied that the others had fled, he stopped to examine the two bodies. Only then did he realize that he was alone. The rest of Recon was still back in the safety of the jungle brush.

He searched the corpses for intelligence material, but settled for a couple of souvenir cans of American C rations. The labels said that they contained boneless chicken, packed in water.

Dong sat open-mouthed, still amazed at the cowboylike display of bravado, as Christian returned and exhibited his captured treasures. "These came from the village," he announced. "We're going back there."

They followed their trail map back to the village, where Christian, in a voice filled with fury, called out the priest. In the midst of the street, he threw down the damning C ration cans and accused, "We know this stuff came from your village."

"No," the priest said firmly.

"Yes."

"No."

Christian fingered the trigger of his M-16. "Yes!"

The priest paled and whispered, "No."

"Number ten!" Christian raged, pointing an accusing finger, as he uttered the worst Vietnamese insult he knew. "You are number ten [the Oriental designation for "the worst"]. We have to kill you."

"Please," the priest begged. "I will not help them anymore."

There was no way of knowing that the priest would comply with his promise, of course, but Recon, in the position of playing God, could not bring itself to execute a man of the cloth.

They spent a final night in the jungle, encamped near the river. In the morning, Christian separated Recon into two groups, one to stand guard as the other romped in the stream. It was 9 A.M. when Christian radioed the base camp and requested that choppers be sent out to pick them up.

"We're pretty busy," reported a bored voice. "It'll take about four hours to get them ready."

"To hell with it," Christian said. "We'll walk back."

As he switched off the radio, Baker asked, "How far is it?"

"Seventeen clicks."

Groans greeted this announcement, but Christian predicted, "We'll be back by dinner time. Okay?"

It was that last word, the pleasant "okay," that impressed Lowe. Lowe had previously told a couple of commanders to "blow it out your ass," but he realized now that Christian had a very different style, a strange way of "asking" an order. He would tell you what to do, then add that little "okay" so that you had at least an illusion that you participated in the decision. It made a big difference.

Midway through the day Lascano stumbled upon a booby trap. It was an enemy Claymore, fashioned out of a trash can lid, containing fragments of broken glass and scrap metal. The men were lucky, for the Claymore was set to explode away from them. No one was killed, but stray shrapnel fragments caught several of the men. For his part, Lascano was satisfied that he had now qualified for a Purple Heart.

Once Christian determined that none of the injuries was serious, he ordered Recon forward. His own fatigue shirt was crimson across the left side of his belly, but he perceived another teaching opportunity. He strode off on the trail, purposely, silently delivering the lesson that true warriors ignore bullshit wounds.

Lowe, for one, had no wish to be left behind, alone in the jungle. Quickly he took off after the leader, and the others stumbled forward, too.

By late afternoon, they stood at the base of a mountain, perhaps 800 or 900 feet high, blanketed with jungle foliage. "We gotta go around," Lascano muttered.

"No," Christian dictated. "The NDP is right on the other side. We go around the mountain, we're gonna miss dinner. We go over the mountain."

"But there are no trails, sir." This time, Lascano's challenge was delivered very mildly, and with the proper etiquette.

"There's a trail about fifty meters ahead," Christian announced with finality, as though he had a crystal ball in his head. "C'mon, I'll show you." In fact, he remembered from his map study before the mission that there was a trail around here somewhere—he hoped that fifty meters was a good guess.

Leaving the others behind, Christian and Lascano moved forward, pushing their way through the dense foliage. Just about fifty meters forward, they found the trail.

"As advertised," Christian said with a grin.

Lascano scratched his head and determined never to challenge his CO again.

They called Recon forward and made their way easily up the trail and across the mountain. Behind him as he walked, Lascano could hear the murmur of excited voices. How did the lieutenant know the trail would be there?

12

Nui Ba Cam, South Vietnam
August 1968

As Christian continued to take the men out in small groups on training missions, word spread through the battalion that he was turning the shit-burners into an elite fighting unit, and this gave him the opportunity to audition candidates. In particular, Recon was in need of a new medic.

"Doc" Carnavelli, the present medic, had been transferred temporarily to the shit-burners as he awaited a hearing on charges of cowardice in the face of the enemy, arising from his refusal to treat his wounded commanding officer. "I was treating other men, sir," Carnavelli explained. "They were hurt worse. The captain yelled at me to forget about them and take care of him, and I refused." Christian had seen enough of the military to believe the story, and he was amazed to learn that while Carnavelli's former CO had charged him with cowardice, others had nominated him for the Bronze Star for his actions during the very same battle. Now, he was ordered to Long Binh, the massive staging base for U.S. troops, for his day in court. (In the course of time he was exonerated and awarded his Bronze Star.)

Several men sought to join up with the renovated Recon, including James Scott, a medic from Rochester, New York, whom the shit-burners knew well, for he had once been one of them. Christian was impressed that Scotty was an infantryman as well as a medic. Unlike some other corpsmen, Scotty carried a full load of weaponry with him and fought furiously until his medical services were required. The negative was a rumor that Scotty was a pothead.

Another candidate for the medic post was the son of a sergeant major, a small-boned boy who, during a brief interview with Christian, repeatedly tossed his penknife into the ground at his feet and mumbled that he wanted to kill a lot of "dinks."

Some choice, Christian thought: a pothead or a psycho. He chose Scotty, because the men wanted him back, but he warned, "If I ever catch you smoking pot, I'll have your ass."

Another former shit-burner applied for reinstatement. He was a light-skinned Polish-American boy, James Guest, and Christian was not so sure that Recon could afford to take him back. The shit-burners, maligned as they were, had basic potential. They were streetwise kids, and Christian could discern within each of them a core of untapped responsibility. Guest did not seem to fit the mold. In particular, Christian was bothered by the persistent story that Guest, after killing an NVA soldier, had beheaded his victim, brought the skull back to camp, cleaned it of flesh, polished it, and treasured it as a souvenir.

Even in war, Christian theorized, there are certain things that neither God nor man can tolerate, and if you crossed that line, you invited retribution. One of these proscriptions is mutilation of the victim. You had to regard the enemy as an honorable foe, undeserving of desecration. Christian was dubious about accepting Guest back into Recon, partly on the strength of the rumor, partly from his reaction to the expression in the man's eyes.

He deferred a decision, saying simply, "We'll have to see whether or not I like you." But what really made up his mind was this: the men of Recon did not want him back.

Remaining noncommittal, Christian sent the man away, and two days later, while on patrol with his own platoon, Guest stepped on a land mine and was killed. Christian was a believing Roman Catholic, although his faith was more dormant than practical. He was also enough of a patriot to place credence in the belief that God was, if not an American, at least an anti-Communist. He was convinced that God kept the final score in battle, and expected the soldier to live up to certain rules of human decency.

As September approached, Christian reported to his superior, infantry battalion commander Lieutenant Colonel James M. Hanson, that the men were ready. He then confessed to Recon that until now he had kept them in a rehearsal mode. The missions to date had all been contrived, planned to keep contact with the enemy to a bare minimum. Now that phase was over. He beamed at the men and proclaimed, "You are soldiers now. We are Spartans. We will split up into small teams and go out to kill the enemy."

He was delighted to see them return the smile, and nod in agreement.

13

War Zone C, South Vietnam
September 1968

"Notify the tower that we're moving out, okay?" Christian said to Rusty Baker. It was early in September 1968, and the sun was merciless, even early in the morning.

The eight-man Recon patrol stepped forward, past the lookout towers that formed a protective barrier around the NDP. They were in no-man's land now, in the northwest portion of War Zone C, and for the rest of the mission, Baker was to confirm their position with the camp at five-minute intervals, so that everyone else would know where there were. The last thing anybody wanted was to be killed by friendly fire.

Lascano led the way as point man, followed by Baker, Christian, and Pete Andrews. Behind them came Wild Bill Divoblitz, a Baltimore native, with a golden-blond, twirled mustache that earned him the additional nickname of Gabby Hayes; "Gooney" Koenig, a Midwestern, dusty-blond kid; and Jim Lowe, with his ever-present canteen of libation. At rear guard was Spec 4 Milam, a Louisiana good ol' boy with a slow, lilting Southern twang to his voice.

The heat was intolerable. The trudge through the "roam plough," the kilometer-wide swath that bulldozers had blazed around the camp, developed into a silent endurance test for the men. Every step through the uneven earth, the felled trees, the scrubby foliage fighting for survival against the Agent Orange treatments, was a struggle. Baker thought that he was in pretty good shape, but Lascano set a killing pace, and Baker began to wonder if he was even going to make it past the first mild leg of their trek. Five minutes more, he told himself, and we'll be through this plough and into the jungle thickets. It'll be easier to move there, along the trails.

But five minutes passed and they seemed no closer to the jungle cover. Baker was nearly at the point of admitting his exhaustion when a sudden heavy rain began to fall, blessed, cooling. He raised his face toward the heavens, let the pure water cascade over him, and silently thanked a merciful God.

Christian loved the rains; they made for good hunting. All sound was muffled. In the silence of the rain, you could walk right up to a man and cut his throat or strangle him, and no one else would know.

Once in the jungle, Christian located a trail and the men moved forward quickly, wordlessly. Only a few feet past the roam plough the world became a secretive, sinister place. The enemy could be anywhere. The men knew that by trudging along the enemy's very own trail, chances of contact were increased at least tenfold.

They marched at a steady, sturdy pace, ahead for several clicks without a break, until, sometime after the rains had passed, Christian stopped them at a fork. He pointed out footprints in the mud that resembled the tire tracks of a jeep. In fact, they were tire tracks, for tires were the source of the soles of the Ho Chi Minh sandals worn by the NVA. These were fresh; the enemy had passed here only recently.

"We are hunting," Christian lectured in a whisper. "We are hunting other human beings, the shrewdest animals in the world. We are hunting someone who has reason and brains, and they are hunting us. But they can make mistakes, and we want to learn from those mistakes. These tracks," he said, pointing with the barrel of his M-16, "are mistakes. They'll lead us right to the enemy."

Recon trudged forward, following the tracks, edging further away from the safety of its own forces.

After a time, the trail widened perceptibly, a clear signal that they were approaching an area where troops were concentrated. Christian was pleased; intelligence reports had indicated the possibility of an enemy base camp just ahead of their present position. They moved now with even more stealth, creeping up on whatever lay ahead. To a man, their hearts beat faster.

Radio contact with HQ grew fuzzy, a combination of the effects of distance, terrain, and atmospheric conditions. Christian knew that it was time to split his patrol in order to maintain his lifeline with the base camp. He decided to leave four troops here to man a relay station. Up ahead, at a bend in the trail, he saw a canopy of trees that formed a secure and advantageous post.

But as Recon reached this spot, the men were surprised to find a small pile of clothing—enemy uniforms—along with Russian-made weapons, four AK-47 rifles and a pair of RPGs (rocket-propelled grenade launchers). From a short distance away, off to one side, came the sounds of men at play. Weapons at the ready, Recon crept toward the noise.

"I can't believe we're doing this shit," Baker muttered, as he parted the elephant grass to peer through at four North Vietnamese troops, clad only in bikini briefs, who splashed happily in cool, spring-fed water. By happenstance, a bomb had carved out a crater in the midst of a stream, forming a pool.

These four must have strayed outside the perimeter of the base camp for an impromptu swimming party. In another time and place they would have been simple teenagers, romping in a pond. But this was Southeast Asia in 1968; who knew how many Americans these boys had already killed?

With hand signals, Christian indicated that he and two others would deal with the prey. His choices were instinctive. Lascano was the bull, the heavy who could overcome on brute strength alone. Pete Andrews was the cat, swift and cool.

The three men stripped, grabbed their field knives, and slipped silently from the cover of elephant grass into the water at a point shaded by trees. They kicked off from the bank and caught the NVA troops by surprise. Christian thrust his knife into the naked abdomen of one man and twisted it. He heard a muffled cry and caught a quick glimpse of terror in the dying man's eyes. Within moments, all struggle ceased. He pulled his knife out with a quick, backward tug, and the body of his victim slipped beneath red-clouded water.

Only then did he glance around to see that Andrews had taken care of one of the others; Lascano had killed two.

Back on the bank, naked, high on adrenaline, Christian whispered quick instructions. Baker would stay here with his radio, along with Divoblitz, Koenig, and Lowe. Christian would lead the other three ahead.

Baker took a twenty-five-foot section of Claymore wire and tossed it over a tree limb. The jerry-rigged antenna immediately improved the quality of his reception on the Prick-25.

Christian, Andrews, Milam, and Lascano dug through the pile of enemy uniforms, pulling on ill-fitting shirts and strapping on ammo pouches. They hefted the Russian-made weapons and grinned over their booty. These were valued trophies of war. Andrews was especially pleased with the liberation of the grenade launchers. The newer model RPG was equipped with so-phisticated electric-eye sighting gear. It held the potential for creating great havoc.

"Let's go," Christian said.

Not far from the bomb crater, the trail widened enough so that the four men could walk abreast. The dirt here was thick with the tracks of Ho Chi Minh sandals.

The four-man Recon patrol flitted past piles of fresh human feces at the side of the trail, along with the residue of toilet paper, U.S. Army issue.

They rounded a slight bend and found themselves staring directly into the perimeter of an enemy camp. Beyond stretched an operations base that appeared to be formidably huge. Dozens of NVA troops lolled around here at the periphery, some of them playing cards, others simply relaxing against the side of a bunker, taking in the sun. One man was cutting the hair of another. None of them appeared to be carrying weapons.

Their lack of concern with security was an indication of the poor job U.S. troops were doing in War Zone C. The enemy felt safe enough to relax its defenses, to swim in bomb craters and lie in the sun. They would be easy prey. Christian realized that he could not have planned a more effortless combat engagement.

An enemy soldier glanced up, saw the four men approaching in NVA uniforms, toting Russian weapons, and raised his hand in greeting.

"Look, guys," Christian whispered incredulously, "they're waving at us. They must think we're their friends who went swimming. Fuckers need glasses." The moment of surprise was at hand. "Start waving," Christian commanded. Then: "Start shooting!"

Andrews dropped to a knee and fired a grenade from one of the captured RPGs. He scored a direct hit on the bunker.

Three heavily armed grunts and a cowboy officer raced forward, screaming rebel yells, their rifles blazing away at an unsuspecting foe. Fourteen enemy soldiers were cut down quickly. They lay on the ground, dead and dying, before any of their companions realized what was happening. The survivors took to their heels, jumping up and across the berm at the edge of a perimeter trail, running for their lives toward the more protected inner areas of the base camp.

Andrews was exhilarated by the success of the brief contact and was ready to rush forward, into the main body of the camp.

"No!" Christian snapped. He sifted the evidence quickly. The trail was wide, the footprints thick. "There are too many of them. We've got to pull back." As quickly as the attack had begun, it was ended.

Recon retreated before the enemy could regroup and mount a counter-attack. The men raced back to the radio relay station, picked up their four comrades, and moved quickly to a post a few clicks distant, walking on the brush at the side of the trail to avoid leaving footprints of their own.

As they set up camp to await the night, Christian ordered Baker to call for a B-52 strike on the coordinates of the enemy camp. Somewhere in Thailand, air crews scrambled, preparing to assault the area, dropping their murderous explosives from 40,000 feet.

The shit-burners waited, straining their ears to hear the aircraft approach, even though they knew the bombers would be too high to signal their presence. Forty-five minutes passed before they heard the first dull thud. The sound grew steadily into the reverberating symphony of death that all U.S. combat troops referred to as "rolling thunder."

Even at this distance, Recon could feel the earth vibrate. The men glanced around at one another, squinting to see in the darkness, thankful that their commander had not screwed up the map coordinates, awed by what they had accomplished.

In the morning, Christian could sense a dramatic change in his men. They strode up the trail with a bit of a swagger in their step as they moved back toward the area of the enemy base camp to link up with the "battalion-minus" force (four combat companies) and lead them in to conduct a bomb damage assessment. For this mopping up mission, Recon was merely to be a subordinate unit, under the command of the CO of Bravo Company.

It was another sultry day. Before long, they paused for a quick break. "Thirsty, sir?" Lowe asked Christian, offering his canteen.

In the jungle this was a redundant question. Christian nodded, accepted the canteen, took a vigorous swig, and choked as the gin burned into his throat.

"You're supposed to sip it, sir," Lowe advised.

Christian glowered at him.

Recon stalked the trail warily, unsure of what lay ahead. Baker was attempting to raise contact with Bravo Company, which had to be near, when a sudden barrage of rifle fire assaulted Recon's flank. Bullets tore into the underbrush and ricocheted off rocks. The men scrambled for cover and pulled their weapons to their shoulders, searching for a glimpse of the enemy, ready to jump up, scream, and charge. It was all real again, that ghastly prospect of instant death. How many are there? Andrews wondered. Christ, *where* are they? How can you shoot someone you can't see, let alone charge at them?

Baker raised Bravo Company and Christian grabbed the radio. As his eyes checked his men, noting no casualties, he reported. "We've just come under fire. . . ."

The Bravo Company commander responded immediately, his voice revealing the excitement of the hunt. He said, "We've just encountered. . . ."

Christian heard confusion in the background, and instantly he realized what was happening. "Get your guys off our ass!" he shouted into the radio, "Or we're gonna shoot back."

The assaulting rifle fire ceased abruptly. After a few moments, the radio voice said, in a subdued tone, "Sorry."

Janney saw deadly fire in Christian's eyes, but the lieutenant suppressed his rage. It was better to deal with these issues after the mission was over. "We're going into the enemy camp," he reported over the radio.

The Bravo Company captain bristled at this, for he wanted to be the one to lead the way. He called Christian over to his position, where they argued over a map, debating their location. Christian soon realized that the supposed commander of this mission had no idea where he was. Still smarting over the "friendly" barrage of rifle fire, he stalked off, declaring that Recon was breaking from its assigned position as point for Bravo Company. "We're going to the enemy camp," he repeated, and added over his shoulder, "We'll see you there, if you can find it."

Recon moved ahead quickly, soon passing the bomb crater where it had claimed its first four victims, and on toward the camp.

It appeared to be deserted. The enemy had probably anticipated the B-52 strike and abandoned its position, but you could never be sure. At the outer perimeter, where they had gunned down fourteen soldiers yesterday, all was quiet. Now they would move across an elevated trail and into the main body of the camp.

Christian poked his head over the berm and froze. His nose was inches away from a Claymore, a parting gift left by the NVA troops. His right arm was entangled in wait-a-minute vines, so dangerously close to the trip wire that he dared not attempt to pull back. He turned his head slightly, mouthed the words, "Don't move," and felt as if his heart had leaped upward from his chest. "I'll get my head blown off if anybody moves," he whispered.

His left hand reached gingerly to his belt, his fingers groping for the Claymore wire clippers that hung there. Struggling to exercise control over his muscles, to eliminate any unnecessary vibration, he inched the tool upward to the wire. About him, the jungle was as silent as death. Even the birds seemed to be holding their breath. Is this my last moment? he wondered. Gritting his teeth, he severed the fuse of the electrically detonated charge and waited for oblivion.

I'm still alive, he realized. Slowly he let the air out of his lungs. He wiped perspiration from his brow, and ordered the men forward, cautiously.

Cries of "goddamn," "shit," and "what the fuck" flew from the lips of the shit-burners as they viewed the scene of yesterday's fight, and the most vocal of the expletives came from the four men most responsible for this carnage. The camp, hidden by dense jungle, was surprisingly huge. Recon found itself striding through a ghost town with a circumference of at least a mile. It was a complete enemy rendezvous point outfitted with elaborate mess halls—some with cooking equipment still set up—a full-size hospital, and a recreation center. It was one of the largest NVA base camps ever found in South Vietnam. Had they known its magnitude yesterday, would they—a four-man unit against hundreds or thousands—have dared to attack?

The realization of what Recon had accomplished brought a growing sense of boldness. If the enemy had left a contingent behind to wait in ambush, the patrol would already be decimated, so they moved through the camp quickly, victorious pirates in search of booty.

By radio, Christian reported to the Bravo Company commander that Recon had reached the enemy operations center.

"How the hell did you get there so fast?" the commander questioned. "Goddamn it, I was supposed to be there first."

Christian stifled a chuckle, knowing that Bravo Company was probably becoming more entangled in the jungle with each passing minute.

Andrews found a hootch wallpapered with posters of Ho Chi Minh. He riddled one of them with bullet holes, and had turned his gun on another when Lowe yelled, "Hold it! We send this stuff home for souvenirs. We can make some money off of it, man." Lowe yanked several posters from the dirty walls, folded them up, and stashed them carefully in his backpack.

The two men wandered outside and considered a North Vietnamese flag that lay placidly against its pole, limp in the stagnant heat. Lowe grinned, pulled it down, and added it to his souvenir collection. As he ran Recon's tiny twelve-by-fourteen-inch souvenir American flag up the pole, his face beamed with pride, an incongruous display of patriotism from an erstwhile draft dodger.

Baker reported that he had found a fresh grave site, mounded like an anthill, roped off with vines and festooned with spiritual trinkets. Christian respected the way this enemy policed its dead, and had no intention of tampering with the burial ground. But when he reported the finding over the radio, the Bravo Company commander ordered, "Dig it up." Christian protested, but the captain was insistent. There was a note of condescension in his voice as he warned, "The grave could be a disguised weapons cache."

"We're a recon outfit, sir," Christian argued. "We're not equipped to dig up graves."

The radio crackled with the terse reply: "Use your hands."

"Fuck you!" Christian growled.

Dong gasped. Christian was a cheeky bastard, but this was a bit much. No junior officer could get away with this. Then he grinned as Christian turned to show the men that he had released the transmitter button. The captain had not heard the final comment.

"Excuse me, sir," Andrews interjected. "But I don't think you should have said that. You should have said, 'Fuck you, sir!' "

Chuckles turned to frustration as the men dropped to their knees and began the distasteful task of scraping away at the loose dirt of the mass grave. Andrews and Dong dug silently. Baker muttered, "That captain is an asshole."

The soil gave way easily under Christian's fingers. As he dug, he wondered if the Bravo Company commander might be right. This enemy *was* devious enough to disguise a weapons cache as a grave site.

His fingers struck something firm. "Ah, a gun," he murmured. He worked with increased vigor until, suddenly, a human hand, as stiff and cold as steel, poked through the soil. He jumped back. Behind him, he heard Baker retch. He grabbed the radio and called, "Bravo 6, this is Victor 6, over."

"Bravo 6. What's up, lieutenant? Over."

"Captain, they are bodies, you idiot!" This time he left the transmit button depressed as he spat out the words.

They left the buried bodies where they were and turned their attention to the visible corpses that littered the area, the remains of those men unlucky enough to be on the wrong end of a B-52 strike. Working in two-man teams, Recon lugged the bodies on litters to a central point in the camp and tossed them onto a growing pile. The chore was unsavory at first, but, as time passed, the stultifying effects of routine broke the tension. Too much of anything—even death—dulls sensibilities. Recon could respect the memory of the enemy, but not his physical remains. These were no longer human beings; they were simply fragments of war that had to be cataloged for the scorecards kept by the brass.

The men of Recon whistled and laughed as they labored beneath the brutalizing sun. They conducted an informal competition to see who could direct the most obscene remarks at Bravo Company, still lost in the jungle.

Lowe was investigating a bunker when he noticed a tattered blanket tacked up on one of the walls. His senses came alert, for such a blanket was often used to cover a tunnel entrance. As Recon's "tunnel rat," Lowe had checked out these things before, and had developed a method of operation. Pulling out his flashlight and his snub-nosed .38—a gift from his sister—he sidled up to the blanket. Standing off to one side, he reminded himself of the drill: if you see anything move—anything at all—empty your .38 into it and ask questions later.

His left hand, grasping the flashlight, reached over and tugged the blanket away. Immediately he jumped in front of the tunnel entrance and flashed his light down the shaft. There, three feet in front of his face, sat a Vietnamese man, hunched over. Lowe felt his eyes grow as large as silver dollars, but he did not fire. With a shriek, the Vietnamese man crawled quickly away into the tunnel as Lowe turned and ran out of the bunker.

"There's a goddamn gook in there!" he reported to Christian.

Was this a setup? Christian wondered. Had the enemy left a sleeper behind to detonate some secret explosives cache at just the right moment? NVA troops were known for their zealous devotion to the cause. To die in battle was the highest honor; this made it easy to recruit suicide commandos.

Christian reconnoitered. He estimated that the tunnel was fifty meters long, stretching from the tactical operations center in the midst of the camp out to a perimeter bunker. Who could be down there? What could they do about him?

"We have enemy activity in the tunnels," he reported to Bravo Company. "Unknown numbers. Unknown arms and equipment. Suggest we burn them out with Willie Peters."

"You will take them alive," Bravo 6 commanded. Was there a hint of jealousy in the captain's voice? Christian wondered. Was Recon's triumph of yesterday so galling that today's commander was desperate for trophies of his own, prisoners of war whom he could deliver to Intelligence?

Christian tried to explain: "Look, we've got a guy in a tunnel, and I'm gonna kill him. I'm not gonna sacrifice a guy to go get him."

"Don't kill him," the captain ordered.

"What do you mean? I'm just gonna throw a grenade into the tunnel."

"No! I'm ordering you to go into the tunnel."

Christian considered the problem. What was in the tunnel? More Claymores? Men? Who? And how many? He concluded that going into that tunnel was sure to cost a life.

Lowe stepped up and announced, "I'm going in after him." He grinned and suggested, "Let's get this shit over with so we can have some libation."

"Okay," Christian agreed. "First, throw smoke grenades into the tunnel so we can find the end of the damn thing. I'll try to come in the other end and meet you in the middle."

Lowe reentered the bunker and remembered with a shiver all the stories he had heard about the NVA leaving scorpions and snakes behind in the tunnels. He dropped to his hands and knees and began to crawl. Shining his flashlight down the narrow, elongated shaft, he spotted the silhouette of the Vietnamese man, resting on his haunches, a long way off, maybe fifty meters. He called out, using his limited Vietnamese vocabulary, ordering the man to come out immediately.

When the man failed to respond, Lowe heaved purple and yellow smoke grenades ahead into the tunnel. Still the man sat impassively.

Up above, Christian saw colored smoke filtering out of a hole on the surface where a B-52 hit had opened up the tunnel. Armed only with a knife, he dropped inside and began to squirm his way toward Lowe.

The passageway was about three feet high and two feet wide, a difficult place for the small-boned Vietnamese soldier to negotiate and even more formidable for an American. The darkness was total. Christian crawled his way cautiously along the narrow subterranean trail, groping with his hands, listening intently. For many moments, the only sound he heard was that of his own pulse. He waited for a knife blade to penetrate his belly. He thought: My heartbeat is so strong, it's going to give me away.

The smoke made vision impossible and breathing difficult. He estimated that he had traveled about half the length of this hellhole, crawling forward like a blind man, when, suddenly, he touched human warmth. "Lowe!" he growled, "is that your arm?"

"No, sir," came a distant voice from the far end of the tunnel.

The enemy sounded a piercing shriek that echoed off the subterranean walls. He lashed out with arms and legs, pushed away from Christian, and scrambled in Lowe's direction. Christian followed the smaller man as rapidly as he could.

Coughing and sputtering, the man finally crawled into Lowe's arms, followed by Christian.

Cursing at their scrappy foe, the two Americans labored toward the tunnel entrance with their burden. Their chests heaved with exertion. Grenade smoke threatened to eliminate the available oxygen.

When they finally tumbled out into the bunker and then climbed up into the blinding sunlight, cheers erupted from the shit-burners. Lowe, framed in colored smoke billowing from the bunker entrance, displayed the prisoner, whom he held by the arm with a viselike grip.

"Holy shit!" Christian muttered as his eyes adjusted to the daylight. The hard-won POW was nothing more than a blind old man, abandoned by the retreating NVA army. His skin was mottled with purple and yellow smoke powder. He probably weighed less than ninety pounds and looked to be about sixty-five years old, although age was difficult to estimate in a race of people who had lived such a harsh existence.

Lowe released his grasp and the old man dropped to the ground, grabbing crazily at his feet. The toughened skin of his soles was actually smoldering.

"No wonder he was screaming," Lowe said. "He must have stepped on a smoke grenade." Instinctively, Lowe reached for his canteen to douse the fire on the old man's feet, but then he realized that the alcohol would merely add to the man's agony. He borrowed another canteen, and threw water onto the feet of the pitiful, blind old soldier. "What the hell are we going to do with him?" he asked Christian. "We're Recon. We can't take prisoners. Do we have to kill him, sir?"

"No, Lowe," Christian replied. "We'll carry him on our backs to camp. They'll take him to the POW compound."

Lascano searched the man's pockets and "liberated" a cigarette lighter with the NVA 271 designation on it. With a satisfied grin, he pocketed the war trophy.

By the time Recon finished its bomb damage assessment, there was still no sign of Bravo Company. By radio, the captain reported that they were returning to base and Recon was to do likewise. The shit-burners shared a laugh over the obvious but unstated fact that Bravo 6 could not read a simple jungle map—something *they* could all do.

Before they pulled out, Recon placed all the captured explosives and equipment into a bunker. They set plastic C-4 explosive in place, along with a blasting cap and a fuse, and detonated the arsenal. It blew with a satisfying roar.

Christian hoisted the prisoner on his shoulders and strode off. The blind man clung tenaciously to the back of his protector and wrapped his legs around the American's waist.

Only as they neared the edge of the jungle leading to the NDP did Recon finally link up with Bravo Company. The frustrated captain glanced at the frail, blind old Vietnamese man, for whom Lowe and Christian had jeopardized their lives, and vented his wrath. He had spent a futile day lost in the steamy jungle, and he was aware that his men as well as Recon were laughing behind his back. The prisoner was hardly a threat of any kind, but he was the first enemy that the company had encountered all day. The captain asked in a terse and tired voice, "Should we kill him?"

"No, you're not gonna kill him," Christian declared.

The embittered captain regarded the insubordinate lieutenant as if he were a traitor, but Christian simply turned away and addressed the men of Bravo Company. "You men aren't soldiers if you want to kill this poor old guy," he said. "He's just an old soldier someone left behind. Besides, he's a POW and he could be valuable for information. This prisoner is more valuable alive than dead."

Without a further word, Christian carried the prisoner off as, from all around, he heard hostile shouts.

"Fuckin' gook!"

"We should blow your brains out!"

Christian knew that the old codger could not understand the words, but the tone was clear. He also knew that NVA propaganda must have convinced this man that Americans tortured their prisoners. Perhaps it was true. Wasn't this torture?

Halfway across the roam plough, Lascano relieved his lieutenant, carrying the burden the rest of the way.

When they finally trudged back across the perimeter into the NDP and turned their charge over to Intelligence personnel, Christian began to offer an explanation of his capture. But Lascano interrupted, not to countermand his commander; rather, to praise him. He told the story of how Christian and Lowe had voluntarily traversed the scary tunnel, and he suggested that both men should be put in for medals.

Christian was given a reward greater than any medal when the blind old man groped forward, seeking his hand. The ancient Vietnamese soldier mumbled, struggling for vocabulary. "American number one," he said, as he drew the lieutenant's palm next to his cheek.

14

Lai Khe Base Camp, South Vietnam
September 1968

Gunnar Pawlata, nicknamed "Ace" after a tattoo on his arm, possessed an athlete's V-shaped upper torso—broad, muscular shoulders tapered to a wasp waist. His German-born father had fought on this turf as a member of the French Foreign Legion, when the country was known as Indochina, and Pawlata frequently boasted, "My old man got shot in the ass here."

Thus far, Pawlata was morose and frustrated with the conduct of the war. He was a grunt with Alpha Company, which he considered to be so incompetent and wimpish that he referred to it derisively as Alice Company. For one thing, he believed that the unit was too large to accomplish much in a jungle arena. They would move out on patrols nearly 200 strong, bashing and crashing their way through the brush. None of the troops knew where they were going or what they were trying to accomplish. If contact was made with the enemy, only one portion of the company was likely to be involved, and you had to run a gauntlet through straggling soldiers just to get in on the fight.

Nevertheless, it was natural for Pawlata to foster what little sense of camaraderie there was within Alice Company. He grew up in Pottstown, Pennsylvania, where friendship came in small, loyal cliques, and where you defended the honor of your buddies. One day, as he stood outside the Enlisted Men's Club, a contingent of troops from Charlie Company, seeking redress for some real or imagined grievance, came searching for a certain Alice Company troop. Pawlata did not even know the man in question, but he felt his spine stiffen.

"He's not here," Pawlata declared through a jutted jaw, "but I'm here, so I guess you're going to have to deal with me."

Pawlata was on the ground, locked in combat with the largest of the Charlie Company assailants, when Christian chanced to appear. He watched the fight in detached amusement, knowing that behind-the-lines fisticuffs were a necessary outlet for the men destined to fight this war. Pawlata was tall and strong, but his opponent was even larger, and had managed to wrestle him to the ground, where he was pummeling him without mercy. Pawlata chose the only available point of attack, the man's leg, and sank his teeth deeply into flesh. The other fighter screamed in agony, relinquished his hold, and backed off quickly. He gathered his cronies and fled, vowing to return with weapons to finish this debate.

Amid the general craziness of a war zone, such a threat could well be real, and Pawlata decided that the best course of action was to make himself scarce for a time. He rushed off to a wooded area, assured himself that it was free of red ants and scorpions, and sat down to catch his breath. Only moments later he realized with a start that he was not alone.

"I'm Lieutenant Christian," a voice said suddenly.

Pawlata wheeled in alarm, wondering if he was about to be subjected to yet another round of the army's blind discipline.

"Wanna be in Recon?" Christian asked.

"Why?" Pawlata responded suspiciously. He knew the old Recon was just a bunch of shit-burners, but he had also heard that under this new commander the unit was beginning to see some real action.

Christian explained the game plan for Recon, and Pawlata found himself intrigued. Here was a chance to cast his lot with a much smaller unit, where men could bond together as friends and fighters. Recon patrols were limited to no more than seven or eight men at a time. "I think you'd make a good point man," Christian announced. "You could carry a twelve-gauge shotgun."

That was the clincher for Pawlata. Sometimes the M-16, powerful as it was, seemed inadequate to penetrate the thick brush. A shotgun held the potential for creating real damage. He accepted the invitation, and Christian went off to take care of the paperwork.

As he studied Pawlata's personnel file, Christian realized that he had found a skilled but undisciplined fighter. Trouble sought out the man. Pawlata had developed a consuming hatred for those who drew combat pay while remaining in the safety of the base camp. All U.S. troops in South Vietnam received hazardous duty pay, yet only about 10 percent actually saw field combat. To Pawlata, it simply wasn't fair. When he was off duty and drunk—the two always seemed to go together—he spent much of his time picking fights with Rear-Echelon Motherfuckers.

Legends had grown around the man. Some said he hid behind trees— or jumped out of them—to ambush passing REMFs. It was said that his goal in life was to bite off a REMF ear and save it for a souvenir. It was a tactic he had picked up from the Vietnamese, who believed that if you lost a portion of your body, you would not go to heaven when you died. Somewhere in Pawlata's fuzzy mind, he reckoned that loss of an ear would justify the REMFs' combat pay.

Christian thought: he's my kind of man. A nickname leaped to mind, keyed by Pawlata's mythical penchant for attacking from the trees. He's not Ace, Christian thought. I'll call him Ape.

Lowe dubbed him Bluto, after the gargantuan heavy in the Popeye cartoons.

15

War Zone C, South Vietnam
September 1968

The battalion was ordered to go on a coordinated mission aimed at clearing out a large, entrenched enemy force in the same northern area of War Zone C in which Recon achieved its initial success. The area was designated as a "free kill" zone, meaning that it was certified as being empty of other friendly troops and civilians. Anyone they saw, they could shoot to kill without hesitation.

Three choppers flew Recon to a clearing two clicks away from the suspected position of the enemy encampment and hovered six feet above the ground in an arrowhead-shaped phalanx, called a Christmas tree formation, as the grunts dropped to the ground. Other gunships, Cobras, blazed away with automatic cannons at the surrounding brush. Recon met only modest return fire from an enemy rearguard element.

The men of Recon moved through the elephant grass toward the jungle forest, firing their M-16s from the hip, laying down a channel of lead to clear the approach. They were already well past the drop zone when other choppers arrived to deliver Pawlata's old cohorts from Alpha Company, designated as the main assault force.

Working carefully, clipping the trip wires of Claymores left behind as booby traps, Recon edged forward along a trail. Alpha Company remained a respectful distance behind, taking its own route through the jungle thickness. They would set up a perimeter behind and around Recon and wait until they were called in.

As Recon reached the edges of the enemy base camp, the rear guard of NVA troops cut its losses and fled. There must have been a security leak, Christian concluded, as he stared into the deserted jungle fortress. It appeared that most of the enemy troops had evacuated the night before. By radio, he reported to the battalion that the camp was empty, and Recon was going in. There was nothing to do now but survey the camp, confiscate what supplies they could, and destroy the rest so that they would be unusable if the enemy tried to return for them.

Inside, Recon discovered a supermarket of enemy supplies—vast stocks of weapons and ammunition and stores of white plastic explosives and blasting caps. The amount of paraphernalia left behind was an indication of the urgency of the enemy's retreat. It did not seem likely that they would kill any NVA troops today, but they would cut deeply into Charlie's supply line.

Andrews came upon a tunnel and decided to take care of it before anyone ordered him to go inside. He dropped a Willie Peter down the shaft, but the tunnel was more shallow than he expected, and fingers of hot phosphorus blew out. He screamed in pain, ripped the shirt off his back, and pounded out smoldering fires.

Christian and Lascano had set about the task of inventorying the booty in the ammo dump when a gleeful whoop sounded from the far end of the camp. A couple of the men had happened upon an underground bunker containing a large store of what appeared to be marijuana. Word

of the bonanza spread almost instantly. Within moments, every man of
Recon was on the scene to help decide what to do with this precious
contraband.

Christian flicked his Zippo cigarette lighter to illuminate the scene in
the windowless cellar, carved out of hard earth, its walls fortified by sandbags. Soft orange light flickered upon bricks of brown-green weed, dried
and compressed. Recon gazed in delicious awe, as if it had stumbled upon
Ho Chi Minh's personal candy store. The men viewed this serendipitous
find as a just reward offered by the gods of war—a sort of cosmic repayment
for their assigned role as combat point men.

"There must be a ton or more of it," Christian muttered.

Knowing their commander's abhorrence of drugs, no one was brave
enough to make the first move toward the stash. They waited for Victor 6
to decide what to do.

Christian gave orders to Rusty Baker: "Radio the battalion."

Baker moved up the stairway of the bunker, sat on the edge, extended
the short-whip antenna of the Prick-25, and thrust it out into the open air.
He raised battalion headquarters, but just as he identified his unit, his words
were cut off by a sudden, ghastly flash of hot, yellow-white light that knifed
in through the entranceway of the bunker, illuminating the faces of the
young men of Recon. Instinctively, they threw up their forearms to cover
their eyes. The light was followed almost immediately by a thunderous,
eardrum pulverizing blast that bounced off the bunker walls and caromed
about wildly.

Baker tumbled down into the bunker, seeking haven from the unfathomable roar, as the universe outside erupted with the sound of a further
barrage of demoniac explosions. Dong felt the sandbagged bunker walls
quiver from the shock waves, threatening to bury them alive. The men,
cast into an incomprehensible inferno, alternately prayed and swore in
disbelief and confusion.

Christian guessed the truth immediately, and cursed out army communications. A B-52 strike is not a random event. This one was probably
scheduled the night before, and someone had missed the message that the
enemy had already fled and Recon had moved into the camp. It was a
classic screwup, and now Recon was caught in a "free-kill" zone, terrorized
and awestruck with the knowledge that they were about to die on the wrong
end of their own bombs—all because of someone's stupid mistake. Christian
grabbed Baker by the collar and screamed instructions into the radioman's
ear.

With shaking fingers, Baker screwed the long-whip antenna onto the radio and shoved the wire upward, out of the bunker and into the flashes of the carnage above.

He shouted into the transmitter, "They are bombing us! We are sitting under a B-52 strike. This is no shit, guys! Get these fucking birds off us."

No one else could do anything except wait in impotence for the moment they would never know.

The hell came in waves, relentlessly. First the infernal flash, then the numbing concussion and the deafening roar. Will they ever be able to identify our bodies? Christian wondered. A direct hit would tear every one of them to shreds and incinerate the bits that remained.

Measured by Lowe's watch, the attack lasted only a few minutes, but every man in the bunker knew that hours passed before the deepest silence in the world descended upon the camp.

When it was over, the men of Recon emerged from the bunker, blinking, in shock and awe. All about them were huge, fresh craters, gutted out of the earth, littered with grotesque hunks of shrapnel, still red-hot. Christian reached battalion HQ by radio and sent out an acid-tongued message to whomever was responsible for the B-52 raid, heedless of rank. Only simple dumb luck had prevented the men from death on this crazy day.

It was many minutes before anyone could move about or talk freely.

Scotty finally broke the tension with a maniacal laugh, an ironic comment upon the course of life in general, and war in particular. Others joined in, gleefully and totally savoring the accident that granted them continued existence. If they had not discovered the marijuana and gathered, to a man, in the bunker, parts of them would now be strewn about the camp like so much trash.

Calming himself, Christian called battalion headquarters once more to report what they had found. Recon was ordered to burn the marijuana on the spot.

The troops were heartbroken, especially Pawlata.

It was a petulant procession of young men who carried the bricks of marijuana outside and piled them high. Christian considered the needs of the moment and pretended not to notice that some of the men stuffed their pockets full of weed. The air still reeked from the smell of cordite. What did it matter if a bit of marijuana added to the aura?

Lascano tossed a couple of Willie Peters into the pile of drugs. The hoard smoldered for a few minutes and then caught, and as flames shot skyward and the sweet smell of pot wafted through the South Vietnamese jungle, most of the Recon troops edged their way to a downwind position.

*   *   *

The enemy base camp was too large to police in a single day. After Christian visited battalion HQ and made several new enemies with his bitter tirade about the B-52 strike, Recon and Alpha Company returned the next morning to continue the task of searching out and destroying the enemy's stockpiles. On this September day they discovered a cache of thousands of gas masks, an indication that the enemy was contemplating some sort of chemical attack. Several RPGs were also in the bunker. When Christian reported this, a colonel, already flying in a chopper to survey the area, sent word that he was dropping in to take a look.

When he arrived, the colonel fondled an enemy gas mask and stashed it in the chopper as a personal souvenir.

Christian conversed with a major, the colonel's aide. The visitor wanted to see an enemy Claymore up close, and he was insistent. Christian did not wish to delay the operation at the whim of this ordnance officer, but the man held superior rank, and he complied. He and Divoblitz descended into a bunker where they had cached the enemy arsenal. On top of the pile was a huge Claymore, the size and shape of a trash can lid, heavy from its load of explosives, concrete, and trash metal. The two men struggled to drag it out into the open. As they labored, Divoblitz suddenly lost his grip and the heavy booby trap crashed to the ground, scraping Christian's leg, gouging out a hole so deep that he knew it would leave a permanent scar.

The ordnance major ignored this incident and set about inspecting the Claymore, noting the Vietnamese technology. The killing weapon was simply a primitive concrete slab with a backing of explosive, filled with jagged metal and an electrically charged blasting cap set to detonate the full complement of dynamite. It also bore a fresh coating of Christian's blood.

Glancing into the bunker and noting the voluminous pile of weaponry, the major muttered, "Hmmm. How are you going to get rid of all this stuff?"

Christian said that he intended to blow it up.

"How are you going to do it?" the major asked, a tone of condescension entering his voice.

"With C-4 and a blasting cap," Christian replied. "That will detonate this Claymore, and the Claymore will fire the rockets, the mortars, the other Claymores, and everything else."

The major glanced at the primitive mine once more and pronounced,

"Can't be done. I could stand on top of the bunker when you try to blow it, and I wouldn't even feel it." He noted pointedly, in front of his colonel, that he was trained as an ordnance expert.

Christian regarded the man and surmised that he was another in the endless line of "green breads" whose experience in combat was limited to stateside classrooms and the textbook maneuverings of chicken-shit war games. He doubted that the major had any idea what it was like to sit in a bunker and sweat out a B-52 attack. Nevertheless, in front of his men, he felt humiliated by the major's condescension.

Divoblitz and Christian dragged the Claymore back into the bunker and placed it at a strategic point, where its heated, jagged shrapnel would rip into the pile. Christian ordered Divoblitz away, and told him to "get everyone out." For a moment he considered inviting the major to stand on top of the bunker, but thought, for once I'll hold my tongue.

"Let's haul ass out of here," Janney said to the others.

As Recon took off, Christian grabbed a block of C-4 white plastic explosive, broke off a chunk, and set it on top of the Claymore. He uncoiled a fuse and lit a small piece to establish a burn speed. Then he cut a length that he estimated would give him ten seconds, and fixed it into a blasting cap and then into the C-4 plastic explosive. He lit the end of the fuse with his cigarette, jumped out of the bunker, and ran for cover, counting silently as he sped away. As his count reached nine, a sudden concussion smashed into his back and threw him face forward to the ground. Behind him, the doorway of the bunker spewed orange-white fire. This was followed by an epic roar. Nearby, trees with trunks two and three feet in diameter leaped from the earth.

Christian arose, dusted himself off, sniffed the gunpowder in the air, and viewed with appreciation a crater carved into the jungle floor, equivalent to the damage caused by one of yesterday's B-52 bombs.

After the dust settled, the colonel came to inspect. Then he turned to his major and declared, "The next time you tell a combat soldier that you can stand on top of an exploding bunker, you'll stand there."

The men of Recon smiled approvingly, as did the officers of Alpha Company.

16

Nui Ba Cam, Night Defense Perimeter, South Vietnam
September 1968

Shirtless, relaxing on his cot in back of the orderly room HQ, Christian assessed what he had accomplished with Recon thus far, and he was pleased. The men had a few successful missions under their Sam Browne belts. Word had spread through the battalion that this strange platoon, the shit-burners, had somehow turned into a fearsome fighting machine, capable of operating behind enemy lines in its own special way. Troopers like Ernie May, a pacifist by both stature and disposition, would now unthinkingly tear off into the jungle, run down a fleeing enemy soldier, tackle him like a linebacker, and kill him.

Each day Recon stalked the enemy, reported on his movements, sniped at his flanks, decimated his smaller units, and called in support fire on his larger elements. Recon was helping to turn the tables here in War Zone C. They were shit-burners no more, in title or reality.

But Christian had no idea how far the word had traveled until he glanced up from his cot and saw Janney standing there with a smirk on his face. He was Recon's champion newshound, an impish sort who jumped at the chance to spark a bit of diverting dissension. He reported, "Marinelli's back."

Christian grabbed his bayonet, headed outside, and found the big, red-haired Italian-American talking excitedly to his old buddy Jim Lowe.

As Christian approached, Marinelli grew quiet, wary. He knew he could be in deep trouble. After completing his five-day R&R, he had returned to the base camp at Lai Khe, but had not bothered to journey out here to the NDP to rejoin Recon. He pitched in to help with a few behind-the-line details, but was adamant about not returning to Recon to serve under the crazy new lieutenant, even though he was officially AWOL. Then he began to hear stories, indicating that the lieutenant was actually fashioning Recon into an efficient, proud unit. Something told him it was time to return.

The two men picked up where they had left off. Without so much as a nod of recognition, Christian thrust his bayonet into the ground, right between Marinelli's boots. "Where've you been?" he asked.

Marinelli said nothing. His glance fell down to the bayonet, then rose back to the eyes of the bare-chested young lieutenant. He waited for Christian to speak.

Christian set out the guidelines. "If you mean to come back, you've got to realize that I'm in charge here," he said.

"I can't believe this," Marinelli grumbled to no one in particular. "I can't believe I'm back and that I'm with you. I just can't fuckin' believe this."

Christian waited in silence.

Finally Marinelli continued sheepishly, "Everybody tells me they are having so much fun, in combat, I mean. I don't want to be in the rear anymore."

"You wanna go AWOL, I don't give a shit," Christian said. "I knew you were gone and I didn't think you were ever coming back. I didn't report you, you know."

The big man nodded solemnly.

"Just do the job," Christian said. Then he prophesied: "By the time I leave here, Recon is going to be remembered. We're having fun, yeah, but we're also doing a job." He repeated, "You wanna go AWOL, I don't give a shit."

Marinelli shook his head at Lowe, as if to ask, what's with this guy?

Christian regarded this man carefully, and decided not to tell him how much he really did want him back. As the toughest troop in the outfit— until Christian arrived—Marinelli had been a spiritual leader of the shit-burners in their concerted rebellion against authority. The lieutenant wanted to continue that rebellion, but channel it into energies that were wartime assets. He knew that Marinelli could be an invaluable ally, or a more fearsome enemy than the NVA.

"The shit-burners are the talk of the battalion," Marinelli admitted.

Christian waited him out.

The big man finally swallowed his pride sufficiently to ask, "Can I come back?"

Christian held his stern gaze for only a moment longer. Then he broke into a grin and extended his hand.

17

War Zone C, South Vietnam
September 1968

Christian and Lascano met with personnel of the Intelligence Battalion, serving the entire First Infantry Division, and were briefed on a special secret mission that Recon was to conduct in concert with a tank cavalry unit. They were to be airlifted by chopper to a rubber plantation, where they were to shoot on sight any human being not wearing a U.S. military uniform.

The most asinine part of the briefing, in Christian's view, was a stern warning not to harm the rubber trees. The U.S. Army would have to pay the French plantation owner for any damage to his trees. Great, Christian thought, kill the people but don't mess with the trees.

When they reached the rubber plantation, they were surprised to find peasants working busily, boring holes into the trees, harvesting rubber just like maple syrup. The peasants took time away from their work to smile and wave at the visiting Americans who, if they followed their orders, should have gunned them all down.

Suddenly Baker noticed a group of about twenty armed men in black pajamas, heading unhurriedly in their direction. They, too, were chatting with the peasants. Christian grabbed the microphone of the Prick-25 slung across Baker's back and radioed the base camp. "Are there any friendlies in the area?" he asked.

Before he could get a response, the peasants suddenly disappeared, and bullets ripped all around Recon. Christian and Baker hit the ground with a thud, taking cover behind a large, felled rubber tree that was obviously going to cost the army a lot of money. "Screw it, they're not friendly," Christian reported over the radio.

Slugs ripped into the tree in front of them. Before most of the men could gather their wits, they heard an Indian war whoop and lifted their heads to see Lascano tearing headlong at the enemy, zigzagging as he sprayed automatic fire.

"Hold your fire!" Christian yelled out to the others. "Don't shoot or you're liable to hit Jesse."

Recon watched with satisfaction as Lascano proved the truth of Christian's battle instructions. One crazed man screaming and racing directly *toward* the enemy can accomplish miracles. The twenty attackers turned to flee from the maniac, desperately seeking cover.

Lascano ran about 100 meters before he bothered to look around to see how many of his friends were with him. When he realized that he was alone, he suddenly dove for cover behind the largest rubber tree he could find.

Recon hustled forward in small teams, one firing, one moving, until they reached Lascano.

Now the radio crackled with instructions from the battalion. "Do not shoot the rubber trees," commanded an official voice. "Repeat, do not shoot the rubber trees."

Strange sounds came over the airwaves, as if someone back at the battalion was struggling to grab the microphone. Then a new voice came over the speaker, and Christian recognized it as that of the commander of their backup armored cavalry unit. This new voice bellowed, "Fuck the rubber trees!"

Recon held off the attack until the cavalry tanks arrived and routed the enemy, uprooting numerous rubber trees in the process.

18

Bien Hoa, South Vietnam
September 1968

Word came in that the entire fighting arm of the division was to be transferred to the Parrot's Beak, or Fish Hook, section of South Vietnam. It was the first indication that Recon's talents were to be put to special use, as the Army Intelligence colonel had promised.

They flew into Bien Hoa, a major U.S. Air Force facility, where the men were told they had a three-hour layover before they would catch the next plane to Quan Loi base camp.

"Let's find a bar," someone suggested.

Christian slipped into a clean fatigue shirt, bearing on his collar the single silver bar of a first lieutenant and the crossed rifles of the infantry. In the field, he wore "squad bag" clothes with no insignia, for shiny metal served only as a target. But he had an intuition that Recon, let loose in Bien Hoa for three hours, might need someone around who was wearing a visible sign of authority.

Recon headed for the highway, toting an array of confiscated enemy weapons, sniffing the air for signs of alcohol.

The nearest watering hole was a quarter-mile distant. It proved to be an air force bar, and the air force planned to keep it that way. As the thirsty Recon platoon queued at the door, it was impeded by an air policeman, who growled, "Where do you think you're going?"

Christian stated the obvious: "We're going to get a drink."

"This bar's for air force personnel," the AP snapped. "Only. Get the fuck outta here!"

"And whose rule is that?" Christian wanted to know.

"It's the general's rule." The AP stared at Christian's shaved head and his lieutenant's bar and added, "and the general also has a rule about wearing hats, sir. I'm afraid I'm gonna have to write you up."

Christian smiled and said politely, "Well, fuck you. Write me up. Just write me up."

The AP glowered.

"And," Christian continued, "aside from that, you tell the general that if he wants my hat, it was shot off my head about three hours ago and some VC is probably running around with it right now. If the general wants it that goddamn bad, he can go out and get it!" The AP remained speechless as Christian's mouth clicked into automatic fire that rose steadily in intensity. Behind him the men of Recon guffawed as he raged: "And, aside from that, we're *gonna* go into your air force bar and we're *gonna* drink in your air force bar, because we've been out fighting the goddamn enemy and this is bullshit and you can write me up for that, too. Get my name right. It's Christian. C-H-R-I. . . ."

"Take it easy, take it easy," the AP said, glancing nervously at the group of parched fighters who stood ready to back up their commander. "We'll let you in the bar."

"Thank you," Christian replied in a civilized voice. "Thank you very much."

"Just don't cause any problems, okay? And the weapons stay outside."

"Okay," Christian agreed. "You give a little, we'll give a little. No weapons inside."

Lascano volunteered to remain outside and guard the weapons while the others investigated the mysterious innards of a forbidden air force bar. The last time the Indian drank anything in a bar it had a dead mouse in it, and he preferred to abstain from then on.

Inside, the drinks were flowing freely when Baker glanced out the back window, and his cry of "Shit!" brought the others running. Out back, guarded by a chain link fence, was a swimming pool, its placid blue waters shimmering like a mirage in the South Vietnamese sun. Beyond that was a weight-lifting room.

"Aw, this is too much," Christian grumbled. To a man, Recon felt the injustice of it all. For numberless days they had been out in the jungle, often praying for water to drink, and here were a bunch of fly-boys, splashing in it. Christian only had to say, "Let's go," and half of the men moved out with him. The nonswimmers continued to take their pleasure in the bar.

A half dozen Recon troops scaled the fence easily and, in full combat gear, jumped into the cool, azure water. Pawlata, playfully holding Scotty's head under the surface, asked, "What are they gonna do to us?"

Christian laughed and said, "They could send us to Vietnam!"

The frolic was interrupted by a bellow: "What the hell do you think you're doing?"

Christian glanced up to see a man at the side of the pool, wearing only swim trunks, who identified himself as a major. The army lieutenant tried the calm approach first, embellishing only slightly. He explained, "Look, we just came from ninety days of tough combat, seeing the enemy every goddamn day. We've been killing the enemy for you, so you guys can sleep and swim and everything else back here. Can't you give us the opportunity to enjoy ourselves?"

He could see disgust reflected in the major's eyes. The precious air force pool was tainted with the grime of combat and even enemy blood dissolving off the filthy army uniforms.

Christian's voice softened even more. "Come on, major," he pleaded, "we're sorry. The dirt will go to the bottom and filter out. Come on. Forget it, okay?"

Perhaps the major was guilt laden, seeing these true fighters against the background of the easy REMF environment. There was much truth in Christian's words, and he knew it. He acquiesced, mumbling, "Okay, go on. Use the gym, too. Whatever you want."

A collective sense of euphoria encompassed the men of Recon. They were Spartans, warriors. They had challenged the enemy and won, and now they had challenged the U.S. Air Force and won. At the moment, life smelled like a rose.

Some of the men remained in the now-murky water of the pool. Christian and a few others, in sopping-wet combat fatigues, headed for the gym.

Their entrance produced grimaces and nasty, but quiet, remarks.

At the far end of the room Christian noticed a muscle-bound fly-boy, lying on his back, doing bench presses. He walked over to watch for a moment, then proclaimed, "Aw, hell, I can do that."

Such a statement does not go unchallenged in a weight room. The fly-boy was happy to give the upstart young army lieutenant a chance. He relinquished his position to Christian and loaded weights onto the bar. With a grin, he eased it into place across Christian's chest. Christian reached his arms upward for the load, took a firm grip, and said, "Okay."

The fly-boy released the safety clasps.

Christian's arms turned to macaroni. Down, down, down slid the weights until the bar lay heavily upon his chest. His pleas for help produced an eruption of laughter.

Two airmen lifted the bar from Christian's breast and, as he caught his breath, an unexpectedly dark thought intruded. *So I'm not invincible after all*, Victor 6 realized.

Instantly, he forced the dangerous notion from his mind.

19

Parrot's Beak, South Vietnam
September 1968

Parrot's Beak, aka the Fish Hook, is a slab of western South Vietnam named for the hawk-nosed profile it exhibits on a map. It is the closest point of access from Cambodia to Saigon, and thus, in 1968, was the termination point of the Ho Chi Minh trail. If they were not stopped here, NVA regulars could work their way to Saigon with comparative ease. One look at a map provided convincing evidence that the war would be won or lost at Parrot's Beak.

CIA reports were alarming: five well-equipped North Vietnamese regiments were working their way down the trail toward Parrot's Beak and bivouacing just across the border in the safe haven of Cambodia, obviously preparing to launch a major offensive against Saigon. The best and most obvious way to stop them was to bomb the living daylights out of them, but the American political climate did not allow for such a display of muscle. Even so, the forbidden area across the Cambodian border was being softened by a few strategic, but highly classified, B-52 strikes, unpublicized back home.

The second strategy was to clog the nozzle of the pipeline with American troops. Plans called for the First Air Cavalry Division and the Twenty-fifth Infantry Division to place themselves directly in the pathway of the incoming enemy. To reach Saigon, the NVA would first have to get past strategically placed defense perimeters, including the First Infantry Division's three fire support bases: Rita, Dot, and Jane.

Thousands of photos were pieced together like a jigsaw puzzle and laid out on a long conference table in front of Christian and the other officers. Viewed through magnifying goggles, these photos, taken at an altitude of 20,000 feet, showed the NVA preparations in such detail that machine gun emplacements and even tire tracks were identifiable. Here was an enemy massing, ready to wash over the land in waves. The numbers of troops provided awesome evidence that the impending battles would be crucial.

What was particularly galling was the audacity. Secure in their Cambodian haven, the NVA base camps were huge, relatively unprotected, and equipped with all the amenities available to a modern bivouac site. The enemy was sitting pretty, thumbing its nose at America, biding its time. Janney grumbled, "Charlie is well supplied here."

Rita, Dot, and Jane were to be reminiscent of World War I-style entrenchments, foxholes and hootches surrounded by concertina wire. The moment the perimeter was secure, 105-millimeter artillery pieces would be flown in on so-called "Shithooks," Chinook 'copters.

But the enemy did not plan to give the Americans the chance to complete their fortifications. Battalion troops barely had time to circle Rita's perimeter with concertina wire before the enemy was upon them, attacking in waves. The first surge came in heavily armed, but successive waves were not armed at all. These men simply moved in and picked up the weapons of their dead comrades. Scuttlebutt passed among the Americans: the enemy troops were whacked out on opium and did not even realize they were being thrown into a suicide mission.

It reminded Christian of the movie "Pork Chop Hill," which he had seen as a little boy. This was like a chicken shoot. The only question was: did the Americans have more ammunition than the North Vietnamese had bodies?

One of the American news networks learned of the battle, and flew in a film crew by chopper. In the midst of the defensive battle, as Christian was moving troops around, he found a microphone thrust into his face. A reporter queried, "Lieutenant, can I ask you a few questions?"

"Fuck you," Christian replied. "There's a war going on."

The reporter said, "Don't you realize that you're on the news?"

"Fuck you."

The reporter got the message and retreated.

Night fell on an American fire support base encircled by concertina wire laced with the bodies of North Vietnamese martyrs. In the morning, the bodies were gone; the enemy had silently policed its dead.

Within twenty-four hours the battalion had plowed the land surrounding the concertina wire and sprayed Agent Orange defoliant into the edges of the jungle to etch away the greenery and destroy the enemy's cover. The NVA left them alone during this second day, but the tension built to the breaking point.

Sometime after midnight on the second day, a sentry picked up movement in his night vision scope. He fired off a few rounds and the perimeter guard joined in, blazing away at their shadowy targets until all evidence of movement ceased. Morning light revealed the bodies of twenty-two wild boars.

On the third day American B-52s pounded enemy positions just across the border in Cambodia. The bombs fell so close that the ground shook beneath American feet. An errant chunk of hot shrapnel dropped adjacent to Christian, ripping open his neighbor's arm.

The battalion troops spent day after day digging, cursing at the rains that collapsed their trenches, and then pulling ambush patrols or guard duty at night. They had never been forced to dig in before, and their eyes carried a common message: this is real strange shit.

The enemy, for the first time in Recon's experience, had heavy artillery, and they began to use it at night. They first fired off an illumination round, green or yellow, for the benefit of forward observers who were hidden somewhere just outside the perimeter. The Americans watched these much like fireworks. Enemy artillery, large mortars, and 122-millimeter rockets "walked" across the rice paddies until a forward observer determined that the fire base was bracketed. When a red round exploded overhead, it meant that the guns were zeroed in and the enemy was ready to fire for effect. Invariably, a few of the men from Alpha Company thrust their limbs out of the trenches, into the nighttime rain of bombs and mortars, hoping for a broken bone and the resultant trip home.

One week passed in this stalemate position.

Home was a hole dug out of dirty clay. During the morning the sun baked it into dust that clung to the body like a gritty, terra cotta rash. In the afternoon and evening torrential cloudbursts came and went. With the onset of each shower, men jumped out of the trenches, stripped hurriedly, lathered their bodies with liquid soap, and plastered their heads with shampoo. Slow bathers were sometimes caught at the end of the storm, standing naked and covered with suds, their feet caked in mud, forced to wait for the next shower.

For Dong, it was always worse at night. Once, he was awakened by a whirring sound and glanced up to see green tracer bullets skimming barely above his forehead. He dared not move a muscle until the attack subsided. Nature was almost a more formidable enemy. Every night the rains pelted his face, disturbing his sleep. Sometimes he woke with a mouth full of water.

At night, anything might come crawling along—snakes, wood leeches, rats, or perhaps scorpions stretching a foot in length. Lowe once swatted at a giant scorpion with the blade of his trenching tool and the tenacious monster grabbed the steel blade and held on!

Each night Marinelli prayed to the mosquitoes: I don't care where you bite me, just stay away from my ears. You get into my ears, you drive me crazy.

Some of the men fashioned impromptu tents out of their ponchos and risked lighting small fires with C-4 plastic explosives, just to keep warm. They had to remember to stick their heads out of the ponchos periodically to avoid asphyxiation from the fumes.

One night it all got to Andrews so badly that he stood up in his trench amid a dank downpour and shook a fist at the heavens. "God, you come down here!" he screamed. "I'll blow a Claymore in your face. Stop that rain, goddamn it. Stop it!" Marinelli pulled him back down, as Andrews muttered, more softly now, "What did I do, God? Please stop this rain."

This is eerie, Lowe thought. He realized: I'm scared as hell. He awaited his upcoming R&R in Hong Kong.

Christian, too, grew skittish, sitting here in a defensive posture; as he had told the CIA, he preferred to play offense. He wanted to move Recon out, away from the target area, where they could melt into their own private milieu, the jungle. He dared not transmit to his men his own growing sense of dread—that the war, at least their part of it, was moving to some sort of inevitable conclusion that he did not wish to think about.

For the first time the young lieutenant felt real apprehension for himself and his men—indeed, for anyone whom the NVA considered to be an enemy. He realized in his gut that not all the Recon boys would make it through.

In the midst of the general malaise, it was Marinelli who suggested a morale booster: the former shit-burners needed a new nickname, one that befitted their present status. Christian liked the idea immediately. He rolled words around on his tongue, seeking an appellation that would combine the proper sense of invincible, yet honorable, warriors. Spartans! he thought. It should be something with Spartans in it. Or maybe Crusaders.

The next morning Christian took a chopper ride to conduct an aerial reconnaissance mission. After viewing the enemy activity from the air, he proposed to the battalion commander, Colonel Hanson, "Instead of waiting for them to come at us, let's sneak out of the back of the fire base, walk around through the jungle, and cut them off from behind."

Hanson checked with his superiors, and they all agreed to let Recon give it a try, so long as the men did not cross the border into Cambodia. These were to be probing engagements. The enemy obviously was using scouting patrols and forward observers to zero in, setting up Rita, Dot, and Jane for the kill. Recon would scout the enemy's scouting teams.

Upon his return to Rita, Christian found Recon waiting for him. Marinelli yelled out happily, "We got our name, sir. We got our name!" The matter was all decided. Henceforth, Recon would be known as "ChrisTian's Butchers," with a capital "T" in "ChrisTian."

Christian was taken aback. He had expected something more traditional, something that sounded like a football team. Butchers? ChrisTian's Butchers? That sounds awful, he thought.

"You sure you don't want to make it Christian's Crusaders, or something like that?" he asked.

Marinelli ignored Victor 6 and rambled on excitedly. He and Lascano had spent the morning designing a logo for their floppy hats, and he displayed the prototype. It was a skull and crossbones with the word "ChrisTian" lettered in white, except for the capital "T", which was black. The skull wore a helmet, bearing the number 6 in honor of their leader.

It's awful, Christian repeated to himself. But he had to admit that it sounded better than shit-burners.

20

The South Vietnam/Cambodia Border
October 1968

The newly christened Butchers found a clear pool of stream-fed water on the border between South Vietnam and Cambodia. Christian realized from his map that it was slightly on the Cambodian side, but he did not care. "Here," he whispered. "This water is going to pull the enemy here." He pointed to a clearing on a small rise overlooking the pond, indicating that it was the perfect place to spend the night.

They laid an ambush of Claymores and Willie Peters, pulling trip wires taut across the jungle path. Every one of the Butchers knew that booby traps were outlawed by the provisions of the Geneva Convention, but the VC and the NVA used them all the time. As long as they did not tell the brass what they were doing, who cared? Being a gentleman could get you killed in a war like this.

When all was ready, the Butchers moved up to the elevated clearing, but they discovered that Pfc Thiery, a skinny ex-lifeguard from New Jersey, had defecated in the midst of their ambush site. Marinelli decreed that this action was not consistent with the revamped image of ChrisTian's Butchers, and forced him to clean it up.

It was after 2 A.M. when a Willie Peter exploded below them, sending white-hot streamers of burning phosphorus radiating in all directions. These tripped the Claymores.

It was over in an instant, and then the jungle grew silent, except for the ghastly moans of a suffering NVA troop.

Everyone wanted to put the victim out of his misery, but Christian commanded in a whisper, "Don't shoot. If there's anybody else out there, you'll draw a grenade. There's nothing we can do but wait. It's war," he reminded them. "We'll do what we can in the morning, and then we'll get the hell out of here."

Throughout the night the horrible moans continued. Then, just before dawn, more Willie Peters detonated. Some of the enemy had come to rescue their suffering comrade, and they, too, were blown away.

The Butchers' eyes were wide as darkness lifted by degrees. They counted six victims, dead or dying.

The ambush was small, but successful. The NVA had not suspected that the Americans would venture from their havens, and the action put them on notice that there was at least a small group of Americans who were willing and able to bring the fight to them, even if they had to cross the border to do so.

21

Parrot's Beak, South Vietnam
October 1968

Christian divided the men into two teams, allowing half of them to stand down at any given time. He, on the other hand, determined to go out on every mission. The Butchers moved quickly into a smooth rotation, one team, fighting one day, partying the next, with equal amounts of vigor.

Unlike most commanders at this level, Christian was adamant that each man should know the purpose of the work, and he briefed the men prior to each mission, sharing with them the information provided by Intelligence. By now the Butchers had honed their senses. They, too, could sniff out the enemy, and they realized that this ability was linked to preparation, not magic.

Their job was guerrilla warfare, harassment, and interdiction, doing to the enemy what the enemy was doing to the remainder of the U.S. Army.

Andrews was enjoying himself immensely, and he took an action none of the shit-burners would have dreamed of a short time earlier. His thirteen months in South Vietnam were almost up, but he voluntarily extended his stay "in country" for another year. When his mother learned of this, she wrote Christian a scorching letter, accusing the lieutenant of twisting her son's mind. If anything, Christian thought, Andrews had blossomed here. South Vietnam was his natural habitat and war was his avocation as well as his profession. What could Long Island offer Pete Andrews? Only vaguely did Christian wonder how Andrews—and all the rest of them—might be able to apply their special skills back home, after the war.

For a time, the Butchers felt they were the only ones in this war who were really "kicking ass." The men stuck back at the fire bases were aware only of an inordinately large number of firefights and enemy kills reported by the Butchers.

Christian tried to promote a team spirit by giving the guys in the back credit whenever he could. One day, while scouting near the border, the Butchers came upon three enemy bodies, torn apart by artillery. What remained of the head of one of them was imbedded into a tree trunk. Many other units would have claimed the kills for themselves, but Christian radioed back, "Well, guys, it looks like the score for today is artillery three, NVA zero. One fellow is sitting on a piece of artillery, but you've got his head stuck in a tree."

The artillery crews loved it; no one else ever seemed to give them credit.

. But others harbored resentment. Near the end of their first week of reconnaissance missions, Baker radioed back to the battalion, "We're in a firefight."

"Yeah, sure, another one," came the dubious reply.

Lascano heard that. "Press the button," he said. Baker held down the transmission button, opening the circuit. Lascano placed his rifle alongside the radio transmitter and let loose a barrage of fire. Now the battalion believed.

In fact, the Butchers were in a bit of trouble, seriously outnumbered, pinned down, low on ammunition, and facing the possibility of being overrun within minutes.

Christian called for a barrage of white phosphorous artillery that would set the jungle on fire. "What coordinates?" Baker asked.

"Give them our coordinates," Christian bellowed. The enemy was virtually on top of them; what difference did it make?

Minutes later, burning phosphorus rained down upon friend and foe alike, but the Butchers sat tight while the enemy broke and ran.

On the trail back to the relative safety of the camp, Christian swiped with his arm to push a large branch out of the way, and dislodged a camouflaged boa constrictor from its perch. As the huge reptile slipped off its branch in front of him, Christian fell to a sitting position and emptied an entire M-16 clip into it. The men watched as the snake collapsed into a lifeless pile in front of them.

Later that afternoon, the Butchers hiked into camp, laughing, already "libating" with cans of warm beer. Other troops in the battalion regarded them all warily, especially the young lieutenant with the dead boa constrictor wrapped around his neck like a scarf.

*   *   *

The Butchers' raids persuaded the brass to send out a few other reconnaissance patrols, and no one seemed to pay much attention to which country
they operated in. Meanwhile, the bulk of the division's troops remained
sequestered in their trenches, waiting in tense expectation.

Correspondence passed between Christian and his CIA contacts in Saigon. The lieutenant detailed each significant mission undertaken by the
Butchers, to keep "the general" and his cohorts apprised of his work. For
their part, the CIA officers reassured him that they were laying plans for
the grand mission to assassinate Ho Chi Minh; they would call for him
soon.

Whenever he could, Christian stole a half day to return to Quan Loi
base camp to promote these exchanges of information. One day, in mid-
October, during a chopper ride back to the perimeter, he fantasized about
the future. He manned the assassination squad in his mind, adding a few
of the Butchers—Marinelli, Andrews, and Pawlata—to his original team.
These were the men who were about to undertake the final mission to end
the war.

As he jumped off the chopper, Christian was pleasantly surprised to
see some of the Lurps, his old friends, nearby. They had gathered around
a radio. He strode over to say hello, to catch up on the news, but his
beaming grin was met with looks of sadness and anxiety.

All ears were tuned to the field radio.

Christian heard a recognizable voice crackle in over the radio. It was
Sergeant Washington, one of the first friends he had made in Vietnam, out
in the field with half his troops. They were in trouble.

"We're surrounded," came Washington's plaintive cry. "We need help
fast. Send in a chopper!" He barked out map coordinates.

Christian watched another lieutenant check a map and radio back the
bad news. "We can't send a chopper," he said. "You've crossed over into
Cambodia."

This is such a stupid way to fight a war! Christian raged internally.

"Send a black chopper," the radio voice pleaded. "We need help
fast!"

"Can't," Washington's lieutenant replied. A black chopper was simply
an unmarked helicopter. The CIA operated a few of them in the area, but
they fooled no one, for only one side had choppers. Troops referred to
them as "Air America." At any rate, not even a black chopper was available.

Washington's lieutenant tried his best to help. "I'll try to guide you out of there," he promised.

Tense minutes passed. Over the radio Christian and the others could hear the sounds of warfare, remote and full of echoes, but disturbingly real. Some of the Butchers gathered around also. It was as though they were listening to a broadcast of the Super Bowl on the Armed Forces Network, but this was no game.

They watched the rookie lieutenant check his map and radio back instructions. More minutes passed as the men waited for word to see if the trapped unit could extricate itself.

Memories flooded over Christian as he listened to the other lieutenant manipulate his men as if they were puppets. He remembered a happy party, not too long ago, with Washington. He was a black man from Montana, just a kid, really, but athletic and intelligent, a bit wild, but a good soldier. He had finished his thirteen months in Vietnam, then had volunteered for another tour of duty. In between, he went home for thirty days and spent much of that time hunting moose. Now he was the hunters' prey.

Too late, Christian glanced at the map and realized that the other lieutenant had screwed up. He had given his men the wrong compass heading, sending them, not back toward the border, but directly toward the enemy deeper into Cambodia.

The radio crackled. Washington's distant voice cried, "Please, please, dear God. We're all gonna be killed!"

Then the radio went silent.

Colonel Hanson ordered Victor 6 to give map reading lessons to the other officers. He also played tapes of Christian's radio communications for the others to hear. "Listen to how calm he is," the battalion commander said. "You can't even believe he's in combat. That's the way you instill confidence. That's the way you get the job done."

On the inside, however, Christian was anything but calm.

Every morning the army brought a Catholic priest out into the field to celebrate Mass. As the stand-off at Parrot's Beak continued, the service grew increasingly popular, attended by many who were not Catholic. Even Marinelli came. Everyone wanted God as a good luck charm, and that meant that they were growing more concerned. "This is the body of Christ . . ." the priest intoned, and Christian wondered: Mass in the morning, murder in the afternoon. How long can we keep this up?

He faced an unalterable truth. The Butchers were proving the old military cliché: the better you did your job, the more work they threw at you. They were *too* good, so good that the brass could not resist the temptation to send them off on ever more perilous missions, pushing them deeper and deeper into uncharted territory and unknown situations. He thought: it's building to a crescendo, to some sort of ghastly grand finale.

22

Cambodia
October 1968

Day by day the Butchers worked their way further into Cambodia. It was lonely business. Isolated from the support of their own forces until they could make their way back to South Vietnam, they had to be self-sufficient. This was the worst part, Dong thought. You knew you were across the border. You knew you were taking a gamble.

They did what few other American troops dared to do; they walked the enemy's trails in the enemy's territory, often meeting the foe eye to eye, when it was a simple question of who had the quicker trigger finger. Their single most effective weapon was the element of surprise.

They became adept at turning the enemy's guerrilla tricks back on himself. By now, any of the Butchers could spot a booby trap twenty yards away, and they loved finding them, for it was a sign that Charlie was close at hand. Often they were able to maneuver around the enemy, launch a surprise attack, and spook NVA troops back into their own booby traps.

Before long, the Butchers' upper torsos were decked out in captured enemy uniforms—shirts of olive-tan, lighter colored than U.S. uniforms, and wide suspenders honeycombed with a latticework of handy pockets. They carried captured enemy ammo pouches filled with captured enemy ammo to use in captured enemy weapons. NVA pants and footgear were too small to wear, but they made good souvenirs.

The Butchers laid lethal ambushes that annihilated far superior enemy forces. They pinpointed the locations of huge enemy camps, calling in artillery strikes and B-52 raids. The people of the United States were unaware of the secret war in Cambodia, but the North Vietnamese troops were reminded daily. They grew increasingly frustrated and fearful of the small band of men that terrorized them and often left behind—affixed to their kills—the insignia of ChrisTian's Butchers.

What had been hell for the shit-burners was heaven for the Butchers. Their expertise and Christian's uncanny knack for the proper balance between caution and recklessness made this the best of all possible wars. A growing tally of enemy kills was not counterbalanced with casualties to themselves, other than a few assorted nicks and bruises.

The men reacted differently to the spectre of their kills. Baker often grew sick to his stomach. Thiery wondered if the presence of the dead remained with them, haunting their midst. Pawlata wanted to cut up the bodies so that the Butchers could live up to their name. Andrews sometimes mumbled, "If you drink the enemy's blood, you'll gain his wisdom."

In the jungle one evening, the Butchers set up an ambush on a major Cambodian road. The approach to their position was protected by Claymores and Willie Peters. As night fell, they took a last cigarette break and wolfed down some food. Christian scheduled the guard rotation. Each man would lose at least one hour of sleep.

Darkness brought the blessing of cooler air and the curse of night sounds. Creatures of the jungle announced their presence with a variety of shrieks and murmurs. Small reptiles scurried about, around, and over the men. By now, every man was expert at swatting silently at an unseen lizard or scorpion.

When there was no moonlight over Cambodia, you could not see your hand in front of your face; it was one of those nights. Christian's Sea Wolf zodiak watch passed from man to man as the guard changed, every hour on the hour. The illuminated dial seemed to compromise security in the pitch-black night, so the men attempted to cup their hands over the face of the watch as the minutes ticked past silently.

In the fullness of the night, the sleeping Butchers woke in unison, their animal senses aware of the faint but ominous sound of jungle brush breaking underfoot. Somewhere out there in the darkness, beyond their perimeter of Claymores, a tree limb swished.

Suddenly a missile of some kind fell in their midst. It did not explode, but the heavy *thunk* caused every heart to race. More objects fell among them, heavy, round, but nonexplosive. No one could comprehend what was happening. Either Charlie had gotten his hands on a supply of dud grenades, or he was throwing rocks!

Instinctively the Butchers fired back at the unseen enemy. The ebony jungle night blazed with bursts of white-orange light and the staccato roar echoed and reechoed off the mountains.

When the brief firestorm subsided, the Butchers heard long, low-pitched, gasping moans, the all-too-familiar sounds of anguish. Those pitiful lamentations continued intermittently throughout the remainder of the long night. Each groan sent a chill up the spine of every Butcher, giving rise to private nightmares. To a man, they wanted to move forward and put the enemy out of his misery, but no one dared venture into the darkness, lest he be caught in his own booby trap.

They waited out the night.

As the first fingers of light moved across the mountains, the Butchers found their makeshift camp littered with coconuts. A few men crept out, warily, to investigate, and discovered the shattered bodies of three orangutans.

An unaccountable sense of sadness encompassed them. They did not mind killing lower forms of life, for food and even for recreation. They loved to kill the enemy, who sought to kill them. But this was different. In death, the orangutans looked eerily manlike, and innocent.

The bulk of the month passed in a fog. Christian was in the jungle every day. He felt like a marathon runner, gliding along in an easy routine. One mission seemed to mesh into another.

On one occasion, the Butchers found themselves playing a deadly game of cat-and-mouse with a larger contingent of NVA troops, running down jungle trails, stopping to blast off a few rounds of ammunition, running again. Suddenly Christian stumbled upon a well-hidden Claymore. He heard the roar and felt himself thrown to the ground.

He was dazed, but he knew he should be dead. He looked down at the source of his pain, to see that the Claymore had blown away his combat boots and left his feet torn and severely bleeding. His flesh looked like raw hamburger.

Worse, the noise of the explosion pinpointed the Butchers' location. A large enemy force pressed in toward them.

Christian hurriedly tied C-ration packages around his feet, fashioning impromptu sandals. Then he and the Butchers raced back toward South Vietnam with the enemy in pursuit.

They had run about a kilometer when Christian stopped at a bend in the trail and ordered, suddenly, "Hold it. Set up here, okay?"

Lascano grinned. The Indian did not like to run from the enemy.

Minutes later a contingent of NVA regulars rounded the bend, hurrying to catch the Americans. They were cut down quickly in a mixture of automatic weapon crossfire and war whoops.

Once more the Butchers raced for the border. Near the end of the desperate eight-kilometer jaunt, Christian passed out from pain. The men carried him, finally, into the safety of the fire support base.

An air force doctor examined the lieutenant's shattered feet. Not only were they torn by the Claymore, but the skin was rotting away from fungus and acute ringworm infection. Christian had slogged through too many rice paddies. "You can't wear boots. You'll have to stand down from combat," the doctor ordered. "Take your Purple Heart and go home."

"I don't need a Purple Heart," Christian pleaded. "C'mon, Doc, don't put me in for a Purple Heart." His face brightened with the glimmer of an idea and he said with a grin, "I'll just have to find an extra large pair of Ho Chi Minh sandals on patrol. They'll be easier on my feet. I won't wear socks and my feet will dry and heal. Please?"

The doctor acquiesced with a sigh.

23

Cambodia
October 25, 1968

Christian rested his healing, but still-sore feet and regarded the bleak vista of the defoliated forest in front of him. Agent Orange was doing the trick, killing the jungle greenery that provided such good cover for the enemy. Judging by its effect on the trees, he knew that it was powerful.

The Butchers had worked their way into Cambodia along a primitive network of roads, and had circled behind the enemy's supply line. Now they waited in the forest to see who might come along, half of them keeping an eye on this portion of the Ho Chi Minh trail as the other half roasted cans of Spam over C-4 explosive.

Just as someone thrust a helping of the hot, processed meat at Christian, a shot cracked the silence, coming from somewhere in the rear. As one, the Butchers hopped to their feet. Combat craziness was now their natural instinct, and they raced forward in the direction of the report, up the enemy-held trail, surprising their attackers with an immediate, reckless counterattack. The enemy fought only briefly, then fled, leaving behind one critically wounded soldier.

Scotty rushed to him and knelt for an examination. A bullet had entered the man's belly, but there was no exit wound. From the evidence, Scotty concluded that it did what it was intended to do—tumble about the gut, ripping into vital organs.

The American medic began to apply CPR, assisted by Lowe. There was an honorable incongruity to the deed. Moments before, this young man had tried to kill them all. But it was the Butchers who triumphed; a bullet from Wild Bill Divoblitz had struck him down. Now, with the battle over, murderous anger disappeared quickly. Yesterday's business was death; today's business is life.

The Butchers radioed for a MedEvac 'copter to meet them once they moved back in the direction of the border. Dong and Thiery placed the limp, shattered body of the NVA trooper on a portable stretcher and hoisted it between them. Then the Butchers ran for an opening in the jungle canopy, where a chopper could land. At the moment, it seemed supremely important to save this young, alien life.

The unit moved with its own efficient, deliberate form of speed, traveling as fast as possible while, at the same time, scouring the terrain in front for any signals of danger. Scotty raced alongside the stretcher, monitoring the vital signs of his patient as best he could under the circumstances. Suddenly he yelled, "Stop!"

Dong and Thiery placed the stretcher on the ground and stood watch as Scotty and Lowe resumed CPR. They worked with passion, Lowe pounding the chest with controlled fury, Scotty bending to place his lips over the silent mouth of the enemy. Perspiration fell from his brow and mingled with the enemy's blood. The rest of the Butchers watched, and whispered encouragement.

After many minutes Scotty sighed, rose, and announced, "He's dead."

"Cancel the chopper," Christian ordered. He regarded the fallen soldier and thought, he's just about my age, nineteen or so.

The Butchers gathered close, freshly awed by the spectre of death.

Christian searched the young man's pockets, found a thin wallet, and flipped through it, looking for intelligence information. He was surprised to realize that the young man was not a North Vietnamese citizen at all. He was Chinese, sent by his government to fight a foreign war. The fact hit home to the Butchers, for they, too, were fighting someone else's war.

The wallet carried photos of the young man's family, and, as Christian

leafed through them, he suddenly realized that the jungle had grown unaccountably silent. Each Butcher, in turn, looked at the strange Asiatic
faces in the photographs and saw a mother, a father, a wife, a girlfriend,
a sister, a brother.

Christian slipped the wallet back into place in its bloodstained pocket.

Pawlata was the first to speak, to break the mood of melancholy. He
asked in a whisper, "Can I make sure he's dead?"

"Yeah," Christian murmured, realizing suddenly how weary he had
grown of the spectacle of misery and death.

Pawlata borrowed his commander's bayonet. With one quick thrust he
skewered the chest of the Chinese soldier, then hoisted him up off the
ground. The body slid off the blade and fell back to earth with a thud.

Andrews repeated the ritual.

Baker turned his head and vomited. He and a few of the others walked
up the trail to escape the scene.

Scotty knelt beside the young man whose life he had tried so valiantly
to save. With no explanation, he took out his canteen cup and began to
drain the enemy's blood into it. It trickled slowly.

Christian knew what was afoot.

Scotty and Andrews had discussed this frequently, with rising passion.
It seemed important to some of the Butchers that they codify their actions
into a philosophy, something that would justify it all to themselves later,
in saner times, should they live to experience them.

The core principle of the emerging philosophy was: *war is honorable*.

The Butchers characterized themselves as true Spartans, the ultimate
warriors, committed in their hearts to driving this enemy all the way back
to Hanoi—and even on to Moscow, if necessary. At the same time, it was
important for them to view the enemy in the same light. It was just as
honorable for the NVA to approach with equal vigor the task of driving on
to Saigon. They were Spartans, too.

The amateur philosophers had carried the theory to logical but far-flung
conclusions. The honorable participants in warfare would be forever and
inextricably tied to one another. No matter what happened to the survivors
in the hazy years of the future, that bond could never be broken. They had
faced one another in mortal battle; some had walked away; some had not.
It was an inviolable responsibility of the survivors to keep alive the message
that their foe had died honorably *and not in vain*.

Scotty and Andrews theorized that it was actually possible to carry
home a measure of the enemy's spirit and valor. To do so, they would have
to undertake one simple, ghastly ritual. Now was the time.

Scotty kindled a small fire and boiled the enemy's blood in his tin cup. He let it cool, and then offered it around. Only three men sipped: Scotty, Andrews, and Christian himself. The others watched, solemn observers at this parody of Holy Communion.

We are the ultimate warriors, Christian thought, as he tasted the warm, bitter liquid. We make the rules. We rain steel from heaven.

Pawlata refused the cup, but he now became a scientific animal, and the body was his subject. He had always wanted to see what damage a shotgun would do at close range. Would it, or would it not, blow off a man's head? He took his shotgun, placed it at the dead man's temple, and fired a double-barreled blast. The gun roared with abominable fury. The body recoiled with the shock of this latest insult. Pawlata stood back, muttering, "Wow!" The man's head had exploded like a pumpkin. The brains were now raw, red meat, but the head was still loosely attached to the neck.

"Can I try, too?" Scotty asked.

"Yeah," Pawlata said. Divoblitz grimaced as he heard the second shotgun blast; it was his bullet that had brought the man down.

Christian walked away from the macabre scene, struggling to justify it to his conscience.

The men dragged the body to a bomb crater for an impromptu burial and Christian uttered a simple eulogy: "He died honorably."

The Butchers spent that night in the jungle, with their thoughts as companions. In the morning, the hike back to camp was silent, solemn. Each Butcher thought: we didn't do that. It wasn't us.

Christian remembered a few disturbing conversations back home with a woman named Theresa, a friend of Peggy's. Theresa smoked grass, wore love beads, and marched in antiwar protests. She was a walking "Peace Now" placard and she had tried to argue him into a corner, demanding that he explain why he was willing to travel halfway around the world to kill people who had never done anything to threaten him. It was an uncomfortable moment, and he had stumbled for an explanation. The best he could come up with was this: his father and mother had both fought German nazism, Italian fascism, and Japanese imperialism. Now it was his turn to fight communism. If your country tells you to, you go off and fight an "ism." What more did you have to know?

To the politicians who decided whether or not to commit U.S. forces to battle, this was not even called a war. It was a "conflict," just as Korea had been a "police action." To the growing number of protesters back home it was an immoral act committed by their own fascist government.

To the veterans of other U.S. wars it was a disgrace—because America was not winning it. To the generals it was a great and enjoyable chess game; they might not admit it openly, but career officers believed they needed a bit of war now and then to keep them sharp.

But what was war at this level? Take a tattooed kid from Brooklyn or a burned-out druggie from Pottstown or a martini-drinking draft dodger from Colorado, throw a rifle into his hands, point out an "enemy"—and he will pull the trigger. If you're nineteen or twenty-three, unsophisticated, naive, and apolitical, when your country—which you believe to be the greatest country in the world—tells you to fight, you fight. Wars have always been thus.

At this level, Christian thought, war is simply *kids killing kids*.

The taste of the enemy's blood turned sour in his mouth, and remained with him as his mind spun: the Butchers were frustrated by the limitations of this silly war. The brass allowed them into Cambodia, then refused to send in a chopper to rescue them. That typified the stupidity of this whole campaign. There was an enemy out there, uncounted hundreds of thousands of troops who were specifically trying to kill them. How could you put limitations on the defense of your own life? Why would you want to?

Yesterday's activity was grisly play, but perhaps it was necessary. It made no difference to the lifeless victim; dead is dead.

Christian tried to rationalize it all with the thought: this is wrong, but it is also, somehow, very right.

The unspoken statement did not wash. With a shivering spine he remembered James Guest, the former shit-burner who had asked to rejoin Recon. Christian had refused him because of his knowledge that Guest had desecrated the enemy by taking a skull as a souvenir. He had been unable to shake the fear that Guest was living under a cloud, that divine retribution must surely come to him. Two days later Guest was killed.

Now, in their passion, the Butchers, too, had violated their own private code of honor. They had broken their own rules.

Or were they God's rules?

And if they were, what did God intend to do about it?

24

Parrot's Beak, South Vietnam
October 26–29, 1968

Christian turned twenty years old on October 26, 1968. He told no one that it was his birthday, for this would have brought inevitable questions about his age, but he coveted a gift, some sort of glorious victory in the field. He and half the Butchers spent the entire day hunting, but they made no contact.

The birthday present came the following day in the form of a classified letter from the CIA. Finally, incredibly, "the general" had accepted his fanciful proposal for a clandestine mission with the objective of assassinating Ho Chi Minh. A special agent had been assigned to coordinate the operation, and he would be in contact, soon, to work out the details.

Christian dared not share this information with anyone, but he hinted to Pawlata, Andrews, and Marinelli that they were about to be singled out for a mission of extreme, even historic, proportions.

All three were excited at the prospect of high adventure and extra pay. Whatever it was, they knew that the escapade would entail a critical degree of risk and probably place them in a sphere of combat from which they could not be extricated easily. Pawlata reasoned: over here, you could lose your life any day, anyway. Here was a challenge none of the three Butchers could sidestep.

That afternoon the Butchers moved out from the rear of the fire support base and infiltrated the jungle from the flank.

As they hiked a trail, still close to Rita, they encountered a telephone. An enemy forward observer must have been directing artillery strikes from there. From the telephone, a wire played out along the ground. Pawlata, walking point, picked it up and followed it back along the trail. It eventually led to a tree, and up the trunk to a platform holding a Chinese-manufactured radio station. The Butchers pulled the equipment from the tree and radioed for a chopper to come pick it up. As they waited, they relaxed. Feeling safe this close to camp, Dong set up his own radio and tuned in to Hanoi Hannah to hear the latest in good old American rock and roll.

Pawlata sat in the jungle, killing time in idle conversation with Andrews, when he heard a slight noise off to his right. He glanced up to see, in the brush only a few feet away from him, an NVA troop taking the cap off a potato masher grenade. In one graceful movement the big American swung his shotgun around and blasted the enemy soldier into oblivion.

Fire erupted on all sides. Pawlata pumped his shotgun with such abandon that Christian yelled, "Whoa! you're gonna kill me and Max, you dumb shit."

The Butchers realized that they were surrounded by a force of far superior numbers. If the enemy became aware of that fact, they would charge quickly, to annihilate the Americans before they had a chance to call in support.

"Open your LAWs!" Christian yelled. Quickly, each man readied his light antitank weapon. As Christian ordered half the men to kneel and the other half to stand, Pawlata grinned with the realization of the plan. The Butchers leveled their antitank weapons at the enemy and, upon command, cut loose a coordinated barrage. The effect mimicked incoming artillery and caused the enemy to panic.

Now Christian had the relative leisure to call in high explosive white phosphorous artillery. He radioed back to base camp in a calm voice, saying, "Look, guys, we're running out of ammunition. I hate to tell you this, but we can sure use some help out here."

Janney marveled once more, both at Christian's cool demeanor and at his skill at calling in artillery; he directed it within fifty meters of their own position. The attack decimated the enemy, and showered the Butchers with bits of spent shrapnel as well.

The action was so close to fire base Rita that battalion photographers were able to preserve it on film.

Troops of Delta Company rushed out to extricate Recon from the trap, but before they arrived, the Butchers had charged through clouds of phosphorous smoke and routed their foe. By the time Delta appeared on the scene, the enemy had fled.

The lieutenant in charge of Delta's first platoon was greeted by a group of laughing troops, chanting "Butchers, Butchers, Butchers!" He asked, "What happened? We thought you would all be dead."

Marinelli saluted him with a can of warm beer.

"Where is Lieutenant Christian?" asked the befuddled platoon commander.

"Oh," Marinelli explained in a matter-of-fact tone, "he took Pawlata and Andrews with him to chase the enemy back to Hanoi. He was screaming at them to come back and fight."

Indeed, the three Butchers were pursuing a cowed enemy force that left behind a trail strewn with hastily abandoned equipment and discarded Ho Chi Minh sandals.

That night, after the three men returned safely with a supply of souvenirs, a colonel called in Christian and announced, "Chris, your men want you in for the Medal of Honor, and your whole outfit is going to get medals for what you did today."

The Congressional Medal of Honor? The flattery made Christian's mind reel, but he knew that being nominated for it was a far cry from actually winning it. Most of the time it was awarded posthumously. Anyway, he reasoned, winning medals was not what the Butchers were all about.

That night Scotty provided a more palatable reward, sneaking away from his trench to liberate a supply of fresh eggs from the mess tent.

The Butchers feasted on omelets.

At 1000 hours on October 29, nine of the Butchers headed into Cambodia once more. Marinelli was held back to hassle with the supply sergeant for Recon's rightful share of rations, dry socks, and equipment. Janney was confined to the aid station, recovering from injuries to his legs. Dong was felled by a malaria attack. Lowe was on his way to Hong Kong for R&R.

It was a sunny day, unusually pleasant, but Pawlata was overcome with a feeling of foreboding. "How 'bout pulling point today?" he asked Milam. "I'll take up your slack."

"Sure," Milam agreed.

25

Cambodia
October 29, 1968

They swept northwest for about two hours, broke for lunch, and then pushed due north. They were looking for the trail that Christian, Pawlata, and Andrews had infiltrated the day before, but, instead, they found a new, unknown pathway, carved through thick underbrush. Fresh footprints indicated that it was likely to lead them to action. Pawlata relieved Milam at the point and led them forward.

Two hundred yards ahead, the trail was blocked by massive anthills, standing taller than Pawlata's six-foot frame. He peered around the edge of one of them and suddenly ducked back. He flashed an open palm toward the others behind him, then closed it and opened it again. About ten men, he indicated silently. The Butchers melted into the jungle.

"Hold your fire," Christian whispered, trying to form a plan. The Butchers crouched, each heart beating with the now-familiar excitement of the hunter waiting for his prey. But as the forward elements of the enemy appeared around the side of an anthill, Pawlata let off a premature round from his shotgun, and, suddenly, gunfire was everywhere.

The Butchers charged and the enemy pulled back quickly, retreating about seventy-five meters. Then, as if by signal, the NVA troops stopped and quickly assumed defensive positions. Almost immediately additional hostile fire assailed the Butchers from the flanks and the men realized, too late, that they had been suckered into an ambush.

Charlie probably knew, from the relatively light volume of fire, that the opposing unit was small. Attack elements moved into place silently and efficiently. Within moments, the Butchers were pinned on all sides by an enemy so close that they could look them in the eyes. Baker tried to raise the battalion on the radio, but could not get through.

"Keep trying," Christian insisted.

Baker succeeded in making contact and reported that Delta Company, the closest available unit, was on the way to help. But they were not in the immediate area and would be a long time coming.

The cover was good. The enemy could not see the Americans well. For some time they probed with automatic weapons fire, but most of it zapped harmlessly into the jungle floor. Christian was beset by a quandary; the normal strategies would be difficult to employ here. How can you charge in the direction of the enemy when the enemy is all around you?

The Butchers were in trouble this time, and they knew it. They appeared to have stumbled onto the outskirts of an enemy camp, engaging a foe that was both ready and eager to take them on. These were skilled fighters, commanded by someone who knew what he was doing.

Small arms fire kept them pinned effectively until the enemy could move more substantial firepower into place. Nearly an hour passed as the enemy toyed, luring harmless fire from the Americans; the Butchers' supply of ammunition grew dangerously low.

Christian worked the radio, seeking artillery support, even as the enemy's own artillery, augmented with mortar rounds, bracketed the Butchers.

They smelled their own deaths. This almost appeared to be a planned slaughter, set by one of Ho Chi Minh's most skilled strategists. The Butchers looked to Victor 6 for help, and drew courage from his calm demeanor on the radio.

Christian waited for the enemy to show his hand, to target himself. Then the Butchers would charge—win, lose, or draw, they would settle this issue.

Suddenly grenades crashed in from overhead and murderous machine gun fire zeroed in. Adam Gonzalez took a bullet in the foot. Pawlata stood up to hurl a fragmentation grenade and felt something slam into his backside, making a strange *thunk* sound. He felt a tingle, but no pain. Looking down, he was surprised to realize that he had been hit with a barrage from a thirty-caliber machine gun. "Shot in the ass, just like my old man," he moaned, as Scotty dressed the heavily bleeding wound. He grimaced against the pain and suddenly shouted, "Fuckin' bastards!"

The machine gun that stitched fire into Pawlata's buttocks was located in a fortified bunker only thirty feet in front of the Butchers' position. Christian's combat instincts now took over; he knew that someone would have to knock out that gun quickly or it would kill them all. He grabbed an M-26 grenade, pulled out the arming pin, and held it tightly with his left hand. With his bayonet in his right hand, he leaped to his feet and raced directly toward the bunker, praying that his timing would be exact. Once he released his grip on the pin, the grenade would explode in seven seconds, and that was too much time—time enough for an alert enemy to toss it back outside. As he neared the machine gun nest, he slipped his thumb off the pin and counted silently, ". . . a thousand-one, a thousand-two. . . ."

He reached "a thousand-five" by the time he arrived at the bunker. Tossing the pear-shaped, fist-sized grenade into a one-by two-foot porthole, he rolled on top of the concrete structure, crying aloud, "a thousand-SIX!"

Lying spread-eagled, his eyes closed, he heard the sound of a quick explosion, as if he were standing alongside a truck as it backfired. The force of the concussion caused the top of the bunker to vibrate.

He felt momentary elation, but when he opened his eyes he found himself staring directly into the barrel of an AK-47. The Act of Contrition leaped to his lips to herald the moment of his death. An enemy soldier squeezed the trigger, but the gun misfired with a *clunk*. Christian yanked the gun barrel out of the way before the soldier could try again, and used its leverage to pull himself to his feet.

On top of the bunker, the enemy assumed a karate stance, yelling, "Yee, Yaw!" as he raised his hands, ready to strike.

Christian was startled, but he was also angry at the realization of how close he had just come to death. Adrenaline coursed through him. His roundhouse right caught the enemy on the side of his left ear. The man fell back and Christian leaped on top of him, searching for a lethal hold on his neck.

Behind him, Christian heard the Butchers cheer and, unthinkingly, turned to acknowledge them. As he did, the enemy squirmed free and ran off into the jungle, back to his compatriots.

Rage welled within Christian. He screamed at his men a slogan that he and all the troops had learned by rote in basic training, but that had never seemed more appropriate: "What is the spirit of the bayonet?"

"To kill!" they roared.

The Butchers were on their feet now, shrieking, firing as they ran, mowing down the surprised and shocked enemy. They were not only destroying the foe, but annihilating his battle plan as well. Pawlata, despite his wounds, blasted away with his shotgun. They overran the NVA position and dispatched some of the NVA troops with Willie Peters and hand flares.

Fresh machine gun fire interrupted their frenzied battle cheers. Still more troops had moved out from the nearby camp, and they had another machine gun trained on the Americans' position with deadly accuracy.

"I want two volunteers to move up with me and cover me," Christian said, struggling for oxygen. Two men quickly assented. One was Milam, and the twang of his southern accent added a strange element of gentility. Working swiftly, they opened the telescoping barrels of two light antitank weapons and heard them lock into place with a distinctive click.

Cautiously Christian lifted his head up from cover to look around. A burst of machine gun bullets tore past his face—so near that he could feel the heat they gave off—and lodged into the trunk of a tree at his side. He felt intense fear, but forced it aside. "You guys stay here," he commanded. "I'll take out the machine gun."

He jumped from the cover of the berm, already firing one of the LAWs. His aim was true. The antitank missile tore the machine gun installation apart but, simultaneously, the last burst of fire from the doomed enemy emplacement ripped into the tube of his second LAW, sending shrapnel through his right hand. The concussion spun him around and onto the ground. He landed on the firing mechanism, which detonated and sent a fiery missile out into the jungle.

The back blast of the weapon caught Christian in the belly and crotch, peppering his abdomen with burning gunpowder, but he did not feel the wounds at the moment. He lay on the floor of the jungle, staring in the direction of the enemy, and saw an orange-red flare glowing through the bush. He thought it was a hand flare, and he shouted, "Wow, these sons-of-bitches are running out of ammunition, too!" At the time, he failed to realize that the flare came from the rocket fired from his own antitank weapon.

As the bullets raced around his body, he heard Lascano, behind him, yell, "You rotten motherfuckers, you hit Victor 6. My Victor 6!"

Scotty raced forward, oblivious to Christian's screams: "Get back! Get back!"

The medic dropped to his belly. Working swiftly, he wrapped a field dressing around Christian's right hand, promising, "We'll get them, sir. Don't worry, we'll get those motherfuckers."

Scotty crawled back to the rest of the force, pinned down behind the berm. The Butchers held their fire for a moment, so that Scotty could jump to safety. But as he rose, a round of enemy fire stitched a pattern of crimson holes across his back.

Christian scrambled to him as fast as he could and cradled the young medic in his arms. "C'mon, Scotty!" he cried. "Make it, make it, goddamn it. We're gonna beat the bastards. Hang in there!"

Fighting tremors that shook his body, Scotty mumbled in pain, calling out for his family.

"Hang in there," Christian repeated, trying to make it sound like an order. "You're going to make it."

In response, Scotty murmured, "My mother is such a good. . . ." His words were cut off by a violent shudder.

"You're going to live," Christian commanded, "Okay?"

But Scotty was still.

Amid flying bullets Christian called back to the rest of the Butchers behind the berm, "Scotty's dead."

There, in the midst of battle, the small squad of Butchers lost its composure. Their friend was gone. They grieved for him, but they also mourned for the entire unit. They had been invulnerable—until now.

The enemy interrupted their despair. Charlie, sensing correctly by the reduced fire that the Americans were low on ammunition, moved in with practiced skill. Large elements of NVA troops had worked their way around to the back. Victor 6 wondered: where is the goddamned help from the goddamned battalion? He grabbed the radio and ordered the artillery to drop even closer, to freeze the enemy movement.

Pawlata, his backside red with blood, was surrounded by a small mountain of spent shotgun casings. With his ammo gone, he fired a flare, scoring a direct hit into the face of an onlooking enemy assessing the battle from his bunker.

During a pause in the American artillery barrage, a black chopper appeared overhead and braved a hail of enemy fire to drop a number of fifty-caliber ammo boxes, loaded with M-16 magazines. The operation was necessarily hurried, and the aim was off: the boxes fell on both sides of the lines and killed two of the NVA troops on impact.

The moment the chopper retreated, artillery rounds flew overhead, again keeping the NVA pinned down.

The battle wore on, and assumed a repetitious litany. At times the enemy was content to pick away from a distance. On occasion, some gathered the courage to charge the small American force. The Butchers repelled these assaults with a dwindling supply of grenades and waited, grim-faced, for the inevitable moment when the enemy would coordinate a lethal charge. Once, Christian glanced at his watch and realized that they had been fighting for more than three hours. He thought: Pearl Harbor only lasted two hours.

Baker called out from cover. Delta Company had arrived in the area, but was unable—or unwilling—to break through the enemy ranks that encircled the Butchers. Christian crawled over to Baker's position, grabbed the radio, and yelled into it the message that he, by himself, was going to break through the lines and drag Delta back with him. "Just don't shoot me," he said.

He jumped up, exposed, and raced toward the enemy's rear position, yelling and screaming his head off, reminding himself that it is very difficult to hit a moving target. Wait-a-minute vines hampered his progress, but he kept running; to stop meant death. Ahead of him his eyes registered the surprised, fearful gaze of an Oriental face. The man had a gun trained at his belly, but his trigger finger was frozen by fear. With a fierce rebel battle cry Christian leaped over him, stumbled, scrambled to his feet, and ran on.

When he finally reached Delta Company he was a fearsome apparition. His fatigues were full of holes and covered with coagulating blood—his own and Scotty's. His face, streaked with camouflage paint, was also reddened with blood. He suddenly realized that his right arm hung uselessly at his side.

With venom in his voice he railed at Delta Company, ordering them forward toward the enemy to save the Butchers. He could see fear in the face of the company commander, so he worked on the first sergeant. He grabbed his radio and broadcast a message back to the Butchers, loud enough for many of the Delta troops to hear, "Hold your fire. Delta's coming in on the enemy from behind."

Forced into action, Delta began to move.

The enemy, feeling sudden pressure from the rear, turned and showered Delta with fire. This was a different enemy, Christian knew. These NVA troops were primed for a fight. By now they probably suspected that they had the Recon unit pinned down—the men who left Butchers' patches at the sites of their kills—and they wanted them badly. What we need, Christian realized, is a few rounds of artillery fire, carefully pinpointed to fall on the enemy located between Delta Company and the Butchers.

He found Delta's forward artillery observer, a black second lieutenant whose eyes were wide with fear. From his bloody mouth Christian commanded, "Call the artillery in closer."

"No, sir," the observer replied. "We can't call it in that close." He knew about these crazy men. These were the idiots who called artillery in on themselves.

Now blood appeared behind Christian's eyes. He was not a prejudiced man, and he was used to fighting side by side with all Americans, but this was no time to be polite. He turned the barrel of his M-16 toward the artillery officer and growled, "Drop the artillery twenty-five meters, nigger."

The observer was so startled that he yelled into his radio, "Drop twenty-five, nigger, repeat, nigger, drop twenty-five."

Only minutes later, the artillery screamed in. Victor 6 watched NVA bodies disintegrate, and he knew that the battle was turning. It was the enemy's battle, turf, and plan, but it was the Butchers' victory.

By the time the artillery barrage ceased, most of the enemy troops who remained alive had fled.

Slowly, the Butchers and Delta Company inched toward one another, mopping up. When they linked together, Pawlata, frustrated, ripped a machine gun from the hands of one of the Delta Company soldiers and sprayed fire toward the remnants of the enemy. He shot so furiously that one of the hot, expended cartridges leaped from the magazine and imbedded itself in his arm.

From his safe vantage point back at the battalion, a superior officer ordered over the radio, "Check the enemy dead for maps."

Christian responded in a voice laced with exhaustion: "Look, I've got one man dead and everybody else wounded. We just want to get the hell out of here."

"Check for maps," the officer repeated.

"Shit," Christian reported to the Butchers. "We have to check for maps."

A sudden shriek captured everyone's attention. One of the Delta Company troops, seeking a souvenir, had grabbed a piece of shrapnel, and the steaming metal had burned into the flesh of his hand. He dropped the shrapnel onto his leg and screamed in fresh pain, "I'm hit! I'm hit! Call a chopper. Get me out of here." It was Pawlata who handled the situation. His rear end was soaked in blood. His eyes were still blasted away from the effects of the more than four-hour firefight. He limped up to the Delta Company troop, who was writhing on the ground, and stood over him, with his M-16 pointed at the man's face. He muttered, "You fuckin' walk or die. No one gets carried back, except for Scotty." The man leaped to his feet.

They worked quickly, despite total fatigue, to search the enemy dead for intelligence materials so that they could get out and back to medical care. Christian came upon an enemy soldier with one leg blown off. He appeared to be dead. Routinely he searched through the man's pockets. As his hand touched the man's chest, he felt the beat of the enemy's heart, still strong, and a strange phenomenon occurred. Perhaps the past months had altered the young lieutenant more than he knew. Kids killing kids, he thought. I've had enough killing. I'll let him live.

He moved forward, but he was halted by the sound of a sudden scream behind him. He turned in response and felt a sharp pain as the spared enemy's knife sliced into his arm. The two men wrestled violently for several minutes, until Christian was able to strangle the life out of his attacker with his left hand.

As soon as they crossed the border back into South Vietnam, Christian and Pawlata were helped into an evacuation chopper. The entire lower half of Pawlata's fatigues was red with clotted blood, but the Ape did not seem to be in pain. He sat quietly, glaring, as two wounded enemy prisoners were strapped into the seats across the narrow aisle.

Scotty's body was stashed on the floor.

As they took off, a deep sadness settled within Christian's heart, not just for Scotty, but for all the Butchers. One of us is dead, he thought. We're not virgins anymore. Then he vowed: I'll put it back together. I'll make this work. His eyes settled on the two men sitting across from him, tiny Asians with fear-filled eyes, and he felt the sense of awe and respect with which he always regarded an honorable enemy.

Pawlata did not share the sentiment. "Motherfuckers!" he raged at the two cowering prisoners. He turned to Christian and proclaimed, "We can't

have this shit, sir. We can't have this . . ." he gestured at the two POWs
". . . *shit* riding along with us, with Scotty. I'm gonna throw the fuckers
outta here."

Pawlata lunged for one of the prisoners, and Christian, wounded and
weak, had to restrain him and shout some sense into his ears over the noise
of the chopper engine.

•

26

Quan Loi Base Camp, South Vietnam
October 29, 1968

At the base camp, even as the battalion commander was vowing to rec-
ommend Christian for his second Congressional Medal of Honor in two
days, Marinelli and Janney waited for the chopper. They had followed the
encounter on the radio. They knew that one of the Butchers was dead, but
they did not know who.

The mournful Butchers laid Scotty's body next to the hospital tent,
and then stood around as Christian, Pawlata, and others received treatment. A priest arrived, and intoned the Last Rites over Christian's bloody
body.

Janney, who could barely walk on his injured legs, babbled that he was
going to get his M-16 and go out to get the gooks who did this.

"Don't be a fool," Marinelli said.

Their eyes met and asked each other the unanswerable question: Why
weren't we out there to help today?

Others prepared another chopper, to rush Christian and Pawlata to the
Evac Hospital at Long Binh. There was more than grief in the air. There
was palpable horror.

Is this unique? Christian wondered in a morphine-induced haze. How
often does it happen that you can put together a group of guys from Louisiana, Georgia, Michigan, South Carolina, Ohio, Texas, New Jersey, California, New York, Pennsylvania—from all across America—and get a
unit like this? How do you face the end of all that? Was this the end?

The Butchers looked at one another and repeated silently: *This is some
bad shit.*

27

Long Binh, South Vietnam
October—November 1968

In the Twenty-fourth Evac hospital at Long Binh, battered young men were hoisted, one by one, onto hard, cold, green tables while medics conducted quick examinations and called out the nature of the physical damage—head injury, sucking chest wound, multiple abdominal lacerations. This was the ghastly moment of triage, when someone was forced to make an immediate life-and-death decision over each patient. If a cursory examination determined that you were probably going to die, your carcass was shunted to the side so that scarce resources could be applied to those who *could* be helped.

In between examinations, the tables were hosed down.

Pawlata's injury was diagnosed as a mere flesh wound to the buttocks. Surgeons would be able to stitch him up and send him back to the war rather quickly.

Christian's case was far more severe. He tried to concentrate, to comprehend what he heard. Apparently he was going to live; the battlefield priest had jumped the gun when he administered the Last Rites. But the ulnar nerve in his right hand was severed, and it could well mean permanent paralysis in the extremity. He had sustained shrapnel hits throughout the lower abdomen, a knife laceration in his left arm, and a deep wound in the upper back. By the time they finished counting, medics found more than 100 holes in his body.

Even with an extra hole added to his buttocks, Pawlata was ambulatory almost immediately. He was assigned to a bed adjacent to Christian's, but he spent little time in it. He preferred to roam the halls, proclaiming to anyone who would listen, "My old man's not gonna believe this. I got shot in the ass. In the left side of the ass. Same place as my old man."

The gunshot wounds to Christian's back caused him some discomfort, as did the shrapnel in his side, feet, and legs. But it was the injury to his right hand—the severed nerve—that most concerned the doctors. He was ordered to remain in bed with his right arm elevated, and the inaction stifled his spirit.

Pawlata wrote a somewhat garbled letter to Peggy Christian on November 1. He detailed the battle, and then added:

"I can and will say to any man alive, I will lay down my life for him if it were necessary because I don't have that much to look forward to in life.

"But your husband has a very good life in front of him, a beautiful and considerate wife, I say this for the reasons behind his ravings of you. And I know he is a very fortunate man and will be happy once he returns to your side. . . .

"I'm getting somewhat soft in my writing this letter and it's a thing I cannot afford to do over here.

"But once I return to the US I hope to be as fortunate as he. I've 5 months left over here for 2 years in this godforsaken country, and I know I will return to battle communism until this land has been liberated.

"It just goes to show that man can never be free of war, for he must fight for what he believes in. I know I am writing this letter for your husband who is unable to do so himself, so I'll do so. Your husband says he loves and misses you greatly, and he says he's mad at me for not allowing him to read my introduction of myself to you.

"But pay no attention to me, because I'm just a crazy and mixed up individual. We may go to Japan on a convalescence and recuperation deal, but I don't believe your husband holds any interest in the matter, because he is just as anxious as I to get back to the rest of the guys in the platoon. . . .

"Your husband says he is a groovy guy and this place doesn't do a thing for him. A place that you can't even purchase any libation in, because we're patients, is pretty bad. . . .

"Your husband will write a few lines on the back of this page, but I warn you it will look like a chicken digging for his first worm.

"Sincerely, from one of your husband's men.

"Ape Pawlata."

On the back of the page, printed left-handed so that it resembled a second-grader's scrawl, was a cryptic note:

"Dear Peg,

"I don't know what Ape told you, but I am ok. I hope the army didn't notify you, for I know you would have snapped out. I just scratched my right hand and my back. . . ."

*   *   *

X-rays revealed that bits of shrapnel remained within Christian's right hand, causing swelling and preventing the ulnar nerve from mending. Christian was frustrated, thwarted in his attempts to comb his short hair left-handed. He worried about trying to go through life without a usable right hand. So much for his fantasy of becoming a carpenter.

Doctors declared that his only hope of regaining any use of that hand was delicate neurosurgery, first to remove the shrapnel and then to join the severed ends of the nerve. Even then it was a long shot. This was intricate work far beyond the capabilities of the Long Binh staff, requiring the attention of specialists at the U.S. military hospital at Camp Zama in Japan. What's more, Christian's innards were suffering from a parasitic invasion that needed expert attention.

Pawlata, however, was healing nicely; a doctor announced with a grin that he was sending Pawlata's ass to Cam Rahn Bay for a brief recuperation before it returned to the field.

This news saddened both men. It seemed important to them that they remained together as a signal to the world that Chris'Tian's Butchers would rise again. Unfortunately, Pawlata was too healthy to accompany Christian to Japan.

The next morning, Christian slipped Pawlata a worm-filled sample of his own feces. "Thanks for the shit, sir," Pawlata said. It was his own ticket to a fantasy vacation in Japan. As soon as they read the lab report, doctors determined that Pawlata was suffering from the very same parasitic invasion as Christian, and cut him a new set of orders.

28

Camp Zama, Japan
November 1968

At Camp Zama, the two Butchers were separated. Christian was sent to the officer's ward to await surgery, and he found, all around him, terrible signs of war. He befriended a man named Burt, whose face had been annihilated by a chunk of shrapnel. A single eye was the only remaining usable feature. Bit by bit, surgeons were reconstructing Burt, taking a piece of flesh from here or there, stretching, stitching, molding it into a new face.

By the time Christian met him, Burt had a handmade nose attached to the upper reaches of his forehead; surgeons were waiting for the right time to move it down into its proper position. All of this could have been done back in the States, but an army psychiatrist opined that it was better for Burt to deal with the incredible physical humiliation here, rather than at home.

For the first couple of weeks at Zama, Christian behaved reasonably well; his goal was to get patched up and return to South Vietnam, either to rejoin the Butchers or to embark upon the assignment to assassinate Ho Chi Minh. He endured four separate operations under general anesthesia, one to patch the holes in his back and the others to begin work on rehabilitating his right hand.

Lying in bed day after day, he had much time to philosophize. He was twenty years old with a pregnant wife eager for him to return home to America. Why did he not want to go? He had not counted on the allure of this war business. Why did the damnable countryside of South Vietnam actually seem *safer* than Bucks County, Pennsylvania? It was because he was good at war, he realized. He excelled at war, and therefore he was comfortable in the job. But what could he excel at back home? He stared at his useless right hand and asked himself what good a one-handed carpenter is.

Even so, he conjectured, he was probably better off than most of the Butchers. Some of the men had things going for them. Janney came from a moneyed family and had a college future. Lascano, at least, had a tribe waiting for his return. But what about guys like Pawlata, Marinelli, Andrews? They were fighters, killers, *good* killers, but sooner or later they were going to be civilians. How could they find outlets for their special skills back home?

As Christian mused, Pawlata partied. He viewed his fictional case of worms as a once-in-a-lifetime opportunity to enjoy the forbidden pleasures of the land of the geishas. He slept away the days in his hospital bed, building his strength for a nightly trip over the wall to the red light district in Sa Gamiono. One night he found himself cowering behind an array of trash cans, tracked by a suspicious MP and his guard dog. The dog, moving well ahead of his master, sniffed out the would-be AWOL. Pawlata killed the animal with his bare hands, and made good his escape.

On another occasion Pawlata was in a USO club, shooting pool with two other soldiers and a woman companion. The game degenerated into a fight. Pawlata managed to break a pool cue over the head of one of the other men before the Air Police arrived, subdued him, and threw him into the rear of a patrol car. He promptly kicked the locked door off its hinges, whereupon the APs attacked him with their clubs.

"I'm pretty sore," Pawlata admitted to Christian the next day. "I really don't remember too much of what happened."

The Ape crammed a great deal of party time into a concentrated period, and this was fortunate for him. Doctors were amazed at how rapidly his parasite infection cleared up. As previously promised, they shipped his scarred ass back to South Vietnam.

Word circulated through the officers' ward that Christian had been nominated for the Congressional Medal of Honor, not once, but twice. He capitalized on the celebrity it bestowed.

He befriended a happy-go-lucky crowd and was drawn into their adventures. As his strength returned, he adopted Pawlata's strategy for postponing a reckoning with the future. Most evenings found him and his friends at the nurses' BOQ (Bachelor Officers' Quarters), playing, singing, drinking, and spinning the bottle. Life in the officers' ward began to resemble a frat party.

One day an army physician, Lieutenant Colonel Terrence, was examining the movement in Christian's hand, maneuvering it back and forth to check the range of motion. Suddenly he stopped, made a face, and asked, "Did you brush your teeth today?"

His head pounding from a hangover, Christian had no patience for this sort of conversation. He replied in kind, snapping out the question, "Did *you* brush your teeth today, asshole?"

The physician kept his cool. He asked, "Well, did you use mouthwash?"

"Yes, I used mouthwash."

"You were drinking last night," the doctor pronounced.

"Yeah, how did you know that?"

"Your stomach told me." Terrence surprised Christian by supplying a bit of medical advice. "What you have to do," he whispered in a conspiratorial tone, "is not just swirl the mouthwash around. You've got to swallow some of it, because all your pipes stink and, if you're not careful, some of these other doctors are going to figure out what you've been up to."

Christian adopted the practice immediately. He also adopted "Doc" Terrence as his new partner in crime. Terrence was about to be rotated back into South Vietnam and had his own reasons for throwing caution and decorum to the winds. He was, if anything, a more enthusiastic patron of the bottle than the lieutenant. They spent most every evening together, Terrence signing the papers that made Christian's absence from the ward legal, Christian providing the introductions to his circle of bubbly acquaintances. Some nights Christian returned from the revelry so blitzed that Terrence had to help him figure out which bed was his.

Christian knew that he was acting like a brassy, cocky, son of a bitch, but he did not care. How was the army going to punish him? Send him back to South Vietnam? That was exactly what he wanted.

29

Lai Khe Base Camp, South Vietnam
November 1968

Shortly after Christian and Pawlata were evacuated, a wave of NVA regulars overran two of the battalion's three fire support bases. The battalion pulled back to Lai Khe, abandoning the terrain to the North Vietnamese. Even as army spokesmen claimed that the entire Parrot's Beak campaign had been a great success, Lieutenant Colonel Hanson was rotated from field command, replaced by a new colonel who was determined to stamp the battalion with his own seal of glory.

Pawlata returned to Recon to find many of the old guys still there, but replacements had been added. One of the new men was outrageous enough to fit in immediately. He was a hulk of a soldier, nicknamed "Tiny." In no time, Tiny and Marinelli had become the closest of friends.

The Butchers were entrusted to a new commander, who had all the swagger and bravado of his predecessor, but none of the necessary savvy and/or luck, not to mention experience. He had heard of Christian the moment he arrived in the battalion and he realized immediately that the only way to replace a legendary cowboy-soldier was to create a legend for himself. Fresh out of Ranger School, he declared in a southern twang, "You guys can just call me the Lone Ranger."

Oh, no! Marinelli thought.

"Now I want you guys to go clean your shootin' ahh-rons," the Lone Ranger ordered.

"What a clown," Dong muttered.

At first, Marinelli could not quite define the difference between Christian and the Lone Ranger, but his senses told him it was vital to do so. For one thing, you don't pull a nickname out of thin air; you earn it. He waited for the neophyte to call Lascano "Tonto," and wondered how many teeth the Indian would allow the lieutenant to keep. But nicknames were a minor issue. The big thing was the gut feeling. No matter how foolhardy the mission, with Christian you *knew* you were coming back. Marinelli did not feel that same confidence as he set foot into the field on his first mission with the Lone Ranger, and the misgivings intensified when the new lieutenant attempted to call in artillery on a suspected enemy position. He missed by a good two clicks.

Morale deteriorated quickly. The Butchers found themselves fighting among one another over trivialities. One night Marinelli and Lowe went at it, and decided to settle their affairs by means of a duel: full beer cans at six paces. In pitch-black darkness, they stood back to back. Janney acted as arbiter, counting out the paces. Both combatants attempted to cheat, turning at the count of five and hurling their weapons. Both missed, but both claimed victory. Marinelli, still boiling mad, picked up a handy plank and smashed it into Lowe's skull.

Janney rushed Lowe to the aid station, where medics diagnosed a concussion. As they treated him, Lowe's wristwatch sounded the alarm. Lowe sat bolt upright, spat blood, and called for his martini-filled canteen. Throughout the night, Janney played nursemaid, frequently assisting Lowe to his feet so that he could vomit outside the hootch. Lowe repeatedly swore off drinking. But he felt better when he woke in the morning, and reached immediately for his stock of martinis.

On November 25, the new commander took the Butchers out en masse and, on an isolated jungle trail, Marinelli, Lowe, and Janney decided to put the Lone Ranger to the test, to see how he would react to real contact. Lowe, walking point, emptied a clip from his M-16 into the jungle, firing at a nonexistent enemy. The next thing Janney saw was the face of the Lone Ranger, running hell-bent toward Recon's rear. So much for his courage, Janney thought.

Later, on the same patrol, they encountered a cache of old rusted equipment, weapons, and booby traps. Logic dictated that this enemy ordnance be destroyed immediately, but the Ranger was unsure whether to do that or to attempt to tote the stuff back. He did not even have the sense to settle the issue over the radio. Instead, he marched the Butchers back to the fire base to report his find, whereupon the colonel ordered Recon to return to blow up the cache.

He's gonna have to get over this indecisive crap, Marinelli thought. *That* was the difference. Christian might not always make the right decision, but he made it immediately, so that you could act. Fumble around too much and you give the enemy time to spot you and set a trap.

Evening was already closing in as Recon retraced its steps. Nearing the site of the equipment cache, the Lone Ranger ordered half of the men to stay put as he went forward with Marinelli, Pawlata, Janney, Wild Bill, and the new man, Tiny. They were ready to blow the pile when gunfire erupted behind them.

"Oh, shit!" Marinelli yelled.

The Butchers raced back toward their comrades, Willie Peters at the ready. They approached from the left flank and took up positions. Marinelli knelt next to Janney and squeezed the trigger of his M-16, but the gun jammed.

Cursing his gun, Marinelli moved to the left, for better cover, to see if he could fix his weapon. Janney was reaching for a fresh clip when, suddenly, a grenade exploded at the very spot Marinelli had just vacated. Janney screamed and held his right eye.

The next thing Janney knew, Marinelli was cradling him in his arms, screaming, "Are you alright?"

"I think I'm hit," Janney moaned.

"No shit!" Janney's face was covered in blood and Marinelli asked, "Can you see?"

"I don't know," Janney admitted. He kept both eyes shut against the pain and added, "I don't want to find out."

Gooney called in artillery on the enemy and dispersed them quickly. With the brief firefight over, Marinelli hoisted Janney on his shoulder and ran for a chopper area.

The arrival of a MedEvac chopper spooked what was left of the enemy—they feared gunships. Marinelli got Janney on the chopper and Wild Bill scrambled in also; he was hit superficially in the back. Marinelli yelled to the others, "Let's get the hell out of here!"

The Butchers raced for camp, desperate to beat the approaching darkness. As they ran, Marinelli grew ever angrier at the Lone Ranger's inept leadership. Janney had probably lost the sight in one or both of his eyes and Marinelli himself had come within a whisker of death. Why? Because the new commander did not have the balls to make a decision.

By the time they reached the base camp, Marinelli was so furious that he muttered out loud, "I'm gonna kill him."

"Max!" someone counseled, "you better watch what you're saying."

"I don't give a shit," Marinelli retorted. "I'm gonna kill that son of a bitch."

The next thing he knew, Marinelli was in the lieutenant colonel's tent. The "old man" growled, "What's this I hear? You want to kill your platoon leader?"

Marinelli fought for penitence. He mumbled, "That's only words, sir. From being aggravated."

The commander was grave. "I'm warning you," he said softly. "If anything happens to your lieutenant, you know where you're going? LBJ."

Marinelli nodded. Long Binh jail. "I'm sorry, sir. I apologize."

The apology was not enough for the old man. He decided that he had to break up Recon, no matter how great a reputation it had acquired. He transferred Marinelli and Pawlata to the main body of Headquarters Company, where they were kept busy filling sandbags and pulling guard duty on the towers. Gooney went to Alpha Company. Dong went to Charlie Company and found everything so disorganized that he was afraid the man next to him might well shoot him by accident if they ever got near a battle.

Janney lost the sight in his right eye and doctors removed nine pieces of shrapnel from his left eye; he was out, rotated home.

The battalion commander then gave the Lone Ranger an infusion of fresh blood, and a mission to fashion a new Recon even more efficient than its predecessor.

30

Camp Zama, Japan
November—December 1968

Lying in his hospital bed, Christian read a series of letters from the Butchers. Pete Andrews wrote on November 27:

"Dear Lt. Christian:

"Hope you're feeling better than when I saw you at the 93rd Evac. Milam and I are back in Lai Khe now eating and drinking beau coup to get our strength back. Ever see a toothpick tote an M-16, well, that's what I look like. I don't know what Milam and I will be doing. It seems he and I are out of jobs in Recon. Sound fucked up, well it is!

". . . they gave Recon to some 90-day wonder who can't function very well in contact. The guys told me he wanted to take off and leave the wounded behind.

"Anyhow the whole battalion (except Recon, 106's, and radar) came into Lai Khe to spend Thanksgiving. Devil 6 went out to the NDP and when he saw Recon unshaven, dirty, just plain gross he said, 'Send the animals in!' Later the colonel sent orders down to have Recon dissolved and disseminated through the line companies. So when you get back if you want to lead Recon again we would appreciate it if you would try and get us together again. I admit we lacked a lot of military spit and polish, but we were some fightin' mother-fuckers when the shit broke loose. If you can't get us back together as Recon maybe you could give us some help getting into the PRUs with you as our leader." The Provincial Reconnaissance Units, an arm of the CIA, were elite assassination squads.

"I don't know how many of the guys would transfer to the PRUs," Andrews continued, "but speaking for myself I would much rather blow away some Gooks than burn myself out busting jungle with a battalion that doesn't realize its own stupidity for dismembering the best unit it had. . . ."

Jesse Lascano wrote:

"Lt. Christian Sir:

". . . about the Recon Plt. well, they split it up. Because we had a Lt. that couldn't call artillery and couldn't read a map so nobody wanted to go out with him . . . everyone around here have hopes that you come back anytime so please come back real soon. . . ."

From Adam Gonzales:

"All the men in Recon want you back Sir. There's no more recon plt. but I'm pretty sure you can get it started again. If you do try and get the old guys back again. We all like to kill and you know it. We need a good leader like you to go and fuck with Charlie."

From Ape Pawlata:

"Victor 6 . . . when are you going to come back so we can be like before?"

These were love letters, and they brought tears to Christian's eyes. He tried to express his feelings in a long epistle to Peggy, written on December 3:

"Dear Pegs:

". . . Let me tell you about my state of depression. I am not referring to your mail or any mail from home. I received mail from all of my old men (my boys). I tell you, my stomach got all knotted up and I felt like crying. I can't explain my feelings of hurt on paper just like I can't write

David Christian's mother, Dorothy, as a young soldier in the Women's Army Corps, serving with General Douglas MacArthur in the South Pacific during World War II.

Brothers Douglas *(left)* and David Christian share a washtub in 1949 in Croydon, Pennsylvania.

Daniel Christian *(right)* at the age of ten, giving his brother, David, his first official salute on David's graduation from Officers Candidate School, Fort Benning, Georgia. Seven years later, Daniel joined his two older brothers in the military and, like them, became a disabled American veteran.

Members of Christian's Butchers and Delta Company after enemy contact in War Zone D, 1968. *Crouching, left to right:* Staff Sergeant Limmer; Rusty Baker (*in mask*); Spec. 4 Milam; Jim Lowe; Ernie May; David Christian; a Delta Company soldier. *Standing:* members of Delta Company examining captured weapons and supplies.

Twenty-fourth EVAC Hospital at Long Binh in 1968. *Left to right:* David Christian, Gunnar Pawlata, and an unknown wounded soldier.

Peggy Christian with "Colonel Rusty," a CIA liaison officer, in the Ginza, Tokyo, 1968.

A few of Christian's Butchers in War Zone C, South Vietnam, 1968. *Back row, from left:* Alton B. Smith and Spec 4 Johnson. *Center, from left:* Max Marinelli and Pete Andrews. *Front:* Jesse Lascano.

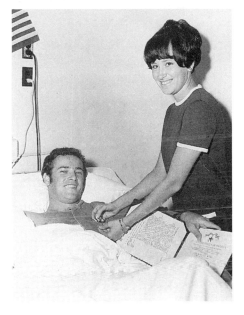

Peggy Christian pinning on Dave's Silver Star in a bedside ceremony at Valley Forge General Hospital, Phoenixville, Pennsylvania, 1969. *(U.S. Army)*

Valley Forge General Hospital, 1970: David Christian receives the Bronze Star and a Purple Heart.

Dave and Peggy after an awards ceremony at Valley Forge General Hospital, 1970.

David Christian II with his father at the dedication of the Vietnam Veterans Plaque at Arlington National Cemetary in 1978. It was the first and only such plaque paid for with U.S. tax dollars. *(Kent Martino, U.S. Department of Labor)*

David Christian upstaging President Jimmy Carter on the steps of the amphitheater at Arlington National Cemetary on Veterans Day, 1978. Instead of leading the Pledge of Allegiance as he had been asked, he delivered a speech about the plight of veterans. *(Kent Martino, U.S. Department of Labor)*

A 1979 meeting of national Vietnam veterans' leaders. *Left to right:* David Christian, veterans' activist; Bobby Muller *(seated)*, founder of Vietnam Veterans of America; Joe Zengerle, then assistant secretary of the Air Force; and John Kerry, a leader of Vietnam Veterans Against the War (now U.S. senator from Massachusetts). *(Forrest "Rusty" Lindley)*

David Christian, then employed by the Carter administration, criticizing President Jimmy Carter's veterans' policies at a meeting of state and national representatives in Tulsa, Oklahoma, in 1979. *Left:* Oklahoma Governor David Boren, (now U.S. senator from Oklahoma). *Right.* Austin Kerby, national employment director of the American Legion.

David Christian with Congressman James Florio (now governor of New Jersey), discussing veterans' issues at the Blackwood, New Jersey, home of Veterans of Foreign Wars in 1980.

Four disabled Vietnam vets receiving New York's highest award, the Conspicuous Service Cross, for completing the Skylon International Marathon from Buffalo, New York, across the Peace Bridge to Niagara Falls, Ontario, in October 1980. *Left to right:* David Christian, Scott J. Whitting, Colonel Bo Gritz, and Jim Donohue.

Buffalo Mayor James Griffin *(right)* presenting David Christian with the key to the city in October 1980. The mayor's brother, Thomas Griffin, is on the left. *(Bob Fisk)*

Guest speaker David Christian (wearing his infamous Panama hat and cowboy boots) at Memorial Day services on board the U.S.S. *Olympia* at Penns Landing, Pennsylvania, May 26, 1980. *(Temple University Library/Bulletin Newspaper)*

David Christian at a veterans' demonstration held in 1981 to urge then Secretary of the Interior James Watt to allow the building of the Vietnam Veterans Memorial.

A meeting at Constitution Hall in 1982 to promote the Vietnam Veterans Memorial in Washington, D.C. *Left to right:* Jan Scruggs, founder of the Vietnam Veterans Memorial Fund; David Christian, veterans' activist; actor James Stewart; entertainer Wayne Newton; and Dan Jordan, Agent Orange activist.

A 1982 briefing in Hawaii on the status of MIA/POW issues with
Lieutenant General Robert W. Sennewald *(center)*, then U.S. deputy
commander in chief of the Pacific Command. With him are *(left to right):*
a Hawaiian Vietnam veteran (name unknown); Lillie Adams, who served as
a nurse in Vietnam; Ernie Harris, a Vietnam veteran; David Christian;
Peggy Christian; and Vietnam veteran Steven Molnar, director of Hawaii's
Veterans Outreach program. *(Patrick K. Smith, Pacific Command)*

David Christian at a news
conference about Agent Orange
held at the state legislature in
Austin, Texas, in 1982. *Left:*
Dan Jordan, a leading Agent
Orange activist. *Right:*
Pennsylvania State
Assemblyman John Cordisco.

David Christian autographing
programs for members of
Chapter 210 of Vietnam
Veterans of America during
a public parade in Doylestown,
Pennsylvania, 1984.

At the National Polish Shrine of Czestochowa in New Britain, Pennsylvania, on the occasion of a presidential visit in 1984. *Left to right:* Elise Du Pont, congressional candidate from Delaware; David Christian; then President Ronald Reagan; Cardinal John Krol; and Richard Thornburgh, then governor of Pennsylvania. *(The White House)*

A gathering of the campaign staff in Levittown, Pennsylvania, 1984. *Seated, from left:* congressional candidate David Christian and campaign manager Ari Flescher. *Standing, left to right:* Kevin Roth, Kathy Gettis, Rick Wiest, Joyce Snyder, Tom Price, Kenneth Mayo, Sandy Capella, and Tony Burns.

Dave stops to give K.C. a cold drink during a 1984 ''Christian for Congress'' parade in Quakertown, Pennsylvania. *(Pete Belmonte)*

A meeting of ''Christian for Congress'' supporters in Trevose, Pennsylvania, in 1984. *Left to right:* Phil Sawyer, former President Gerald Ford, John O'Leary, Ginny O'Leary, and David Christian.

The Christian family at home in Washington Crossing, Pennsylvania, 1984. *Left to right:* Coleen Ann, David, David II *(standing, at rear)*, K.C., Peggy, and Maureen.

Vietnam veterans' activists Joseph Buscher *(left)* and David Christian meeting in 1986 with U.S. Senator John McCain of Arizona, one of the longest-held POWs in Vietnam.

Liberal Democrats Tom Bell of Georgia and Roland Mora of California show up to support an old friend in his 1986 bid for office.

Some of Christian's Butchers with dignitaries at the 1986 reunion in Bensalem, Pennsylvania. *Standing, from left:* former Secretary of State Alexander Haig, Max Marinelli, General William Westmoreland, James Lowe, and Dennis Going. *In front, from left:* David Christian, Sam Janney, and Gunnar Pawlata.

Family and friends of David Christian with Senator Robert Dole in 1986. *Seated, left to right:* Pam Gabral, David Christian, Coleen Ann, and Dave's younger sister, Gloria. *Standing, left to right:* Joyce Snyder; Agnes Armstrong; Peggy's mother, Margaret Todd; David II; Peggy; Senator Dole; Bill Snyder; and Charlie Lerch.

David Christian with his daughter, Maureen, at Rockefeller Center's skating rink, Christmas 1987.

David Christian with Lieutenant Colonel Oliver North at the Pennsylvania State Fair in Philadelphia, May 29, 1988.

David Christian with Drew Lewis, former secretary of transportation *(left)* and Henry Kissinger, former secretary of state, in 1988.

Pennsylvania Attorney General Ernie Preate *(right)* at an informal meeting with Dave and Peggy Christian in Newtown, Pennsylvania, in 1989.

U.S. Congressman Larry Coughlin of Pennsylvania *(center)* introducing David Christian to President George Bush at Willow Grove Naval Air Station, Willow Grove, Pennsylvania, on October 30, 1989. *(The White House)*

Burying the hatchet in Washington, D.C., 1989. *Left to right:* U.S. Attorney General Richard Thornburgh, U.S. Senator Arlen Specter of Pennsylvania, David Christian, and President George Bush. *(The White House)*

The American business delegation to Cambodia entering the country from Vietnam in January 1990. *Left to right:* Dr. Charles Simone, noted nutritionist and cancer specialist; Cham Prasidh, deputy minister to President Hun Sen, who supervised the Americans' safe passage across the border; David Christian; and Joseph Jingoli, Jr. *(Pat J. Deon, Sr.)*

Phnom Penh, Cambodia, January 1990: members of the American business delegation and the Cambodian government display the new Cambodian flag that symbolizes neutrality. *Left to right:* cabinet member Long Visalo; Joseph Jingoli, Jr., Vice President Kong Som Ol; David Christian; Dr. Charles Simone; Pat Deon, Sr.; and cabinet member Him Smceuk.

Revisiting Saigon—now Ho Chi Minh City—in January 1990. *Left to right:* David Christian; Joseph Jingoli, Jr.; Pat Deon, Sr.; and Dr. Charles Simone.

my feelings of love for you. I'll send you a couple of letters and maybe you'll be able to understand.

"I don't know what to do, or which way to turn. I'll admit I am lost. I love you and I would give my right arm if I could be with you this Christmas. I know it is impossible, but I can still dream.

". . . I put my old flop hat on tonight and I looked in the mirror. I must say I am ready to go back. I don't understand this stupid war, and I am not justified in saying whether it is right or wrong. I do know one thing . . . I feel as though I am there for a purpose."

31

Penndel, Pennsylvania
December 1968

Half a world away, Peggy Christian shed deep tears over Dave's letter.

She was a strong young woman. She had to be, to carry her husband's baby along with the burden that his life was in jeopardy every moment of every day. And she was an intensely practical person. What she could not comprehend was Dave's eagerness to return to the fight. She had all the medical information in front of her, forwarded by the U.S. Army. It was bad. The right hand might be useless forever. All he had to do was say the word and he would be shipped home and mustered out of the army. How could he possibly think about returning to the war? Why would he want to?

Peggy was living with her parents as she awaited the arrival of the baby. She spoke with them long into the night, wondering what she could do to pound some sense into her obstinate husband.

Together the family decided that it was time for Peggy to act.

32

Japan
December 1968–January 1969

"You know, you're getting into a lot of trouble here," the voice said.

Lying flat on his back in the hospital bed, Christian did not bother to glance at the man. He assumed that the voice belonged to another in the long line of doctors who probed at him constantly. Doc Terrence was the only one who was human. "Fuck you," he snapped.

A cool silence warned him to pay attention.

He turned his head and stared into a pair of steel-cold gray eyes, and he sensed a note of humorless urgency. The man stood ramrod-straight, tall, slim but muscular, bald as an egg. He wore the uniform of a full-bird colonel.

"You may call me Colonel Rusty," the stranger whispered. "The general sent me to see you."

Christian struggled to a sitting position. He mumbled an apology. "Sorry. Didn't realize who you were."

"Can we talk?" the man asked curtly.

"Sure, just give me a minute to get my act together."

Christian eased his aching body out of the bed, wondering whether the pain was more from injury or hangover. He wrapped a robe over his back-slit hospital gown, slipped shower clogs onto his feet, and followed the tall man into the corridor.

Colonel Rusty adopted a steady pace, and Christian followed.

"Do you still want to do the mission?" Colonel Rusty asked in a barely audible voice.

"Can we? Can we make it come about?"

Christian's enthusiasm was obvious, but now there was a sticking point. He had to prove to the CIA bigwigs that he still possessed both the physical ability and the spiritual courage to pull off the mission.

"How can I do that?" Christian asked.

Colonel Rusty considered the question for an extended, dramatic moment, as if he had not come prepared with the answer. Then he advised, "You have to write a letter." The letter should be sent to the general, he said, and it must declare that Christian, despite his injuries, was more determined than ever to run the mission that would bring about an end to the war. "Prove to him that you are tempered—like steel—by your wounds," he suggested. "Can you get out of here this weekend?"

Christian nodded; Terrence would see to that.

"Come see me in Tokyo. I'll help you write the letter. And we'll talk."

Several men wandered about Colonel Rusty's hotel room, clad in sheer, tight, black bikini briefs. Indeed, that was all that Colonel Rusty wore. Could he be a switch-hitter? Christian mused.

Nothing was said about Colonel Rusty's friends and their skimpy apparel. The man simply got down to business. He sat at his typewriter, cranked out the letter, and told Christian to sign it in a tone that was more command than request.

"Now enjoy yourself in Tokyo," he said. Again it was a command. "We'll wait for the response."

"Okay."

Colonel Rusty spoke cryptically. "Do what you want in this great city. As long as you're here, I'll be your eyes and ears."

The moment he returned to the hospital ward, Christian had a telegram thrust into his hand. It declared: "Arriving Tokyo, 1600 hours, 21 Dec. . . . Love, Peggy."

"Holy shit!" was all he could say. He glanced around, searching for a calendar. "Hey guys," he called out, "what's today's date?"

"The fuckin' twenty-first of December," someone called out. "Four days 'til Christmas."

"Holy shit!" Christian repeated. Peggy was due to arrive that very afternoon, in a matter of hours, expecting to find her bullet-ridden husband at death's door.

Christian bolted from the ward, headed for the train station, and hopped an express back to Tokyo. He stopped briefly at the Hotel New Japan to make a room reservation for the night, bristling at the exorbitant $22.00 charge. Then he flagged a cab and ordered it to Tokyo International Airport.

Peggy stepped off the airplane wearing a smart herringbone coat with a Chesterfield collar. Her short, dark hair was freshly styled. She managed to make her way to the baggage claim area. Many minutes passed as she watched one suitcase after another come on the baggage platform. When the last of it appeared, she fought hard to forestall tears. She was very pregnant and very confused in an alien land. She knew that she had to remain strong, but the emotional strain of the long trans-Pacific flight had left her with a head spinning full of questions. And now the airline had lost her luggage! It was a trivial annoyance compared to her concern for her husband, but it brought her close to the breaking point. She located a wiry, animated airline official and struggled to communicate her problem.

Suddenly her husband stepped from behind a pillar, smoking a Japanese Hi-lite cigarette, and offered, in his best Bogart impersonation, "Can I help you, Ma'm?"

Peggy did not expect Dave to be conscious, let alone standing in the airport terminal. His freshly grown amber mustache stymied her for a moment. Then she burst into tears and fell into his arms. "What are you doing here?" she cried. "I thought you were in the hospital." In frustration and relief, she beat her clenched fists against his chest.

Christian was overcome with excitement. She was a round-eyed woman, *his* round-eyed woman. He was filled with amazement at the mysterious course of life. In some ways he hardly knew Peggy. They had met in March, less than a year ago, and had fallen in love quickly—two starry-eyed youngsters who thought they were ready to face the world together. He was impressed with her courage, to fly halfway around the world to be at his side even though she was pregnant. But he knew that there was much more he wanted to learn about, and share with, this woman.

The next day, they traveled out to the hospital, and the first sight tormented Peggy. Christian realized how quickly he had become accustomed to the sight of broken human beings. In the halls of Camp Zama, men hobbled around carrying plastic arms and legs on their shoulders. The images were deeply troubling to a sheltered American woman who had never dreamed that she would see war.

Christian took his wife around Ward 6 to meet his buddies, First Lieutenant Joe Wecker, a wounded paratrooper, and Chris, aka "The Brain," who worked calculus problems to pass the time. Doc Terrence offered a rosy prognosis and commented on what a fine example Peggy's husband set for the other patients.

In the hallway, they ran into Burt.

"Hey, Burt!" Christian called out happily. "Look at your nose. It's looking real good."

Peggy grew nauseous. Burt's nose was in the midst of his forehead, over a single eye.

Troubling topics entered their conversation. Peggy announced that Dave's old friend Tony Verano had died of a drug overdose.

"Geez," Christian said, "we used to skip school together." Tony was a big, strapping kid. Why did he do that to his body? Christian wondered. These were eerie times. Here he was at war, where people shot at him every day. Back home safe, Tony accidently kills himself. It did not make sense.

Peggy showed Dave a letter she had received from her friend Sherry Hartnett, discussing the war. Like so many other Americans, Sherry was confused. She asked, "Are you for or against the war?" and Peggy found the question perplexing. She *was* supportive of the war that her very own husband was fighting, and yet she could not quite explain to Sherry— or to herself—why.

The rumblings of antiwar discontent were growing far stronger "back in the world," she told Dave. The Christians were young and, for the most part, apolitical. The reality that many Americans would take issue with their own government's strategies was supremely confusing. After their wedding, before he had left for South Vietnam, Christian had declared to Peggy, "Women have to have babies and men have to fight wars. It's no big deal."

Now things did not seem so simple.

This was Peggy's first trip to Asia and, once she realized that her husband was alive and very much kicking, she was anxious to see the sights. Together the young couple toured the shrines and temples, attended a performance of the Kabuki theater, and witnessed a traditional Japanese marriage ceremony. Christian endured the sightseeing, but missed the partying.

On Christmas Eve, at Peggy's insistence, they attended Mass. As they walked to the Roman Catholic church in downtown Tokyo, they saw throngs of Japanese participating in an antiwar rally. The demonstrators sat upon blankets and pillows and listened politely to genteel speakers protesting American involvement in Vietnam as well as the compliance of their own country by providing bases for the Americans to use. Christian could not comprehend this phenomenon of dissent.

In the packed church, Peggy regarded her husband out of the corner of her eye as he stood next to her, chanting portions of the Latin litany. Taller than the surrounding Asians, his blond hair shining, he appeared larger than life. He was a remarkable man, this stranger of a husband. She had expected to find an emaciated trace of a formerly vital man. Instead, he was more gung-ho than ever.

Peggy now became the key player in Colonel Rusty's game.

The CIA man knew his quarry. He sized up Christian as a brave, if foolhardy, sort, who could be counted upon to try any crazy scheme and probably pull it off. But he was young and naive, despite his combat record, and he was malleable. Colonel Rusty realized intuitively that it was Peggy Christian, not Dave or the doctors, who would make the final decision on whether or not the man returned to war.

Over a period of two weeks Peggy met the mysterious Colonel Rusty several times; indeed, she could not avoid him, for he seemed to be her husband's shadow. Although Colonel Rusty never told Peggy the exact nature of the impending mission, he made it obvious to her that it was one of supreme importance. He labored to convince Peggy that Dave was needed back in South Vietnam after his hospital stay, and he pointed out potential rewards. Twenty-four hundred dollars a month in tax-free pay was a great deal of money. In return for the extended tour, the young couple would amass enough cash to buy a home and set up housekeeping back in the States.

Colonel Rusty sweetened the pot. He hinted that if the mission proved to be a long one, "his people" would move Peggy to Bangkok or Hong Kong, so that she and Dave could be together one week out of each month. He attempted to convince Peggy that if her husband accepted this extension, he would be in no danger whatsoever. He would simply be training men in combat techniques.

Peggy did not buy the line. She was about to become a mother, and she did not wish to become a widow also. Dave was wounded and vulnerable, and it was time for him to give up this war business, come on home, and begin the process of life. Peggy ached for a home in the suburbs and a quiet, honorable, sedate future. But for a time she held her own counsel.

It was New Year's Eve, when 1968 would turn into 1969, and Peggy was beginning to believe that she had married a lunatic. They spent the early evening hours alone together, but by 11 P.M. Dave was restless. He announced that he wanted to go back to the hospital to celebrate the New Year with his friends.

Peggy was tired and more than a little annoyed at the request, but she acquiesced. Christian hailed a cab and ordered the driver to take them to Camp Zama, about a forty-five-minute drive away.

By the time they arrived at the Officers' Club, the celebration was well under way. Peggy and the handful of wives and girlfriends who were there felt awkward and distinctly out of place. It was impossible for women to infiltrate the camaraderie of these men.

A group of Japanese entertainers attempted a performance of Beatles' songs, but mixed up their "Ls" and "Rs." Christian and his buddies, full of what they called "rocket fuel," jumped to the stage to assist them. They blared out in an off-key chorus, "I rub you, yeah, yeah, yeah. I rub you. . . ."

Other patrons were not amused by the young officers' antics, and when they stepped from the stage, an American military doctor chastised them for their conduct.

Christian's friend Dick Nash responded by throwing the man against the wall, and a scuffle ensued, the Camp Zama Butchers against the world. Shortly after one unidentified, inebriated body was thrown outside, shattering a window, the fight broke up, and Christian and his friends were asked—none too politely—to leave. The band was packing up anyway, so they decided to continue their party back at the nurses' BOQ.

There, after the last strains of a chorus of Auld Lang Syne faded into the early morning mist, Peggy saw an army major, in his dress blues, stand up and call for silence. Then, in a commanding voice, he held his glass high and declared, "It would be a grave dishonor to let this night pass without remembering our fallen comrades in the battlefield." The mood turned immediately somber. Every man rose. They stood solemnly, shouted a Japanese toast: "*Com Pi!*" swigged their drinks, and crushed their glasses in their hands, drawing blood.

The major shouted, "What is the spirit of the bayonet?"

The group roared in unison, "To kill!"

Peggy was appalled. Doctors had labored to salvage what remained of her husband's right hand—he had 120 small sutures on the inside and thirty visible across the palm. Now, he was grinding fresh glass fragments into it.

Suddenly it was clear to Peggy that this ghastly, little-boyish war game must run its course. She could easily get her husband's torn body back home, by refusing to agree to Colonel Rusty's plan. But it would be a hollow body, for the spirit would remain in the combat zone. Her heart ached with the realization that it was *not* over. She had to take the risk of losing Dave altogether in order to have any chance of a normal life after this stupid war.

Early that morning, the first day of 1969, she acquiesced to the plan. With her blessing, Dave would return to South Vietnam.

On January 2, Peggy left for home. She flew back to the States, sitting next to basketball star Wilt Chamberlain on the final leg of the journey.

Her husband, meanwhile, received orders to meet Colonel Rusty in Saigon.

33

Saigon, South Vietnam
January 1969

Shortly after 9 o'clock on a morning in early January, Christian sat in a Saigon bar, killing two hours before the meeting with the colonel. Ceiling fans pushed the tepid air downward. This bar, he thought, looks just like a Woolworth's soda fountain back home. He ordered *bom-de-bom* to slake his thirst.

From an alleyway outside, the too-sweet fragrance of burning incense filtered in, along with the soft reverberations of wind chimes; the Buddhists were praying for peace, mumbling their petitions fervently, apparently unconcerned that their God was taking His own unfathomable time to answer their request.

After a moment, the Buddhists were drowned out by the rumble of a motorcycle speeding along Tu Do Street.

The time passed slowly, allowing Christian to muse upon the good fortune that was about to encompass his life. Working for the CIA carried that beautiful $2,400 a month tax-free paycheck, along with the chance to spend one week a month in Thailand or Hong Kong with Peggy. When it was over, when he was through doing whatever he had to do to win this war, he and Peggy would return to the United States with enough of a nest egg to set themselves up comfortably. It was a dream come true for a fatherless ruffian who had, in his twenty years, lived merely at the level of survival.

Finally it was time to seek out Colonel Rusty in his hotel room. As in Japan, the man was clad only in black bikini briefs. In the dim light, his pale, husky body carried a sinister bearing.

Christian's face fell immediately, for Rusty's forlorn look communicated the message before he stated it.

"We have to put it on hold," he said.

"What?" Christian snapped.

"You can't do it."

"Why?"

"Because the military has just realized that you are twenty years old, and you're nominated for the Medal of Honor—twice. You're going to be a captain. We thought it would be good to play up the medal aspect, but now it's boomeranging.'' He explained that the army regarded Christian as a valuable public relations tool. The brass was desperate to find some common-man heroes in this ugly war, to counter the deplorably bad press back home. Uncle Sam now planned to publicize Christian as the most highly decorated U.S. soldier since World War II hero Audie Murphy, and did not want to risk him in combat.

"Keep the medals," Christian snapped. "I don't want medals. Give me money. I'm cursed by these medals.''

Colonel Rusty shook his head and commented wryly, "This is amazing. You're going to be promoted to the rank of captain and you're not even old enough to drink or vote back home!''

Christian no longer heard Colonel Rusty's voice drone on about how sorry he was and how he was sure everything would work out all right; he heard, instead, the steady sound of rain falling outside. He no longer saw Rusty; he saw, instead, purple bougainvillea trailing down the window outside the hotel room, blurring into a soft, surreal, unwanted dream.

"I didn't come back to Vietnam to play any fuckin' games," he raged. "I came back here to do something that is gonna end the war, and now you're telling me I can't do it?''

Colonel Rusty nodded slowly, impotently.

Christian returned to his hotel room in an army-run hostel located in a residential section of the city. From his window he could see an MP guard standing at his station in a sandbagged sentry booth on the downstairs patio, rain pelting him. He turned, lay down in bed, and stared at the fan twirling overhead. Tomorrow he had to report to Long Binh to find out what stupid REMF assignment the army had decided to hand him.

Just like the army, he thought. Fighting is what I do best, so now they're not going to let me fight.

No! he vowed. This was simply a new kind of battle, and he was going to win it. Somehow he would work out a way to earn that $2,400 paycheck, to regroup the Butchers. The fighting was *not* over.

34

Long Binh, South Vietnam
January 1969

Long Binh, the largest U.S. base in South Vietnam, was a logistical support center etched into the jungle scenery a few miles outside of Saigon. The military metropolis of dust-covered tents and quonset huts stretched three miles across at the center—so large that if the enemy fired a 122-millimeter rocket from the edge of the camp, it would not reach the middle. The base was a temporary home for men and women awaiting reassignment, but a REMF stationed at Long Binh might never see the war.

The early evening sky was turning red over this monster complex when Christian arrived at the Ninetieth Replacement Company, spoiling for a fight. He trudged through dusty streets, kicked at a grubby mongrel that wandered into his path, and searched out his quarters. There, he changed into civvies, slipped a pair of shower clogs onto his feet, and set out on patrol, in search of the nearest officers' club.

But the manager, an obese, belligerent sergeant, refused to let him in without proper attire.

Christian aimed a pointed glance at the button-stretched front of the man's ill-fitting fatigue jacket, and said, "You must be out of your mind. Who the hell cares about dress codes in a war zone?"

"I'm sorry, sir," the sergeant replied, uttering the obligatory "sir" with a pronounced sneer. "But that's the base commander's orders."

"Well, you go tell the base commander to stick his stupid regulations up his ass. Tell him that there is a war going on and that he should be concentrating on winning it." Even as he attempted to shove his way past the sergeant, Christian wondered where these words were coming from, and how far he could take the issue.

The sergeant held him off, and promised, "I'm going to physically remove you from the premises if you don't change out of your shower shoes. Sir."

Christian wheeled, grabbed the front of the man's shirt, and used it as leverage to swing him out of the doorway and down to the ground. The two wrestled furiously in the dirt for several minutes, until the sergeant's weight advantage prevailed. He rolled over on top of the banty-rooster lieutenant and beat his fists against his tormentor's skull. Christian's fingers reached around the back of the man's head and found a hold on the sergeant's mouth. Shoving his fingers past the lips, he ripped at the cheek skin. His other hand applied pressure to one of the sergeant's eyeballs. The victim screamed for mercy and surrendered.

Dusting himself off, Christian realized that he had scored an unpopular victory. The gathering crowd of spectators was populated by the sergeant's friends, and their eyes promised revenge. Attempting to ignore them, Christian sauntered into the bar, reflecting on how his tolerance for violence had grown. The reverie was short-lived, for when he ordered a beer, the bartender adamantly refused to serve it.

Christian's face turned red with fresh anger. He was contemplating his next move when a friendly voice behind him said, "Here's a beer, Lieutenant Christian."

The words emanated from the grinning, bespectacled face of Doc Terrence, also freshly arrived from Camp Zama. "I should have known it was you outside," Terrence said. "I asked the bartender what was going on and he told me that a new lieutenant pulled into town with a bad attitude and that the Sarge was going to clean his clock for him." For the hell of it, Terrence had bet the bartender a beer that the lieutenant, the underdog, would win. "You're drinking a beer that you won for yourself," he announced.

"I'm just in the mood to get drunk," Christian admitted.

"Well, you're in good company."

As Christian drew the beer toward his mouth, Terrence stopped him, and examined the right hand with both professional curiosity and friendly interest. Most of the surgical evidence was fading. Christian would be left with a half-moon scar in the middle of his palm, and that was about it. "The surgeon did a nice job," he muttered. "How does it feel?"

"I have about half the sensation in it that I used to have, I guess," Christian reported. "And I have a constant ache in it, sort of a crimping feeling."

"Might be arthritis," Terrence diagnosed. "Not much we can do about that."

The two friends settled into serious drinking, alternately reminiscing about the good times at Camp Zama and fretting over the uncertain future here. Several more times during the evening, Christian became embroiled in minor scuffles.

A cool dawn was breaking over the countryside by the time Terrence and Christian staggered back to their quarters, serenaded by the distant thumping sound of artillery fire.

The next thing Christian knew it was two o'clock in the afternoon and Doc was shaking him awake, broadcasting the news that the army's new war hero was to be reassigned to assist the Eighteenth MP unit at Qui Nhon, a major base camp between Nha Trang and Hue, on the shoreline of the South China Sea. It was far removed from current enemy activity. "I can't believe it," Terrence roared, holding his sides to contain the laughter, "Lieutenant Christian as an MP!"

Christian was still fighting mad. He jumped from his bed to confront a world that was strangely uncertain and unstable. His tongue was swollen. His mouth felt as if it were full of red Vietnamese clay—during the dry season.

He dressed hurriedly and ran off to spend the afternoon quarreling with assignment officers. These quarrels culminated in a wrestling match with a lieutenant who called Christian the most obnoxious officer he had ever seen. The struggle was broken up by a stern-faced captain who marched Christian into his own office for a lecture on military etiquette.

"For the past twenty-four hours," the captain began, "I've done nothing but review reports about your misconduct. You have turned a rear echelon staging area into a war zone and I want to know why."

For a moment, Christian was able to see reality from the outside. He knew that his uniform was disheveled. He knew that his body reeked. He knew that his act needed cleaning up, and fast. Why was he acting like a spoiled teenager?

He offered a subdued explanation, detailing his disappointment, first at being turned down for a special assignment, so secret that he could only hint at it. After that, he had been told that he was being kept out of the action altogether, and why?—because he was such a good fighter. His frustration grew complete when he learned that he had been assigned to the MPs. "I'm sorry," he apologized, "but I have more Purple Hearts than most of these mouthy characters around here have days in Vietnam. I won't take any shit from them."

The captain was pensive for a moment. Then he said, "Look, Christian, I was a combat soldier and now I'm a desk jockey, so I understand— maybe even better than you. You're due in Qui Nhon in a couple of days and I don't want any more problems from now 'til then. Is that clear?"

"Yes, sir."

"One point. You see, I can't let your actions go unnoticed or else I'll have a morale problem with my troops. Therefore, I will include a formal reprimand in your personnel file."

Christian's grimace was cut short as the captain continued.

"However, you will be personally carrying your records to your next outfit, and that reprimand best not make it there, or else you will be causing me a lot of extra paperwork. And if that happens, then I *will* get a case of the ass. Understood?"

"Yes, sir," Christian shouted. He ran from the captain's office, crashed into the lieutenant with whom he had wrestled minutes earlier, mumbled an apology, and hustled outside, into a sudden monsoon shower.

That evening, after the rain had stopped, he sat in the setting sunlight and contemplated the future. In front of him, a dog bathed in a mud puddle, and he remembered the dripping rain outside of Colonel Rusty's hotel room yesterday.

Was that only yesterday?

How could that be?

He daydreamed, remembering the first time he ever heard about this country. He was a sophomore in high school—not very many years ago —when Mr. Massari, his solemn-faced current events teacher, had announced what he believed was important news. "Prime Minister Ngo Dinh Diem was overthrown by a military coup in South Vietnam." There was intellectual sincerity in the teacher's voice, but his news brought only curious smiles and chuckles from students who neither knew nor cared about the strange-named leader of a backward country so far across the world.

Two years out of high school, Christian thought, and I am fighting a war in a place that I barely knew about. Some of my old school buddies have been killed or wounded here. We Americans are now dying where the Frenchmen died, where the Japanese died, where the Chinese died. What does it all mean?

From the hootch across the road, Jimmy Hendrix music blared. Christian wallowed in depression that clung to him like the mud on the dog's hide.

35

Lai Khe Base Camp, South Vietnam
January 1969

Heavy clouds loomed over the foothills to the west, mirroring Christian's mood, when he jumped off a chopper into the sprawling camp at Lai Khe, set between jungle-covered hills and emerald-green rice paddies. He called Recon HQ immediately and reached Wild Bill Divoblitz.

"Lieutenant Christian is back!" Divoblitz shouted to someone else in the room. Then he spoke into the phone: "Sir, we thought that you'd been sent back to the States. Goddamn, am I glad you're back!"

Wild Bill jumped into a jeep and careened toward the chopper pad. He was in Lai Khe, seemingly, in an instant, greeting Christian with a bear hug and a huge grin beneath his Gabby Hayes mustache. He ushered Christian into the jeep and drove off at breakneck speed toward the new company area, along a road cut through a grove of rubber trees shading them from the sun. It reminded Christian of King's Highway in Haddonfield, New Jersey.

They arrived at the orderly room to find a small group of men waiting outside. They roared "Welcome home, Victor 6," slapped him on the back, and thrust cold beers at him.

Marinelli gave a brief speech. "Thank God you're back," he said. "This outfit is really giving Recon the screws. Now that you're here we can become a proud fighting outfit again." The others shouted their approval.

"What's been happening?" Christian asked.

"We've been on ash and trash details," someone muttered glumly.

The Butchers filled him in, describing how the Lone Ranger had led them into a deadly ambush, destroying their reputation and morale at the same time. Following that debacle, the new battalion commander, in his inscrutable wisdom, had decided to disband the platoon. The men—some of the best fighters in the U.S. Army—were being held back from combat, as frustrated as Christian by the prospect of finishing their time in South Vietnam saddled with do-nothing tasks.

Pete Andrews had been carted off to the hospital, suffering from malaria. The light-drinking Jesse Lascano was made NCO in charge of the Enlisted Men's Club. Marinelli and Milam were relegated to boring duty in the perimeter watchtowers. Pawlata, perhaps the best pure fighter in the platoon, had caused nothing but trouble for Headquarters Company and was now reassigned to the bumbling Alice Company.

Gonzalez told a story to indicate how screwed up things had become: "Last night the battalion was burning trash and the fire got out of control and ignited the dry field around the base camp. The fire spread to the ammo bunker and it exploded. The sky was lit up like the Fourth of July. We were out on a night ambush and we could monitor all the confusion over the radio. It was a real zoo."

"We don't do anything but get drunk and pull guard duty every other night," Marinelli complained. "They're putting together a new Recon outfit now and from what we have seen, they'll never make it. They say they are going to bring back heads just to show they are better than we are."

Wild Bill thrust another beer into Christian's hands and prophesied: "Now we'll get all this shit straightened out, so let's celebrate your return."

A sick feeling grabbed at Christian's stomach. Oh, shit, he thought, they're convinced that I've got orders to return to Recon.

It was late in the evening when Wild Bill ran into the area, gasping, "Victor 6, we need your help!"

"What's up?"

"It's Pawlata."

"Has he been hit?"

"No, sir," Wild Bill replied. "He got real drunk over at the Enlisted Men's Club and Sergeant Lascano kicked him out. Then he went outside and started a fight. The MPs came and he took off. Now he's hiding in the rubber trees."

Christian laughed. "That sounds like the ape man. . . ."

"No, it's very serious. He's jumping out of the rubber trees and biting off the tops of people's ears."

"Cut the bullshit, Wild Bill."

Marinelli said, "Sir, he's serious. This isn't the first time this has happened. He bit a couple of people last week."

"Shit!" Christian exclaimed. "We better go find that nut before he gets shot. Where is he?"

"Over behind Bravo Company."

"Come on."

"Right on, sir!" Marinelli shouted. "Maybe Pawlata will get us into a rhubarb."

"Hot damn!" Milam shrieked.

They simply followed the sounds of the ruckus, pushing their way through a crowd near Bravo Company HQ to find a struggling Pawlata fighting fiercely against the iron grasps of a pair of hulking MP master sergeants.

"Let him go," Christian ordered calmly.

"We can't, sir," one of the sergeants replied. "He is crazy drunk. He'll just snap out at anybody."

"*Let him go!*"

The sergeants dropped their arms. Pawlata responded by slugging one of them in the face, but Christian got the jump on him from behind. He held the man in a headlock, and ripped at his mouth with his fingers.

"I give! I give!" Pawlata shouted in agony.

Christian released his grip and Pawlata's fight turned to sudden drunken joy. "I'm so damn glad you're back, sir!" he screamed. He clasped his arms about Victor 6 and lifted him high off the ground.

"I won't be glad if you break my back," Christian said. "Put me down."

Pawlata complied, and began pumping the lieutenant's hand, repeating, "Welcome home," in an exaggerated slur.

Christian was distracted by a tap on the arm from one of the MPs, who announced, "We gotta take this man in, sir. He bit three people and started a half dozen fights."

"I'll take charge of this man, gentlemen," Christian announced. "You can write in your report that Lieutenant Christian is going to take Pawlata to his commanding officer for reprimand, and I'm sure the battalion commander will follow up on this situation tomorrow."

The MP agreed. "Okay, sir, but be careful with him. He's a wild one."

"Thanks for the advice." Flashing a grin at Marinelli, Christian pulled Pawlata off toward Alpha Company headquarters.

Captain Harrison of Alpha Company was distressed to hear yet another report of Pawlata's misconduct, but he was equally eager to meet the commander of ChrisTian's Butchers.

"Have a beer," Harrison said, thrusting a can toward Christian.

Pawlata reached for it quickly, barking out, "Thanks."

"Not you!" Harrison bellowed. "I think you've had enough tonight. I've gotten quite a few bad reports on you."

"That's why we're here," Pawlata conceded.

Harrison turned to address Christian as though Pawlata was not even present: "Pawlata seems to function very well in the field. However, he just can't seem to draw any distinction between the field and his own camp. He just doesn't know when the fighting starts and stops."

Christian glanced at Pawlata and found the Ape staring at him wide-eyed. Then he turned a knowing glance back at Harrison.

"Pawlata, I think it's time you hit the sack," Harrison said.

"Okay. See you in the morning, captain." He rose, started to leave, then turned and addressed Christian in a tone of deep dejection. "See you in the morning, Victor 6."

When Pawlata was gone, Christian invited the captain to continue.

"Well, a lot of your men have become unruly, unmanageable, and antiauthority since you were MedEvaced to Japan. Pawlata is not much different than the rest of them; he just seems to get into more violent fights. He's up for a couple of disciplinary actions that could result in court martial and reduction in grade. I tell you, lieutenant, if he didn't have such an outstanding war record, he probably would be in LBJ by now."

Christian defended his old group. "A lot of these men were misfits in the States. But they all have heart and, more importantly, guts. They were a crack outfit in combat. Every man could call in artillery, read a map, and even take a leadership role. They probably wanted to share their combat wisdom with their new commanders, and this was interpreted as anti-authority. Maybe I can convince the new battalion commander to reestablish the old Recon."

As he walked back to a cot in Recon's orderly room, Christian muttered to himself, "What a bummer."

Late the next morning, Victor 6 went to the Battalion Tactical Operations Center to meet with the new lieutenant colonel. He pleaded for permission to re-form and rejuvenate ChrisTian's Butchers.

The old man had better things to do with his time—such as figure out how to explain to his superiors that some of his men had let a trash fire ignite the ammo dump. "We have a new Recon now," he growled. "We don't need a Lieutenant Christian or anyone else to establish a second Recon. Besides, we have no room." His voice took on an added degree of iciness as he asked, "Do you have orders assigning you to this outfit?"

"No, sir, I was assigned up north to a rear echelon infantry outfit. I was just hoping to work out a deal if you could only establish a need for me."

"We are heavy with company-grade officers at this time, Christian, so it would be hard to justify any such need."

Christian asked, "How many are seasoned with combat experience?"

"Lieutenant Christian!" the lieutenant colonel roared, "I don't think you are getting my point. I don't have any need for you. Therefore, I suggest you go back to where the army has assigned you before someone classifies you as being AWOL. That stands for absent without leave. You are dismissed, Lieutenant Christian."

The moment he returned to Recon HQ, Christian was confronted by several of the Butchers. Gooney voiced the universal question, "Are we going to get back together?"

"Not while that bastard is your battalion commander," Christian said. He saw faces fall, and he vowed, "I'm going to take the next plane out of this place and see what I can work out with the boys from the CIA." This announcement raised the spirits of no one, but it was the only hope that Christian could hold out. He asked, "When's the next plane?"

"About two hours," Milam said. "But we all have to go out on sandbag detail."

"No problem," Christian said. "I'll join you."

As it happened, the sandbag detail was located immediately outside the battalion commander's tent. There, Christian and the Butchers toiled fiercely in the hot, early afternoon sun, filling bags and singing cadences.

"None of the new officers would ever think of helping us with any of these chicken-shit work details," Gonzalez allowed, as he dumped a shovelful of dirt into the bag that Christian held open.

Working alongside Victor 6, the Butchers got into the job, picking up the intensity of their labor and the volume of their collective voice, singing, yelling, cussing with abandon, until the noise was so obnoxious that the flap of the lieutenant colonel's tent unfurled and the commander himself stepped out to silence them with a cold stare. His eyes met Christian's, and he shook his head in scorn at the sight of an officer belittling himself with menial labor. Without a word, he stepped back into his tent.

"Fuck you!" Christian screamed at the top of his lungs.

The senior officer shot back out of the tent, glaring, wanting to be able to pinpoint the lieutenant as the source of the targeted profanity.

There was a moment of uneasy silence.

Then Gonzalez spoke, his voice beginning in a shaky timbre, but gaining volume and confidence as the words tumbled out: "Fuck . . . you . . . HO . . . CHI . . . MINH!"

Marinelli laughed and echoed, "Fuck you, Ho Chi Minh!"

The others joined in, chanting as one, "Fuck you, Ho Chi Minh! Fuck you, Ho Chi Minh! Fuck you. . . ."

*   *   *

Marinelli drove Christian to the airstrip. Christian shook the man's bear paw of a hand. "See you," he said.

Marinelli held the grip. Tears welled in his eyes. His voice caught as he said, "Recon will never be back together again, sir. It's all over."

As Christian boarded, he turned to flash a final wave. The big Italian-American shouted something, but Christian could not hear over the roar of the engines. He saw Marinelli bang his fists against the steering wheel of the jeep and mouth the words, "No! No! No!"

36

Lai Khe Base Camp, South Vietnam
January 1969

Only days later, Marinelli said good-bye to another friend. He stared at the plastic bag as it was unloaded from the chopper, and, from the size of its contents, he knew it contained Tiny. The other, smaller bag had to contain the Lone Ranger. He looked at Tiny's gear, yellowed with grenade dust, riddled with bullet holes. Tiny's M-16 had a piece of shrapnel imbedded in the stock.

If I hadn't shot off my mouth, Marinelli grieved, I'd have still been with Recon. Maybe I could have done something.

Fighting against a gargantuan lump that lodged in his throat, Marinelli gathered Tiny's personal effects from his hootch. He sat on his own cot and composed a letter to Tiny's mother. What can you say? What can compensate for such a loss? Nothing, of course.

When the letter was finished, Marinelli stuffed it into an envelope, along with an undeveloped roll of film from Tiny's camera.

He wondered if he would ever recover from this war.

37

Qui Nhon, South Vietnam
January 1969

Christian was pleased to learn that his new CO was a feisty sort in his own right. First Lieutenant Tom Crawford complained that the base was REMF heaven. "And the MPs have so many rinky-dink rules that it takes all of my waking hours to keep up the men's morale," he grumbled.

Thus far, Qui Nhon had been relatively untouched by the war, which was precisely why the army's new war hero was assigned there. Nevertheless, said Crawford, there were rumors afoot that the enemy was drawing closer.

For once, the scuttlebutt proved correct. On Christian's first day, NVA commandos blew up the ammo depot. On the second day, they bombarded the Enlisted Men's Bar—an outrage that approached the sacrilegious. On the third day, Christian was called into the colonel's office. "Since you're a seasoned combat soldier, I want you to take a group of men to pinpoint and burn out the enemy's infiltration routes," the colonel ordered. "Talk to Crawford. He'll get you men and supplies."

It seemed like a minor chore, one that involved no enemy contact, so, after he had secured a supply of napalm, Christian broke a personal rule; he did not bother to interview the men he took along on the mission.

The unit hauled a fifty-gallon canister of napalm to the edge of a cliff, overlooking the spot from which the enemy had struck the night before. Christian and a private first class from Amarillo, dubbed with the inevitable nickname Pfc Tex, carted buckets full of napalm down the sharp face of the slope, while others remained above the canister. The two men saturated the elephant grass with the viscous fluid, moved safely off to one side, and ignited it.

Just as Christian and Tex began to clamber up the sandy cliff toward safety, an explosion rocked the ground, possibly from an enemy's rocket-propelled grenade or electrically detonated satchel charge. Whatever the cause, there were flames at their feet, dangerously close to the napalm blanket.

High above, one of the troops panicked. Thinking that Charlie was below—forgetting that Christian and Tex were there—he pushed the heavy napalm canister down the hill toward the already burning fire. Christian heard a shout of dismay from above and glanced upward to see the barrel bouncing down the side of the cliff. He also saw the face of the culprit, white with panic, screaming, "I'm sorry!"

The canister crashed into the burning field and exploded into a wall of fire more than 100 feet high, engulfing Christian and Tex.

Christian heard the roar first—an encompassing blast of thunderous fury. He glanced at his arm and saw flames shooting up inside the sleeves of his shirt. He watched the fabric disintegrate, leaving only charred black skin. Instinctively he threw his hands across his crotch.

He screamed but could not hear his own voice over the roar of the fire.

His feet struggled for purchase in the soft, sandy soil.

He saw a diamond pinkie ring, a souvenir from Airborne school, slip from his finger and fall into the flames.

His lungs cried out for oxygen; the fire seemed to be burning it all away. The deadening effects of shock overtook him and he struggled upward, through hell itself, tapping unknown reserves of energy and determination, until he finally pulled himself to the plateau, out of the flames.

Helping hands lunged at him. They rolled his body across the soil to smother the flames. Vietnamese dirt ground into his raw flesh. He smelled the strangely pleasant aroma of a charbroiled steak, and realized that it was him. His buttocks, crotch, back, arms, and one side of his face were black. Unaccountably, he felt no pain.

A sergeant's face appeared, screaming hysterically, "You gotta go back down! There's another man down there."

Somehow the logic filtered through. Don't send an able-bodied man into the flames after Tex. Send a man who is already burned. It's triage. I'm already dead.

Christian wobbled to his feet. He stared at the inferno wall, and heard the piercing screams of Tex somewhere below. He staggered forward, knowing with certainty that the moment of his death was at hand. He would lose his footing and fall to the base of hell, probably with Tex next to him.

But he would go.

He placed one foot across the threshold of the hill. Suddenly the blackened face of a man who could only be Tex emerged into his field of vision. The man appeared to be screaming senselessly, but he either had no vocal cords or Christian had no ears.

Tex reached out with flaming hands. Christian grabbed the stumps, covered with fiery napalm jelly, and pulled him to safety.

Then he fell back, away from the fire and into oblivion.

38

Qui Nhon, South Vietnam
January 1969

He woke to find himself strapped to a Stryker frame on Ward 5 at the U.S. Army's Sixty-seventh Evac Hospital. He could move only his head. His eyes darted from side to side, asking: What day is it? It must be sometime in January 1969, he thought, unless I've been out longer than I realize.

The memory of the inferno returned, and he thanked God for letting him live.

He regretted that thought almost immediately, for a human being missing 24 percent of his skin is simply a throbbing mass of raw, exposed nerves.

A Stryker frame is essentially a hospital mattress board attached to a pair of large metal ovals, one at the head of the bed and one at the foot. It was designed for patients who cannot turn themselves or be turned in a conventional manner, patients like burn victims or those with broken backs. The unique construction allowed attendants to rotate Christian's blackened body, rolling him from his back to his stomach or vice versa, as a preventive measure against bed sores and associated infections that could attack the unprotected flesh. Every four hours they sandwiched what was left of the twenty-year-old army officer between two boards, lashing him in place, then rotated the Stryker frame on its axis. The attendants tried their best to be gentle, but the slightest movement tore apart Christian's wounds and his nerves. The open sore that was his body quivered in unfathomable pain; he felt—and he was aware that he also looked—like an overcooked pig on a barbecue spit.

At three-hour intervals came the special torment of changing the dressings, part of the debriding process. A corpsman, working with forceps held in a sterile-gloved hand, pulled off a crusty, dried, twelve-inch-square section of bandage, ripping away blotches of dead green skin with it and opening fresh wounds. The pain was excruciating, similar to the agony of a severe toothache, caused by a nerve exposed to the air but intensified a thousandfold because of the multitude of unprotected nerves. The slightest movement of ambient air was torture.

Each time, Christian resolved to be strong. But as the first bandage was torn off, he could feel his pulse rate skyrocket.

"Stop, please stop!" he screamed. "I'm going to have a heart attack."

But to stop was to condemn the patient to the ravages of infection. The corpsman, muttering words of support, pulled a fresh bandage from a saline bottle and draped it over the exposed area. The moment of contact brought intense agony, but it was followed by an immediate sensation of relief as the nerves were once more protected.

As the tedious process continued, the smell of burnt flesh combined with the odor of infected skin to permeate the air with a sickening stench. It took eight of the large dressings and numerous smaller ones to complete the task. When it was over, Christian was a quivering, whimpering mass of bandages.

Over the course of hours, the new bandages dried, capturing more bits of dead, infection-laden tissue. They, in turn, needed to be replaced.

No one required a wristwatch on the burn ward. The passage of time was measured by the rhythmic cadence of the diabolical rituals: rotate the Stryker frame; change the dressings.

As an added indignity, a catheter was inserted into his penis.

During moments of respite, as best as he could from the corners of his eyes, Christian studied the patient in the adjacent bed, a man named Murray. Murray's scalp was shaved bare and his face and neck were covered with brown-black scabs and deep crimson, potlike sores, broken by white gauze bandages over his eyes. Only by the timbre of his voice, screaming for someone to pick the scabs off his face, could Christian tell that Murray was a young man.

In an attempt to quiet him at least for a moment, Christian, through the side of his mouth, asked the universal question of the military hospital ward: "Hey, Murray, what the hell happened to you?"

Murray explained in a surprisingly clear voice that he was injured at the end of his indoctrination course; he had just arrived in South Vietnam: "I was placing out a Claymore, and as I looked through the aiming arm, my partner hit the clacker. All I know is that I woke up in the hospital two days later. What do I look like, Christian?"

"Man, you look fucked up," Christian acknowledged. He had seen— and felt—what a Claymore could do. If Murray had caught a back blast full in his face, it was incredible that he was alive.

"Don't worry," Christian counseled. "They can do some amazing things once they get your ass to Japan. When I was at Camp Zama, I had a buddy who had half his face blown off and they were rebuilding it. When I left him, he had a nose in the middle of his forehead and they were gradually moving it down into place. If you get to Zama, tell Burt that Christian says, 'Hi.' "

"Sure."

The conversation was interrupted by a corpsman, who asked, ''Hey, Mr. Murray, are you ready for me to pick your scabs?''

''Yeah.''

Christian turned his head to avoid watching, and he thought: Murray will probably never see again.

Later that day, three colonels from the Eighteenth MPs came to visit. One quipped, ''Christian, you just can't keep away from these hospitals.'' But the attempt at humor fell flat. Perhaps the greatest irony was that Christian—whom the U.S. Army was ready to tout as the most-decorated war hero since Audie Murphy—had been cut down, not by enemy fire, but by American napalm. He, like Murray, was one of an estimated 40 percent of all American GIs whose wounds were the result of friendly fire. Twenty percent of the deaths of U.S. soldiers in South Vietnam could be attributed to their own forces.

39

Over Southeast Asia
January 1969

Shortly after the aircraft leveled off into a cloudless sky, Christian felt the effects of his most recent morphine injection wearing thin, and he knew that it was too soon to beg for another.

Doctors had ordered him transferred to the 106th General Hospital in Yokohama, an extension of Brooke Army General Hospital in San Antonio, regarded as the finest burn treatment center in the world. Attended by an army doctor and an air force medic, he was the only passenger aboard the C-130 military transport flight to Japan.

The C-130 was the same type of aircraft that had taken him aloft for his maiden parachute jump in airborne school, only last year. To distract himself from the escalating pain, he pictured himself, standing first in line at the hatch, waiting for the signal of the jumpmaster, trying to look the part of the officer ready to lead his men out the door. He was unafraid, or at least bravely hiding his apprehension, but some of the others, behind him, succumbed to nausea.

"Stay in line!" the jumpmaster screamed. "Take your barf bags with you."

Before he knew it, the green light emblazoned, the jumpmaster screamed, "Go!" and smacked him on the rump. He was out in the cold air, 1,200 feet above the ground, floating free. The memory of that cool, heady feeling brought relief now. He tried to keep the moment sharp in his mind.

But an attack of self-pity brought him back to reality midway through the flight. He thought: I've been shot; I've been stabbed. I've received the back blast from an antitank weapon inches from my crotch; I've run barefoot through clicks of dense jungle with my feet bloody and my body full of scrap metal and glass from an enemy Claymore. I'm no virgin to pain, but I've never known anything like this.

Involuntarily he cried out, "Oh, this fucking pain! Doc, give me a pain shot."

"Just hold your horses," the doctor replied, checking the patient's chart to see when the last dose was administered.

Christian could not wait. His mind raced: Only a short time ago I had a beautiful body. I could run, jump, use my arms, my hands. Now I'm twenty years old and I'm a freak. The glum monologue, coupled with the pain, sickened him physically, and he vomited all over himself.

The doctor and the medic helped him to a sitting position and cleansed him as best they could. Then the doctor announced that he would have to change the dressings where Christian had soiled them.

They had only begun the excruciating process when the medic remarked in a shaky voice, "I just never saw a human body burnt so bad." Then he, too, vomited.

Even as he recoiled in revulsion and agony, Christian somehow managed a wry chuckle. He was suddenly back in airborne school, back outside the plane on that first jump, jerked rudely erect as his chute opened. As he sailed along, seemingly suspended in a Paradise of nothingness, he was bombarded from above by a barrage of brown paper barf bags.

Life was like that.

40

Yokohama, Japan
January—February 1969

A macabre symphony of moans, shrieks, and pitiful wailing sounds emanated from Ward 3 of the burn unit at the 106th General Hospital. The noises escaped from grotesquely charred bodies, mingled with the stink of rotting tissues tinged with a charcoal aroma, and assaulted the senses ceaselessly. Here, muffled from the ears of the world, were twin rows of beds and Stryker frames populated with men who described themselves affectionately as "crispy critters." It was an appellation you had to earn by surviving for at least a week.

The Angel of Death hovered over Ward 3; indeed, some said it was the lucky ones who died.

Pain washed over Christian in waves, and made him crazy. He stared at the hospital ceiling and implored: *Please, dear God, let me feel good for one minute. Just one minute. This is not me. This only happens to other people.*

He wondered how the doctors could live with themselves, and finally concluded that they must be sadists. That was the only reasonable explanation for erstwhile healers who caused nothing but eternal torment.

"Nurse, nurse, nurse!" he bellowed.

A nurse came running, asking, as if she did not already know the answer, "Yes, Mr. Christian, what is it?"

"Nurse, please, please, bring me something for this pain—no, wait, has anyone died so far tonight?"

"No, Mr. Christian. I'll get your medication now if you have no other problems."

He prepared himself to receive the blessed morphine injection. Just the knowledge that it was on the way helped—but he was confused when the nurse returned with two small pills in her palm. Where was the syringe?

"Hold on there, Mr. Christian, I'll roll up your bed so you can take these yourself."

"What are you talking about? What the hell are you giving me?"

"Mr. Christian, the doctors took you off intramuscular medication and prescribed Darvon for your pain."

"You've got to be crazy!" he railed. "I'm going out of my mind with this everlasting pain and you're giving me something a woman takes for cramps?" The waves of pain banished any sense of decorum. Christian shrieked at the nurse, "Give me some morphine, and stick those Darvons up your ass!"

The nurse was a pro. On this ward, Saint Peter would have difficulty controlling his tongue. She replied, courteously but firmly, "Mr. Christian, you must take these if you want any relief."

"Nurse, go fuck yourself with those Darvons!"

The nurse stiffened and snapped back, "Mr. Christian, you're going on report. The doctors will see you in the morning."

Big deal, Christian thought, as she stalked off. I could be dead in the morning. Put me on report? Great. What are they gonna do? Send me to Vietnam?

Seeking the respite of sleep, he shut his eyes, but the overhead lights danced beneath his lids like mosquitoes around a flame. Silent tears rolled down his cheeks and splashed onto the pillow. He cried out in frustration for someone to turn out the lights, then panic gripped him. Unreasoning fear told him that if the lights ever went out, he would die. He cried out again for the lights to stay on.

His thoughts sped halfway around the globe. Why did he always cry when he thought of Peggy? He tried to imagine her as a young widow with a baby on the way. Had they told her they expected him to die any day, any moment?

Sometime that night he saw—and felt—himself die. He was motionless, breathless, and wordless when a pair of wisecracking GIs tossed his carcass onto a cart to haul it off to the morgue. But then, suddenly, it was not his body. It was the Chinaman they had killed in Cambodia, the enemy whose blood was now mingled with his own.

He woke up in a cold sweat.

Night passed into day. The lights remained on, and Christian still lived. But morning was even worse than night; medical attention was worse than being left alone.

Morning brought the first dressing change of the day. Grown men shrieked and recoiled at the approach of the cart filled with the apparatus of torture—and their writhing brought added agony and louder screams. Many begged to die.

Christian lay on his stomach, lifting his head despite the pain the movement caused, watching for the corpsman to approach, hoping that it was one of the slower medics who would delay the moment of perdition. He noticed one of the more officious doctors arrive and head toward him with an expression of vengeance in his eyes. Despite his pain, he chuckled silently. He knew that he was about to get what was left of his behind chewed out.

"Good morning, lieutenant," the doctor said coldly. He waved a sheet of paper by the side of the bed, low, in Christian's field of vision. "This report states that you were quite unruly last night. I don't have to tell you that your conduct was not only unbecoming of an officer, but I want to point out that you, as an officer, are setting a bad example for the others."

"Yeah, yeah, Doc," Christian mumbled.

"I'll tell you what, lieutenant. As a favor to you, today I'm going to personally change your dressings. Nurse, give me your scissors."

With a quick, harsh movement, the doctor tore away a dry, coagulated slab of dressings from Christian's burned and nerve-exposed back.

The patient screamed, "Holy Christ! Oh, my God! Sweet Jesus, you're tearing my lungs out. Get away from me. *I can't take this shit!*"

"Come now, lieutenant, act like a man."

"You pompous pig!" Christian roared. "If I had the strength I'd punch your nose through the back of your head."

"Nurse, 150 milligrams of Demerol," the doctor ordered anxiously.

Victor 6 felt himself slipping, slipping, slipping . . . days or weeks or months—he did not know which—passed in a series of disjointed images rising, shimmering, changing color and shape and sound—all against the backdrop of pain so intense and encompassing that it cannot be endured, yet somehow must be.

A sympathetic Red Cross worker shaved his face and then helped him write a letter to Peggy; he tried to be optimistic. He worried that the words were too impersonal, and he hoped that Peggy would read between the lines when she saw the notation: "Dictated to a Red Cross worker, January, 1969. . . ."

His penis swelled to five times its normal size and the doctors told him not to worry; how can you not worry about *that* . . .?

One morning a second lieutenant marine pilot, a patient named Reds, asked, "Hey, Dave, do you know who is out in the front ward?"

"No."

Just then a group of civilians stepped into the ward and Reds exclaimed with awe, "It's Broadway Joe!"

"Who's Broadway Joe?"

"Are you shitting me? Joe Namath's just about the greatest quarterback of the century. He's a superstar. He was one of the first quarterbacks to wear bellbottoms and fancy shirts."

"Big deal," Christian sneered. "I hate bellbottoms, and I don't know much about football." He glanced at the celebrity and added, "And I hate his hairstyle."

"Well, smell me," Reds countered.

Namath made the rounds and eventually approached Christian, asking, "How you feeling, soldier?"

Christian laughed in his face, and Namath smiled back condescendingly.

"Do you have a piece of paper?" Namath asked. "I'll give you my autograph."

"No, I don't have any paper," Christian replied. He had a sudden thought: "You can sign your name on the tape on my chest dressings." Namath did so, and Christian later traded the autograph to a medic in return for an extra morphine shot.

The weeks of January passed in a cloud of torment. Next to the pain itself, time was the supreme frustration. Christian had been wounded before, and always his young body had healed rapidly. But this was torturously slow.

Even after he became somewhat ambulatory, he knew he faced an extended stay here at the 106th General Hospital, and then at another military hospital back home.

One afternoon a patient wearing nothing but a towel appeared at Christian's bed and invited him to join the other "crispy critters" in the shower room, where they turned on all the spigots and sat around on toilet seats, enjoying the impromptu sauna. The hot steam brought some relief from the pain caused by the chilly ward air until Mr. Lang, the physical therapist, discovered them and chased them back to their beds.

How long could a person hold on, Christian wondered? Sooner or later the pain had to end. If it was sooner, that meant you bought relief with death. If it was later, that meant you survived. The heaviest irony of the burn ward was that few were sure which alternative was preferable.

The whirlpool treatments were the worst moments. First, Mr. Lang plucked off Christian's dry dressings with a ripping motion. Then he prodded the screaming patient into a large stainless steel tub where the motion of icy water loosened bits of burned and infected skin. A Japanese papa-san pinched off snips of dead flesh with tweezers. If Christian cried out—and he always did—the papa-san jeeringly called him "baby-san," pulled up his trouser leg, and exposed the scars of his own gunshot wounds, received in Manchuria during World War II. There was no reasoning, fighting, or arguing with the papa-san. If he chose, he could let you slide out of his wiry arms and drown.

Meanwhile, as the papa-san worked with his tweezers, Mr. Lang grabbed Christian's arms and legs and jerked them unmercifully, stretching the fledgling skin.

Christian promised Mr. Lang, "If I ever see you back in the States I'll give you some physical therapy of my own."

Christian's temperature rose to 103.8 degrees; he was diagnosed as suffering from acute melioidosis—a parasitic infection that is a major cause of death in Southeast Asia. He probably picked it up as he writhed skinless in the South Vietnamese earth. Melioidosis is resistant to penicillin and therefore difficult to treat. About 70 percent of its victims die. The treatment of choice was a regimen of intramuscular injections of the drug kanamycin, as painful as rabies' shots.

Moved to the infamous Ward 2, where the survival rate hovered around a mere 50 percent, Christian was greeted by a male nurse whom the other patients called Captain Nice.

Captain Nice tweaked Christian's toe playfully and announced that the last nine patients who arrived here suffering from melioidosis all died.

"Don't worry, he's just goofy," explained the patient in the next bed, a Pfc named Trinkwell.

Christian fell into a labored conversation with the man. Trinkwell had been an army cook assigned to the First Infantry Division, a REMF who had never seen combat. One day his stove exploded, transforming him into a globule of roasted meat. He suffered second- and third-degree burns over 80 percent of his body. He had been here for many months, enduring thirty skin-graft operations. In fact, he was the senior patient on the ward, and he was marked as a survivor.

From the reactions of the attendants, Christian could see that Trinkwell was a five-star general on this ward. He had made it through the unendurable and qualified to reap the rewards. Someone had provided him with a lamb-skin rug to place atop his sheets, to cut down on the intolerable itching. He had earned the privilege to be rude or crass to anyone, regardless of rank, much like the right that a baby has to break wind, or an old person to belch in public. Combat medals meant nothing here. This was a different sort of war.

Each morning two soldiers from the morgue crew, whom the patients dubbed "Mutt and Jeff," arrived on Ward 2 to haul away the men who had died the previous night. Mutt, employing a Gomer Pyle accent, greeted the patients with a cheery, "Who are our customers for today?"

Jeff chimed in: "Yep! who is going for a ride on the Meatwagon Express?"

Mutt enjoyed spooking Christian with comments like "You still here? I thought for sure we would have picked you up by now."

A Red Cross worker delivered a pair of strange letters. The first was from Peggy, and it was a couple of months old, written before she had visited him at Camp Zama. It read: "Dear Dave. I really don't know whether I should be addressing you with the salutation of 'Dear.' I don't know who or what I married. I just received about $1,800 in bills from your old bachelor days at Fort Bragg. Your brother has defaulted on the loan that you cosigned for him and the Bank of North Carolina is now holding you responsible for the $1,100 outstanding . . . aside from that Sears is demanding $160 for past due payments on your television set. The straw that broke my back was a phone bill from North Carolina Telephone Company for $118 for phone calls made by your friend Frank Deeny. Since Frank was killed in Vietnam, they want you to pay the bill. . . ."

Christian listened to the litany and sighed. Once he got better—if he got better—there was a harsh, real world out there. How was he going to handle it?

The second letter was, of all things, a badly mistimed Halloween card from his father, the first he had heard from M.J. since the man ran out on the family thirteen years earlier. The writing was cursory and almost illegible, as if it had been scrawled idly while M.J. was sitting at a bar. It read: "Dear Son, It sure was nice of that Secretary of the Army to write me and tell me that you are a first lieutenant. All my buddies at the bar are proud of you and so is your Grandma. Be careful burning things or else the Secretary of the Army says that death will be imminent. I don't know what that means, but be careful. Love always, your Daddy. P.S.: Keep up the good work."

As she read the card to her patient, the Red Cross worker's face registered shock. Christian deciphered the message, realizing that his father was confused by some sort of official communique from the secretary of the army, proclaiming that the death of his son was at hand. He could see the same message in the face of the Red Cross worker. She, too, along with the secretary of the army, Captain Nice, Mutt and Jeff, and probably every doctor and nurse and patient on this hell-hole of a ward *knew* that it was true. He *was* dying!

"Get out of here!" Christian screamed suddenly. "I'm not dying. I am not going to die!"

A new patient arrived on the ward, an Australian soldier who had suffered third-degree burns on 100 percent of his body. You can't get burnt any worse than that, Christian thought. As the fragile, unconscious form was placed in the bed adjacent to Christian's, Captain Nice confided, "It's a miracle he made it this far. He's not gonna live, though."

"What happened to him?" Christian asked.

"You know how those Aussies love to booze it up? Well, this character was sleeping in the supply hootch and his drunk friends came back from the bar and set the hootch ablaze. They thought it was funny until they heard the screams. The tent roof of the hootch fell on top of him. His body was still burning when he was pulled out."

Christian cringed and exclaimed, "Oooh!"

"Naw, he doesn't even know he's alive," Captain Nice contended. "The doctors will get some good pictures of him. He'll be around for two or three days at the most."

That evening, after the ward grew quiet, Christian maneuvered his body so that he could get a close look at the Aussie. He caught his breath. The man had no ears, no hair, no toes, no fingers, no testicles, and a terribly mutilated face. Despite Captain Nice's claim that he was unconscious, Christian whispered, "Hey, Aussie, can you hear me?"

"Yank, I want to go home." The words were barely audible. Christian leaned closer as the Aussie continued, "I want to go home and see my mother. When I get out of the bloody forces, I'm going into business for myself, but now I just want to go home and see my mother."

"Wow!" Christian muttered, as he lay back in his own bed. He thought: I don't think this guy is ever gonna see his mother. I'm sure it will be a closed coffin.

Am I that bad off? he wondered. Am I so far gone that I don't realize how close I am to death?

In the morning, two doctors stopped by to photograph both Christian and the Aussie for their private case history reports; one doctor poked his finger through a hole in Christian's tongue while the other gleefully snapped a picture. Am I just a learning experience, Christian wondered?

The timeless daze returned, one day merging into another. Christian's mind registered vague impressions: he woke once to find broken glass in his mouth, from a thermometer that he had crushed; he was glad for the sensation of the pain, for it meant that he was still alive.

One day a couple of the Butchers called from a bar, somewhere in South Vietnam, but he could not remember who they were or what they said. He tried to recall the Butchers, to picture them, but it all seemed so long ago.

A nurse grew angry when she lit a cigarette for him and he let it lie idly in his mouth until it burned down and seared his lips. She scolded him as she pulled the butt away, and Christian vowed, "I don't think I want another cigarette for the rest of my life."

The nurse laughed and declared, "Well, that may not be too long."

"Fuck you!" Christian shouted at her retreating back.

How can everyone give up on my life? he wondered. Then he resolved: I'll prove them wrong. I know I will.

A whirlpool treatment was interrupted by a frantic telephone call from Peggy, whose voice emanated from another universe. She complained that she was getting official telegrams laced with dire warnings, and she questioned whether he was telling her the truth in his upbeat letters.

"No, I'm getting better, Pegs," he lied. "I'll be home soon and you can see for yourself." The pain grew intolerable, and he strained to keep his voice calm. "I have to go now," he said. "They are working on me."

"David, I love you," Peggy cried. "I love you. Please get better and come home. Don't go back to the damn war."

"Don't worry, Peggy, I'm coming home."

"Please get better real quick, or else your little baby will arrive before you."

"Yeah." Christian bit his lip, to forestall pain and tears.

Another whirlpool treatment was interrupted by yet another phone call. This was from Linda Guiterez, one of the nurses at Camp Zama, inquiring about his condition. Christian tried to carry on a conversation, but the effort of speaking, combined with his emotional exhaustion and the terrible toll of pain, made him swoon. He dropped the phone, fainted, and fell face down into the water.

He awoke in bed to find a priest standing over him.

"Who are you?" Christian asked gruffly, suspiciously.

"I'm Father Jack Turner."

"What are you doing?" This question was delivered in a tone just beneath a scream.

The priest explained with practiced compassion, "I'm just setting up your nightstand to give you a sacrament."

"Holy Communion?"

"No, Dave, the sacrament of Extreme Unction."

"The Last Rites?!"

"Yes, Dave, you are very fortunate. Many Catholics die without receiving the Last Rites."

"Last Rites? Death? What the hell are you talking about? Have you given up on me, Father? Has God given up on me?" Tears rolled down Christian's face. He stared at the ceiling and cried, "Everyone thinks I'm going to die, but why you? *Why you, God?*" Then he leveled a hostile gaze at the priest and shouted, "Get the hell out of here!"

Father Turner, with a compassionate, professional air, ignored the tirade and lit a candle on Christian's nightstand.

He has the power of life and death over me, Christian thought. And he is continuing the death ritual. "I'm only twenty," he cried out. He tried to bargain: "Father, I'll never drink again. I'll never smoke again."

The priest made the sign of the cross on Christian's forehead.

"I'm only twenty," Christian repeated, as if God had not heard him the first time. "Why?"

"David, David," Father Turner reprimanded, "you are being very selfish."

The words were like a slap in the face, disturbing, but calming. "What do you mean?" Christian asked, more softly.

"You are very fortunate in that God let you live twenty years. He let you marry, and your wife is going to have a baby."

"Are you for real?"

"David, many people are taken from their families at very tender ages. Children die from accidents and diseases. God calls on many people before they ever experience half the opportunities you've experienced."

Christian did not respond.

"David, just look around you. You are lucky. Look at the Aussie; you weren't burned as bad as he was. Look at the dead soldiers who were taken out to the morgue yesterday. God let you live another day. You should be thanking God, but you're being selfish and negative. Thank God for what you have."

Christian challenged, "What do I have, Father?"

"You have today. Thank God for this day, for this moment to share in this last sacrament. With your selfish, bitter attitude you are denying yourself the precious moments that God is giving you. Dream about your family, David, and thank God for the opportunity to dream."

If he had possessed the strength, Christian would have delivered a punch to the father's sanctimonious nose. "You're nuts," he diagnosed. "Fuck you. Leave me alone. Take your God and get the hell out of here."

Even a priest has his limits. Father Turner gathered his candles and ointments, packed them into a leather case, and walked away.

Christian yelled at his back, "Fuck you, Father, I'm going to live."

That night, the Aussie died. In the morning, when Mutt and Jeff came to collect the corpse, Mutt showed a brief moment of compassion, remarking, in his best Gomer Pyle voice, on the blessing that the Aussie had never regained consciousness.

"But he did," Christian contended. "I talked with him. He wanted to go home to see his mother."

"Yeah, sure, lieutenant," Jeff said. "You just hang in there. We have a busy day today. We want you to die on a slow day."

As Mutt and Jeff hauled the Aussie away to eternity, Christian thought, Thank God I'm still alive. The words in his mind caused him to start, to remember his blasphemies of the night before. How could he, here and now, curse God?

He lapsed back into a semi-comatose state.

Father Turner returned later in the day to find a remorseful patient.

"I'm at peace with myself and with God," Christian declared. "You were right. I got to live longer than some of the guys on this ward and I'm thankful. I'm not afraid of death anymore, but I'm still going to fight to live. I think God wants me to prove to him that I want to live."

"That's great," Father Turner replied. "I think you're going to make it. Thank God for the right and the power to fight."

Christian requested, "Father, hold my hand, please."

"Yes, Dave." Something was obviously on the patient's mind and, as the priest clasped Christian's weak grip, he asked, "What is it?"

"I want to pray, Father."

"Any particular prayer?"

"Yes, I like the Lord's Prayer and the Hail Mary." Then a strange thought intruded, and Christian added, "Let's pray for all the other patients on the ward, just for insurance." He answered the priest's quizzical gaze: "You see, Father, I'm not a gambler. Just in case I do die, I don't want to have the sin of jealousy on my soul. If the pessimistic predictions are right and I do die, I want to make sure that I go straight to heaven. No burning in hell or purgatory for me. I've had my fires and my hell. Pray for the other guys and just sneak in a little prayer for me." Christian's voice was childlike as he asked, "That would be okay, wouldn't it, Father?"

The priest beamed. "Yeah, Dave, that will be alright. You aren't being selfish anymore."

The fever broke the following morning, February 5, 1969. The swelling was down, the crisis over. Doctors could not quite believe that Christian's battered body was fighting off the melioidosis infection.

But he *was* improving.

On February 11 doctors announced that as soon as his temperature dropped to 100 degrees, he could go home.

To America.

To Peggy.

To what?

41

Interlude

There are various ways to define the duration of the Vietnam War. The Vietnam Veterans Memorial in Washington, D.C., which lists the names of U.S. dead and missing in chronological order, silently declares that the war began on July 8, 1959, when Major Dale R. Buis was gunned down by VC fire while he was watching a movie at Bien Hoa, and ended on May

25, 1975, when Richard Vandegeer was killed during the rescue of the U.S.S. Mayaguez.

Legally speaking, the war began more than five years after Buis's death, on August 5, 1964, when the U.S. Congress passed the Gulf of Tonkin resolution, committing America to a major role. It can be said to have ended on January 27, 1973, with the signing of the Paris Peace Accord, or on March 28, 1973, when American troop withdrawal was completed. However, it did not officially end until, by proclamation, President Gerald R. Ford set May 7, 1975, as the cutoff date for entitling veterans to certain war-related benefits.

By any measurement, it was the longest continuous period of military involvement in the history of the nation, even though a formal declaration of war was never issued.

During those years, 9.2 million men and women served in the Armed Forces of the United States. Of that total, 2.6 million spent a portion of their time in South Vietnam, including 7,000 female nurses; 1.6 million were involved in some type of combat duty; more than 300,000 were wounded; more than 58,000 were killed.

Sending a young soldier into combat is the most that any country can ask, a truth turned into stark reality by the names engraved on the Vietnam Veterans Memorial. But, although it is easy to acknowledge that the dead made the ultimate sacrifice for their country, there is a tendency to forget how life is altered for the survivors. Survive a war, and facets of the experience will stay with you forever.

This phenomenon was compounded in South Vietnam. In previous wars, a soldier might have participated in one or two or perhaps three major battles. In South Vietnam, thanks primarily to the helicopter, the battles never ceased; combat troops were simply flown from one engagement to another. Postwar studies indicated that the infantryman in South Vietnam saw more battle time than any other soldier in the history of U.S. armed conflict.

Contrary to popular opinion, combat veterans are never a cross-section of American life. This, too, was compounded during the Vietnam War. In the late 1960s and early 1970s, avenues of avoiding the draft, both legal and otherwise, were more accessible to young middle- and upper-income men. By the process of elimination, the disadvantaged sectors of the population fought a disproportionate share of the war for the rest of America. In fact, 25 percent of Vietnam-era veterans came from families whose annual income was $6,000 or less. Additionally, their average age was less than that of World War II or Korean vets.

When they returned home—their normal years of educational and vocational development interrupted—veterans needed schooling, jobs, medical care, marriage counseling, psychotherapy, and substance abuse rehabilitation, yet it seemed to them that the government systematically reneged on its end of the soldier's contract. Simple statistics bore this out. By the mid-1970s, Vietnam-era veterans comprised about 20 percent of all living U.S. veterans, yet only 5 percent of total veterans' benefits were earmarked for them. They were America's lost and forgotten army.

Sympathy did not come from the most logical private sources—the traditional veterans' organizations—and this followed an historic pattern. The American Legion was organized by World War I veterans before they ever returned from France, and it remained stuck in a time warp, unwilling to share the reins of power with World War II veterans. Thus, veterans of World War II swelled the ranks of a younger organization, the Veterans of Foreign Wars. Korean veterans established AmVets to address their special needs. In the 1970s, the leadership cadres of all three groups spurned the newest class of American war veterans.

Worst of all was the social ostracism. The Vietnam veteran returned home to find a country that scorned his sacrifice. To the Vietnam vet, it seemed as if nearly the entire populace was caught up in the peace movement, marching with placards, singing protest songs, demanding an end to the war. Many veterans were sympathetic, and even joined in. Yet even they were confused by the antipathy of the "peaceniks" to the grunts who had fought the war in simple response to the call of their country. Protest against the politicians, sure. Protest against the generals. But how can you hold a grudge against the footsoldiers?

The media portrayed the Vietnam veteran as a social psychopath, unfit to work, beset by marital problems, subject to alcoholism and drug abuse. These *were* growing problems within the morose community of Vietnam vets, but were they caused by the Vietnam experience or the American experience? Were they pathological responses to the straightforward, kill-or-be-killed environment of war or to the unfathomable anger and rejection of their very own countrymen?

Why do we have to take the blame? Max Marinelli often wondered.

Why did the Butchers fight in South Vietnam? Because their country had told them to—it was as simple as that. Did this nation really expect a generation of teenagers to be so politically astute that it would refuse, en masse, to fight a war based on unfathomable motives?

Was Vietnam any less justifiable than the Spanish-American War or the Great War or even Korea?

Perhaps the American people had been conditioned by the clear-cut nature of World War II. Then, the issues were black and white. One could easily identify the good guys and the bad guys. When Korea came along, many Americans found it difficult to understand a war based on a shakier political foundation, and by the time Vietnam rolled around they were willing to stand up and say so.

But even if one granted the possibility that the Vietnam War was wrong, was that the fault of the Butchers or the politicians? Did it make the scar on Pawlata's ass less honorable? Did it mean Scotty died in vain?

Marinelli had questions, not answers

Soon after he returned to America, Martinelli visited Pete Andrews. They were walking together through a bus station parking lot in Hempstead, New York, when a passing car backfired. Both men hit the ground. They glanced sheepishly at one another and laughed, but their amusement was hollow. They knew that it was going to take a long time to adjust to what most of the country defined as normalcy.

The young men of Recon had reached their zenith in South Vietnam. For most of them, the experience was far headier and more satisfying than anything else they could ever hope to do. Coming back home was a shock. They wanted to share their combat high with family and friends, and no one wanted to listen. This society wanted peace, now; it most assuredly did not want war stories.

How can you adjust to that? How can you face the rest of your life knowing that by your early 20s, the most significant part of your life is over, and nobody will let you talk about it?

One week after he arrived back in the United States, Marinelli's cousin got married. Max's father wanted him to wear his uniform to the ceremony but already Marinelli was afraid to display it in public. Too many people accosted him on the street and demanded angrily, "Did you ever kill anybody?" So he wore a business suit to the wedding, but people nevertheless *knew*. He was dancing with a woman, a casual acquaintance, when her father pulled them apart and growled, "Do you know where he's been? I don't want you near him."

One by one the Butchers took up their own private quests. Some did well; others did not.

Dennis Going returned home with a Bronze Star, using his V.A. educational benefits to study electronic drafting at Idaho State University. In his head were memories so vivid that he thought he would never forget them.

Sam Janney, despite the loss of his right eye, could not escape the feeling that he had left unfinished business in South Vietnam. He signed onto a commercial fishing boat, but after it sank and he was almost lost at sea, he opted for calmer pursuit, enrolling in college to study engineering.

Proclaiming himself a civilian the moment he set foot back in the United States, Jim Lowe received an early release from the army in order to matriculate at Western State University in Gunnison, Colorado. He laid plans to start his own excavation company in partnership with his brother Barry. He gave his Silver Star to his mother for safekeeping.

Ape Pawlata searched for a toehold on life. He, too, had been nominated for the Silver Star, but an irate commander, punishing him for his numerous fights, had downgraded it to a Bronze Star with a V for valor. He had a companion Bronze Star to go with it, the Air Medal, a Purple Heart, a pair of Vietnamese medals, and a slew of more standard combat ribbons. But he didn't know what to do with them. Back in Pottstown, Pennsylvania, they did not buy a Mrs. Smith's pie.

All Pawlata wanted was for someone to say, "Hey, we're proud that you went over there and served your country." But no one said it.

The ink was barely dry on Pawlata's membership card in the Pottstown chapter of the VFW before he became embroiled in a fierce debate with a Korean veteran on the merits of their service. After Pawlata pummeled the man, officials ripped up his VFW card.

For a time, Pawlata bummed around Pottstown, unemployed and chronically drunk. Then he landed a position as a management trainee and spent the next year supervising the second shift production line at Mrs. Smith's Pies. He quit there after developing an ulcer, and became a machinist at an auto parts plant.

It was Pete Andrews who seemed to have the most difficulty readjusting to society. Andrews found the weight of his Bronze Star hard to bear. The earliest clue to his emotional state came in 1969, when news of the My Lai massacre broke in the newspapers. The evidence indicated that an entire U.S. platoon, under the command of Lieutenant William Calley, had slaughtered innocent civilians—men, women, and children—in a defenseless South Vietnamese village. Within days, Andrews visited a psychiatrist at St. Alban's Navy Hospital in New York and "confessed" that he and the Butchers had committed numerous war crimes that made My Lai pale in significance.

Marinelli was summoned to St. Alban's, where a psychiatrist told him that Andrews claimed that Recon had slaughtered POWs.

"You gotta be kidding me," Marinelli responded. "No way. It was always better to bring in a prisoner than to kill him.'' Marinelli added sadly, "Pete's just a loonie.''

To Andrews he said, "Pete, you're hurting us all with this bullshit.''

Andrews broke down and admitted to the psychiatrist that he had fabricated stories of atrocities. "I wanted the Butchers to be famous,'' he admitted. "We should be.''

"Not like this,'' Marinelli countered.

For his own part, Marinelli learned that his own Silver Star nomination was downgraded to a Bronze Star with a V for valor by some paper-pushing officer who probably had never been within 100 yards of the wrong side of a bullet. It was galling, and all too typical.

As time passed, Marinelli fell in love. One evening he brought Sandy over to the Christian home in Washington Crossing, Pennsylvania, to meet his old commander. He announced that they were going to be married, and that Sandy had given him direction in life; she had persuaded him to enroll in school.

"What are you going to study?'' Christian asked.

Marinelli's face reddened for a moment, but then he said proudly, "Hairdressing.''

Christian guffawed.

But Marinelli made a go of it. He and Sandy put together a successful business, servicing professional hairdrying equipment.

It was some time later that Marinelli heard from Tiny's mother. She had developed a roll of film from her son's camera, and sent Max copies, because he was in most of the pictures. The grieving mother and the grieving veteran corresponded frequently after that. Marinelli thought it was the least he could do. He still somehow felt responsible for Tiny's death.

In fact, Marinelli carried on a correspondence with a small group of the Butchers, including Christian, Andrews, Lowe, Going, and Janney. Many years would pass before anyone would understand why this particular group banded together.

No one else wanted to hear old war stories, so Christian, Marinelli, and Andrews met frequently, usually in a bar, to relive their exploits and to curse the present. On a couple of occasions Janney drove across country to join them.

They laughed and mused on the effects of memory. Only a relatively short time had passed, but they all tended to have their own versions of small details. Janney realized, however, that the conversations always seemed to center on the lighter side of their ventures.

Christian tried to convince them that there was a way to keep the fight going, but not with M-16s and Willie Peters. "We've got to let the nation know that Vietnam meant something to us," he declared. "We deserved to have an unknown soldier buried at Arlington," he said. "We've got to fight for these things."

"We just can't do it," Marinelli said.

"Yes, we can," Christian snapped.

But the meetings nearly always ended on a sour note; whenever Christian walked away, he felt tired, defeated, nothing more than a drunken soldier.

On April 14, 1971, Andrews wrote to Christian: "I withdrew from college on St. Patrick's Day, and got a job running a computer-run manufacturing machine in a plant. Why? You were pretty close to home when you asked if I had shot any hippies. . . . I got pretty tired out of all that horseshit they were handing out so I started telling people off. Well you know how fuckin' evil I can be if I want to, so while I looked over job opportunities I started putting the shit to the 'subversive' elements which had kept me in the fire for a whole semester. I won't go into sordid details here but believe me that gook you gave to me and Ape near Cambodia was much luckier.

"Anyhow I'm totally clear of all implications and now I'm waiting for some correspondence I've written to be answered. I wrote to the Director of Personnel, CIA, for employment as a mercenary but haven't heard anything yet. Also that I'm saving money and going dry (not drinking, pot, or anything) and planning on bounty hunting (still *legal*) this summer. The biggest hassle is getting a pistol permit from New York State. If nothing else I can get in some target practice on the local Communist party head-quarters!"

After that, there was a disquieting lack of news from Andrews. He had been one of the most vehement about the importance of staying in touch; now he simply disappeared. His phone was disconnected; his mail went unanswered. Marinelli worried that Andrews had finally found life intol-erable. It was only conjecture, but neither Marinelli nor any of the other Butchers ever heard from Andrews again.

In the years following the war, some said that as many as 50,000 Vietnam vets committed suicide. There was no way to prove it, but Christian came to believe that the 50,000 estimate was far too low.

He was forced to face a simple truth: every veteran, to some degree, is a casualty of war.

PART

TWO

Our God and soldiers we like adore
Ev'n at the brink of danger; not before:
After deliverance, both alike requited,
Our God's forgotten, and our soldiers slighted.
          —Francis Quarles,
          Epigram

42

Valley Forge, Pennsylvania
February 1969

The standing joke was that the initials of Valley Forge General Hospital were an acronym for "Very Few Go Home." In fact, the first lesson Christian learned when he arrived there, direct from Yokohama, was that he *was* home. Through a fog of pain he addressed his new attending physician, a captain, as "Doc."

The captain stiffened, and instructed, "While you are under my care, you must address me as *Doctor*, not 'Doc.' Is that clear?"

Christian answered sarcastically, "Yes, *Doctor*, I understand your Mickey Mouse rules loud and clear."

The captain walked away angrily.

"The bullshit never ceases, does it?" Christian commented to a nurse.

"It's just beginning," she warned.

This was reality therapy, and in some ways it hurt Christian worse than his burns.

The more his body mended, the more his mind rebelled. The details of daily life bore no resemblance to his fantasies of the returning war hero. This might be expected, regrettably, from a public caught up in boiling antiwar sentiment, but it was unfathomable on the part of the U.S. Army. Routinely, some officer or another strolled onto the ward the first thing in the morning to deliver a pep talk to the patients, urging them to clean up the ward, to make it glow with spit and polish. The inevitable threat was that some mysterious personage referred to only as "the colonel" might be coming through for an inspection, and, of course, the ward wanted to make a good impression. Beyond that, they should strive to win the weekly Clean Ward Award.

What bullshit! Christian thought. But the only other officer on the ward, a colonel himself, always caught the spirit and shuffled around, pulling rank on the wounded veterans, cajoling them into cleaning. Christian felt the fallout from this; the men hated officers as a breed.

"We don't have to do this," he proclaimed out of the colonel's earshot. "They pay people to clean up for us." He whispered a plan to willing ears.

That night brought the first indication that the war was not over for Victor 6. A raiding party of Valley Forge Butchers waited for the gung-ho colonel to receive his nightly sedative. When the medical personnel left, the marauders unlocked the wheels on the colonel's hospital bed and pushed him outside onto the cold veranda. The colonel woke in the chill of a Pennsylvania spring morning, aching and cursing, but he got the message. Never again did he try to pull rank.

Yet, Ward 8CD mysteriously displayed the coveted Clean Ward Award week after week, even though no patient lifted a finger toward a mote of dust. It was a ragtag Recon platoon that pulled off this miracle, conducting midnight raids to liberate the plaque from its rightful resting place.

43

Princeton, New Jersey
1969

Wearing a dress uniform over his bandages, the old Special Forces green beret on his head, muttering to himself, "What the hell am I doing here?" Christian stood off to one side of the platform and listened to a diatribe presented by another Vietnam veteran, a former enlisted man.

Out in this real world, two wars were still going on, one in South Vietnam and one in the streets of America. The antiwar movement seemed to be gaining steam daily, and its principals had organized a rally at Princeton University. In the spirit of fair play, they invited the U.S. Army to send a representative. The invitation filtered down through channels until it reached Christian's bed at Valley Forge. The army was ready to use its new war hero as an apologist. Christian accepted the invitation to speak, but had no idea what he would, or could, say to the protestors.

He listened with growing anger as the supposed ex-GI told the story of his indoctrination to South Vietnam. The man said that he was sent into the jungle without a rifle, without food and water, and forced to scrape for existence for thirty days. If he survived this training ordeal, he was considered fit to fight the war.

The speech was a whopping lie, and Christian knew it, but everyone else appeared to swallow the ridiculous story.

"Boo!" Christian shouted.

Heads turned. The speaker appeared a bit flustered. He had expected no opposition from this crowd.

"Boo!" Christian repeated. "Boo!"

Catcalls were directed at Christian from all sides. In response, the MC approached the microphone with a glimmer in his eye and said, "Well, it looks as if Lieutenant Christian would like to speak right now. He is Lieutenant David Christian from Valley Forge General Hospital. He is one of the nation's most decorated war heroes." This was greeted with a crescendo of jeers. "Do you have something to say? Come on up here, lieutenant."

"Yes, I have a lot to say," Christian announced into the microphone. The audience turned into a raucous mob, whistling, cackling, booing. Some people sitting near the front threw confetti. Christian allowed them their moment and waited for the noise to subside. Then he spoke, quietly, firmly. "I'm looking out at a bunch of real bright people," he said with sincerity. The compliment caught their attention. "Some of you are a year or two older than me, maybe more. Professors, I know that you're older than I am. So how can you listen to something that is just a lie?"

This brought more catcalls, but they were diminished in volume and duration. Somehow, the audience sensed that this man had a valid point, even though he represented the opposition. With a palpable sense of resignation, the crowd quieted, and allowed him to continue.

"I would venture to say that no one in this group here in front of me could live in America for thirty days without food or water, let alone in a combat zone without a rifle. The man who spoke before me . . ." he waved a crippled right arm to gesture ". . . the only thing that is true about this man is the yellow streak running up his back!"

The crowd reacted with vehemence, erupting in a fierce and frightening burst of jeers, whistles, and screams. But a strange phenomenon occurred. The previous speaker, whom Christian had just labeled a liar, slinked away, off the platform and out of view. His actions provided eloquent support for Christian's argument.

When the crowd quieted once more, Christian proclaimed, "The people who are really getting hurt are the returning veterans. You are hurting us. It hurts me to hear this man giving you such a misperception. Because of his words, you don't like me—and you don't even know me. You don't know what I did for the country. I think it's wrong just to take one side on an issue, cheer for it, and not understand the other side."

The words did not carry the day, but they helped Christian codify in his own mind the inevitable fruits of the peace movement. Whether or not these protestors influenced the outcome of the war, their legacy would surely be bitterness toward the young men who fought it, the country's newest veterans. The protestor would have his say, finish his education, and take his place in the fabric of society, probably earning a good income. The politician would keep his ear attuned to the cacophony of dissent, weigh it, and respond accordingly; Christian had no doubt that the politician would survive. Clearly, the coming years would be hardest on the Vietnam veteran.

44

Valley Forge, Pennsylvania
1969

On August 1, 1969, three months before he was old enough to drink or vote, Christian became the youngest captain in the U.S. Army. Then, as he became more ambulatory, he was given the job of assisting V.A. counselor William Gimpperling. He worked alongside another convalescent, Captain Gerry Rosenbaum, ostensibly to help recovering veterans take advantage of their V.A. educational benefits. It was a front-row seat in the peacetime theater, and he became a concerned spectator as he saw what he believed to be a calculated pattern of injustice in the way wounded veterans were bounced around between the military and the V.A. Now that these men were no longer fit for battle, the military simply wanted to get rid of them as fast as possible, but the V.A. did not want to take them.

He saw the scenario replayed many times. A military "counselor" presented the soldier with the opportunity for immediate separation from the service. This was a golden enticement for most GIs, but it meant the end of military pay as well as military medical care and the beginning of a new bureaucratic battle in the attempt to receive proper benefits and treatment from the V.A. Once the soldier separated from the service, he was dependent on the V.A. for continuing care, and no one bothered to tell him that it might take the government eight months—or more—to complete the necessary paperwork. Thus, the broken soldier was kicked out into the world with no medical treatment, no disability pay, no educational benefits—and no thanks—for an indefinite period of time.

The power structure of the government, it seemed to Christian, was as ambivalent about the war as the public. After throwing these men at the enemy in Southeast Asia, it was only too willing to throw them away on the streets of America. Unlike the protesters, who scorned the veteran for fighting an unpopular war, the military hierarchy seemed frustrated with him for not winning it. They wanted to get rid of the veteran quietly, and in the most cost-effective manner.

Christian determined to stand in the way. In line for a wide array of decorations, including *two* Congressional Medals of Honor, he decided to capitalize on his status. Without asking anyone's permission, he set up a veterans' counseling center within the hospital to assist the troops in processing the cumbersome paperwork for the V.A., Social Security, and the Physical Evaluation Board. His goal was to speed up the arrival of their benefits.

He discovered that his name was getting around. One day he received a phone call from a New York newspaper reporter. She had heard of his exploits, and she questioned him at length. At one point she asked, "What is your philosophy on the war?"

Christian had to ask for clarification, attempting to hide the fact that he wasn't sure what a "philosophy" was.

The reporter tried again, asking, "Well, what do you feel about the war? Is it going right or wrong or whatever?"

Christian declared bluntly that the United States should either fight to win or get the hell out of Vietnam.

Shortly after the story appeared in print, a directive arrived from the public relations office of General William C. Westmoreland, former commander of U.S. forces in South Vietnam and now Chief of Staff of the entire U.S. Army. Henceforth, Christian was not to speak to the press without first going through the office of the army's chief of publications.

The publicity flap resulted in an informal prison sentence. When he wasn't receiving treatment or working at his educational counseling job, Christian was confined to private quarters, a room guarded by MPs.

The army, clearly, did not know what to do with the maverick. From time to time Christian was marched out to the parade grounds to receive yet another medal for bravery. His Medals of Honor nominations were downgraded. Nevertheless, he wound up with the Distinguished Service Cross (the nation's second highest military honor), two Silver Stars, one Bronze Star, the Air Medal (for 25 combat assaults from a helicopter), seven Purple Hearts, the Combat Infantryman's Badge (for being under enemy fire for 30 days), two Vietnamese Crosses of Gallantry (that nation's second highest military honor), and a fruit salad of other badges and ribbons. After each award ceremony, he was marched back to his room, confined with his pain pills.

In addition to honoring him, the U.S. Army billed him for a total of $22.44 in subsistence payments (hospital food) and warned: "Accounts not settled within thirty (30) days normally are transferred to the Finance and Accounting Office for Appropriate Action."

Out of frustration, he asked his friend and coworker Jerry Rosenbaum to help him take his case right to the top. Rosenbaum arranged a photo session that documented Christian's war wounds—repugnant blue-black scars that covered his back and buttocks. On an old manual typewriter he prepared a letter to the commander-in-chief, and sent carbon copies to scores of politicians.

In his letter to President Richard Nixon, Christian declared that he had been proud to serve his country, but, because of his country's disservice to the many wounded GIs, he would feel forced to return his medals unless veterans' treatment improved. He received an indignant reply, not from the President, but from an irate colonel in the Pentagon, who simply pointed out that if Christian had a gripe, he should go through the proper chain of command.

"Do you have to keep fighting the war?" Peggy cried out one day.

His nickname was Pizza, and he was an Italian-American kid from some-where in the Pennsylvania boondocks whose face was shot up. Doctors did a reasonable job of reconstruction, but Pizza still had only half a tongue when he came to Christian's office in the hospital to inquire, in a barely understandable voice, about educational training once he separated from the service.

The more Christian heard, the more he bristled. Pizza's girlfriend was pregnant and, therefore, the boy was in a hurry to get home to marry her. Doctors had advised him to sign his back-to-duty papers, releasing the army from its obligation to provide further treatment. Since he was manifestly unfit for duty, Pizza would simply be discharged from the army, and he could go home to get married.

"You're going to get married and have a baby, and then what are you going to do?" Christian asked. "You've only got half a tongue. The army's not finished with you; they've got to fix you up."

Pizza was confused, and worried about getting home. He mumbled that he would be treated by the V.A.

"That's going to take time," Christian warned. "You are gonna have no paycheck coming in and a wife and kid to support."

Christian grabbed the phone, mumbling that he was going to "kick some royal ass." He called the Office of the Surgeon General in Washington and attempted to plead Pizza's case.

But it did no good. The army turned a deaf ear on Christian, and Pizza spurned the advice, signed the papers, and was released from the army with no immediate benefits.

The only thing that Christian accomplished was to bring himself fresh attention from the brass. An army review board asked Christian to undress so that it could examine the scars on his thighs and back, and ruled that he should be retired on a disability pension. The panel awarded him 80 percent of his current military pay for life, instead of the usual 75 percent. Both the V.A. and the Social Security Administration followed this by rating him as 100 percent disabled. All of this qualified the young veteran for a lifetime pension of about $400 a month, tax free. At the time, it sounded like a great deal of money.

Thus, at the age of 21, Christian became the U.S. Army's youngest *retired* captain.

45

Villanova, Pennsylvania
1970

"PEACE NOW!" signs adorned the campus of Villanova University when the ambassador of the Republic of South Vietnam arrived to speak to Alpha Sigma Mu. It was a special fraternity for Vietnam veterans, organized by a number of undergraduate students, including Christian. The fraternity had invited its guest to present the official South Vietnamese version of the conflict, knowing that it would have its hands full. Only a few weeks earlier, the ambassador had been booed off the stage at nearby Temple University.

Intelligence reports held that a liberal bloc of professors and students were determined to show up in force and heckle the ambassador off the stage.

By now Victor 6 was a seasoned observer of the protest movement. He had witnessed campus demonstrations at a half dozen universities, and noted a phenomenon that went unreported in the press: he always saw the same faces. He concluded that these events were not spontaneous uprisings by individual student bodies; rather, they were orchestrated protests coordinated by professional "circuit-riding" dissidents. Local students did little but listen to the inflammatory orations delivered by the principals of the traveling road shows.

What disturbed Christian most was not the antiwar rhetoric, for the speakers were, he supposed, within their rights to criticize the politicians and generals. But they never addressed the concerns of the privates and Spec 4s and sergeants. No one ever mentioned the worsening plight of the grunts who, rightly or wrongly—did it matter?—marched off to war. Beyond that, they refused to grant basic freedom of speech to their opponents. Today they would.

Fraternity member Bill Hotz was in charge of the defense perimeter. He was a hulk of solid muscle, a former marine corporal who had brought an NVA's ear home as a souvenir. One of Hotz's hobbies was to seek out a long-haired hippie in the cafeteria and drop the ear down on top of his sandwich. Hotz was cocaptain of the university weightlifting team, and he marshaled a force of hefty veterans and weightlifters who stationed themselves at strategic points in the Villanova field house. Thirty minutes prior to the ambassador's speech, Hotz reported to Christian, "We are ready, willing, and able to kick ass."

As the crowd filed in, the Villanova Butchers singled out the obvious leaders of dissent, the professional protesters. They were easy to spot, for they were armed with NVA flags. Hotz grinned at one of them and suggested, "Try to raise that flag. Please, just try to raise it."

There was not a whimper of protest throughout the ambassador's speech.

46

Camden, New Jersey
September 1972

Russell Fairbanks, dean of the Rutgers Law School at Camden, granted Christian a special interview.

When Christian walked in, the dean had the information in front of him: this law school applicant had been the youngest second lieutenant in the U.S. Army and, in turn, the youngest first lieutenant and the youngest captain. According to various reports, he was the second most decorated civilian-soldier in U.S. history.

Twice he was administered Last Rites. He had been shot in the right side of his chest and stabbed in the left arm. The ulnar nerve in his right hand was severed. An antitank weapon had exploded in his stomach and crotch. He had shrapnel wounds in the left side of his chest and in his legs, groin, buttocks, and back. A Claymore had ripped up his feet. Nearly 40 percent of his body was scarred from napalm burns. Today, about two square feet of his skin consisted of keloid scar tissue—rough, raised areas a full inch thick—from split-thickness grafts. He could not bear sunlight for any extended length of time. He was plagued by intense migraine headaches.

He was presently under the care of a neurologist, a dermatologist, and a plastic surgeon at the Philadelphia Naval Hospital. His prescribed medication consisted of more than 100 pills a day—Sansert, Fiorinal, Talwin, Dalmane, Valium, Demerol, Seconal, Benadryl. He could not take rigorous classroom tests while suffering through the worst of his pain, but neither could he concentrate properly while loaded up on medication that brought a host of side effects, such as drowsiness, dizziness, nausea, diarrhea, and blurred vision.

Despite all this, he had made the Dean's List for six of his eight semesters at Villanova, accumulated at B+ average, and graduated with honors after only nineteen months. However, his tests were only one hour long in college and he could endure the pain without medications.

The problem was his performance on the Law School Admissions Test (LSAT), a grueling six-hour examination to determine an applicant's legal aptitude and potential to meet the rigors of law school.

Christian took the LSAT "under protest," explaining in writing prior to the examination that, for physical and psychological reasons, his performance was likely to be impaired. He was subject to an unusual Catch-22: his medication reduced his ability to concentrate, but if he stopped the medication for a test, he would be clobbered with the simultaneous effects of withdrawal and searing pain. He took the test anyway, scored a disappointing 348, compared to a national average of about 500, and was denied admission.

Now he was here to plead his case for special consideration. The dean was a retired lieutenant colonel himself; Christian hoped he would understand.

But this was the same dean who, the previous year, had closed down the law school and canceled all spring exams when the United States openly invaded Cambodia. He had allowed students to graduate without taking their finals, justifying his actions by declaring that the social protest movement was more important than exams.

"The newspaper said you had a hundred holes in your body," the dean said.

"Gunshots, shrapnel, grenades," Christian acknowledged.

"The newspaper said you'd been blown to hell and back," the dean said. He paused, studied Christian's face intently, then added, "You sure don't look like it. You look like Robert Redford."

"What do you want, a basket case?"

The dean said nothing. He merely walked out of the room.

Shortly thereafter, another man entered and introduced himself as Dean Peter Bent, in charge of admissions. He, too, expressed disbelief over the extent of Christian's disabilities. An uneasy silence ensued.

Finally realizing what the man wanted, Christian slowly unbuttoned his shirt. The dean took a pencil and stuck it into the deepest bullet wound he could find. He mused, "You know, I've shot deer, Mr. Christian, less severely than you've been shot. I am amazed that you lived."

Christian cried during the drive home alone, punching the steering wheel in frustration. Who could have known that the pain inflicted on American boys by the enemy was only a prologue to the deeper, sharper pain in the years to come?

Christian was admitted to law school, but placed immediately on academic probation. On the way to one of his first classes, he encountered another student in an elevator, who asked, "Geez, did you meet the warmonger yet?"

"What warmonger? Who's that?"

"The guy who killed all those women and children and got a bunch of medals for it—a real creep."

Christian's gaze turned icy. He replied, "You're talking about me, and I never killed any women or children."

47

Philadelphia, Pennsylvania
1973

After the signing of the Paris Peace Accord, WCAU-TV in Philadelphia scheduled a postmortem debate on U.S. involvement in the Vietnam War. Christian was one of the law students in the audience as an invited observer when, moments before the start of the telecast, the host announced that the prowar speaker, an official of the American Legion, had failed to show. "I know this is a ridiculous question," she mumbled, "but is there anyone here who can speak for the war?"

It was Christian's TV debut. He characterized his opponent to his face as an "anticverything" advocate and attempted to sway the audience with impromptu rhetoric: "If communism isn't bad," he argued, "why is it not working in Berlin? Why is it not working in Cuba?"

"What about China?" the liberal asked smugly. "Look at China."

"Can't," Christian drawled. "The Communists won't let me in to look."

The audience responded with laughter. Christian did not know whether he had persuaded them, but he did realize that he had found a new gig. I'm just as good as these other guys, he thought.

From that moment on, bits of limelight searched him out, and it was not his nature to avoid them. He accepted a speaking engagement at the state convention of the New Jersey Department of the VFW. In Teaneck, he addressed the Allied Veterans of New Jersey. He spoke to high school and college groups across the northeastern corridor, and became a frequent radio and TV talk show guest, pointing out that the war would never really be over until its veterans were reassimilated into society.

He thought: I can handle this. *I can rock and roll!*

48

Camden, New Jersey
1973–1976

As he became more familiar with life on the Rutgers campus, Christian realized that law students were intensely political animals—even more so than the undergraduates at Villanova. Everyone seemed to be active in one or more organizations fighting for a cause. Blacks were organized. Women were organized. The peaceniks were somewhat in disarray, searching for new injustices to address.

Christian helped to organize the Law School Veterans' Association, and realized that he had tapped a raw nerve. The leaders of the traditional veterans' groups were ignoring the Vietnam vets, leaving them at the mercy of an unresponsive V.A. and a public that was downright hostile.

One of the most successful programs adopted by the Law School Veterans' Association was the Military Law Program, which allowed students to serve as apprentices to the Judge Advocate General's Section in the Philadelphia Navy Yard, helping navy lawyers prepare defendants' cases prior to court martial proceedings, "so that guys won't get out of the military with bad paper that will haunt them the rest of their lives," he explained to Peggy.

Christian frequently showed up at military hearings, to speak for the defense. The program was so successful that the Veterans' Club set up a similar service at Fort Dix, New Jersey. For his efforts, Christian was recognized by a Resolution of Honor, bestowed by New Jersey Governor Brendan Byrne during a Veterans' Day ceremony.

Despite a high profile, Christian struggled against a vicious cycle. Physicians at the Philadelphia Naval Hospital maintained his medication regimen; the side effects interfered with his performance in class; as he saw his grades slipping, his headaches worsened; doctors increased the dosage of his medication to counterattack the headaches.

Twice, his grade-point average fell .08 percent shy of the requirements. Both times he was officially dismissed from law school, but readmitted on academic probation. After the second such episode, the Scholastic Standing Committee warned him that this was his final chance.

In August 1975, when it was time to register for his third year, Christian was in the hospital for a skin graft operation, so Larry I. Palmer, chairman of the Scholastic Standing Committee, selected his courses. When he saw the heavy schedule, Christian asked Dean Fairbanks for permission to drop a seminar in modern legal philosophy, but the request was denied.

Knowing that he had to find some way to contend with his chronic pain, Christian sought out a private psychiatrist, Dr. George Hager. The specialist was horrified by the wide spectrum of medications prescribed for his new patient, and by the amount and frequency of the doses. His workup produced the profile of a young man who was angry, frustrated, and confused at his inability to manage pain—he had coped with every other challenge of life, and he felt guilty for giving into pain.

Dr. Hager began psychotherapy treatments, hoping first to get Christian to consider a possible emotional basis for at least some of his difficulties. There were pains attacking Christian that went far beyond the physical effects of war. Once Christian was able to acknowledge this, he could begin to wean himself from the pills.

Meanwhile, Christian pushed on, studying as hard as he could. He lined up a job after graduation with the Public Defenders' Office in Southern New Jersey.

In the early winter of 1976, when he was in the hospital for yet another operation, he learned that he had received a D in the seminar he had asked to drop, again drawing his grade-point average 0.8 percent below the level necessary for graduation. Four credits shy of his law degree, he was out, the first time he had failed at anything. This time there was no appeal.

Rutgers considered this to be a significant event. Officials held a press conference to announce that Christian would *not* graduate. The story went out on the wire services and even hit the *New York Times*. Dean Fairbanks proclaimed, "Not everyone can become a lawyer; it's a difficult profession. Maybe Christian will make a great Elizabethan poet or businessman, but not a lawyer. . . ."

At home, Peggy pulled down the shades and kept the lights turned off for three days, avoiding the press.

She's in shock, Christian realized.

What do we do now?

49

Washington, D.C./Arlington, Virginia
November 11, 1977

Wearing a flashy Panama hat emblazoned with a hot-pink scarf, his feet shod in cowboy boots, garish gold rings gleaming on his fingers, Christian stepped off the train at Union Station in Washington, D.C. He hailed a taxi, and commanded the driver, "Take me to Arlington National Cemetery."

"Today's Veterans' Day," the cabbie pointed out. "Are you nuts?"

"No," Christian replied, wondering if it was a lie. He sat in the back seat, pinning miniature medals onto the lapel of his light blue suit jacket. The driver let him off at the gate and Christian took a shuttle bus to the Amphitheater.

After leaving law school, he had realized that it was his destiny to live on the edge, where he could test rules and regulations. He had to be his own boss. To this end, he had carved out a successful business career. He formed his own firm, DAC Consulting, and envisioned himself as a wheeler-dealer, a broker bringing together people and contracts. His reputation as a war hero and his easygoing way with words proved to be an effective combination. Beyond that, his work with Dr. Hager had enabled him to throw away his store of medications and manage his physical pain. In the process of therapy, he had crystallized a two-point philosophy that provided a natural immunity to the vicissitudes of self-employment.

The first tenet was: nothing matters except your family and your friends. In the years since the war, he and Peggy had grown ever closer. He was the dreamer and she was the pragmatist; he was the Knight Errant, prowling the world in search of injustices that needed righting, and she was the Keeper of the Home Fires. The partnership was mutually nurturing.

By now there were three little Christians running around the house. Coleen Ann was born on March 5, 1969, when her father was still a patient at Valley Forge General Hospital. The moment Christian first saw the tiny redhead, he thought: my mother always wanted a red-haired child; she would have been proud. Coleen is here to replace my mother. She is something sent from heaven.

On August 26, 1971, Peggy bore a son, and Christian had to resist the temptation to name him Recon. Instead, the proud parents dubbed him David, II.

Maureen was nearing her first birthday.

The sober responsibility of fatherhood triggered a myriad of old feelings in Christian, and it insulated him from the slings and arrows of the business world. He knew, quite consciously, that these three little lives were why he had fought in South Vietnam. He had fought to provide himself and the rest of his countrymen with the opportunity to carry on the great American quest.

Aside from Peggy and the kids, what else could possibly matter?

He knew this more forcefully, perhaps, than most American fathers, for he had nearly sacrificed his life in order to enjoy these rewards. To be in a battle and to see it turn in your favor brings a sense of euphoria that can never be matched in civilian life. In war, you toy with life and death. Your heart races as you call in fire from the sky. You see the enemy die, or turn and run. The sensation is nearly indescribable; the closest Christian could come to it was to tell friends, "You feel damn good."

Someone once invited Christian to hunt deer, and he found that he could not do it. He had hunted the ultimate enemy; what could top that?

The corollary tenet of his philosophy was: everything else is bullshit. He had learned that when you say this to most people, it drives them crazy. "What matters," Christian preached, "is making my family and friends happy. Nothing else."

In civilian life, people get tangled up in the minutiae of the day and they assume that you will do the same. Remain above it and you can accomplish miracles. Run directly at the enemy, screaming your lungs out. Scare the hell out of him. It worked in Southeast Asia; it worked in South Philadelphia, South Jersey, and wherever else Christian's business ventures took him.

Life was reasonably comfortable. Army and navy physicians had finally supplied him with the last of the thirty-three operations necessary to put him back together. Although he still experienced constant pain in varying degrees, the migraines were gone. He appeared robust, and he became a focal point of attention from certain elements of government that were, finally, beginning to reach out toward the Vietnam veteran. Because of his stellar war record, resolutions honoring him were passed by the states of New Jersey, Pennsylvania, California, New York, and Oklahoma, as well as by countless county and city jurisdictions.

It's all bullshit, he had to remind himself. To others he demurred, "You're never a hero in your own eyes. If you fall for that trap, you're a fool." He emphasized the point by spitting tobacco juice, a habit he had adopted to compensate for his discarded cigarettes.

The Christians had purchased a canal-side colonial home in fashionable Bucks County, Pennsylvania. From there, Christian set out upon his own private physical rehabilitation program, jogging fourteen miles every morning along the Delaware Canal towpath. His route took him past a cemetery in the state park south of New Hope, and each day, in the quiet dawn hours, he sensed a kinship with the Revolutionary warriors who were buried there.

Sometimes the feeling was disquieting. Were fame and fortune the ultimate goals of adulthood, or should he be doing something more unselfish? Yes, family and friends were all that mattered, but how far did those definitions stretch? He was a privileged veteran, but what about the millions who were not? Were they not friends? Were they not family?

Thoughts like these had led him to become an active member in the Legion of Valor, an organization for holders of the Congressional Medal of Honor, the Distinguished Service Cross, or the Navy Cross, the nation's highest military decorations. He had made new friends with common concerns and, on this Veterans' Day, he linked up with one of them, Captain Art McGowan. McGowan, who had won the DSC in South Vietnam, was what Christian called "the veteran's veteran." He was a tireless crusader for veterans' rights.

As he awaited the beginning of the ceremonies, Christian strutted like a peacock, his rings and medals gleaming in the autumn sun.

McGowan watched, bemused, as Christian was accosted by an army general who demanded, "Who gave you the authority to wear your medals on a civilian suit?"

"The most important person I know," Christian replied with a laugh. "Me."

The general copied down Christian's name and stormed off, muttering, "I'll have your ass!"

Undaunted, Christian and McGowan savored the Veterans' Day ceremonies, and then accepted the invitation for high-ranking brass and civilian officials to gather at a nearby Officers' Club. Most of the revelers massed about the bar, swigging drinks and chowing down on hors d'oeuvres, celebrating the day. By now, Christian had sworn off alcohol, so he gravitated away from the bar and toward a group of gentlemen huddled in a corner. Unexpectedly, he found himself in the midst of several members of President Jimmy Carter's cabinet, trading idle banter with National Security Adviser Zbigniew Brzezinski, Labor Secretary Ray Marshall, and triple-amputee Max Clelland, director of the V.A., and Veteran Employment Secretary Roland Mora.

The array of medals on Christian's chest testified to his abilities, and his glib tongue provided further evidence. "You should be in Washington," Marshall said. "Send me your resumé."

50

Washington, D.C.
1978

During his successful election campaign, President Carter promised Viet nam veterans "an honorable and worthwhile place in our society." He had repeated this promise in a "fireside chat" delivered on February 3, 1977, declaring, "The top priority in our job training programs will go to young veterans of the Vietnam war." But one of his first presidential acts gave veterans cause for concern: Carter issued an amnesty for Vietnam-era draft dodgers. Veterans waited with an air of skepticism to see how he would follow up on his promises to the men and women who had chosen to serve.

Subsequently, Carter established the Labor Department's OUTREACH program to find jobs for Vietnam vets, and earmarked $140 million for it. It appeared to be a positive step, and the government needed someone to spearhead the fight for veterans' employment. Aided by the recommendations of New Jersey Governor Brendan Byrne and Assemblyman Ken Gwertz, Christian landed the post of special assistant for the Labor Department, to be the spokesman for veterans, to try to do something about the astronomical unemployment rate for Vietnam veterans.

His immediate superior was presidential appointee Roland Mora, half Hispanic, half Chiricahua Apache. In the Third Marine Division, Mora had been the senior intelligence officer for U.S. ground forces during the first five months of organized military involvement in South Vietnam. Back home, he had served as a labor organizer for the militant United Farm Workers' Movement. Mora's plan was to target veterans in the ghettos and barrios across America, moving them toward the mainstream of business life. As a result, he had already been singled out as an object of animosity by the traditional veterans' organizations, whose members tended to be mainstream WASPs. Upon this evidence, Christian concluded correctly that he could work well alongside Mora. What he failed to foresee were problems further up in the political hierarchy.

Christian took an apartment in Washington, on 4th St., S.W., overlooking Fort McNair and the Potomac River. It was only a mile from the Labor Department. Every weekend, he commuted home to Peggy and the kids in Pennsylvania.

During his first morning on the job, officials ordered him not to wear cowboy boots to work, so Christian vowed to wear them every day, even if they made his feet ache. As he studied a backlog of paperwork on his desk—the bulk of it letters from veterans seeking job assistance—he spit tobacco juice into an empty CoffeeMate jar and sighed over the government's adamant refusal to issue him a spittoon.

Along with Mora, Christian developed another ally at the Labor Department, a decorated Vietnam veteran named Jan Scruggs who still carried eleven grenade fragments in his body. Scruggs was a wiry chain-smoker who much preferred blue jeans to a business suit and grunts to officers. He, too, was partial to cowboy boots. His job in public relations brought him into frequent contact with Christian, and, as time passed, the two men commiserated over what they viewed as a lack of follow-up by the administration on its early promises to veterans.

One of their pet peeves was the effect of President Carter's pledge to give 20 percent of all federal jobs to women and minorities. On the surface, this was a compassionate plan, but in practice the victims of the plan were not the classic white male workers who dominated federal positions. Rather, they were the Vietnam veterans who also sought positions. To give women and minorities a competitive edge, the President sought to abolish veterans' preference in Civil Service jobs. This long-standing benefit credited a veteran with an added ten points on his or her Civil Service entrance examination, but over the years it was systematically diluted as Congress legislated preference for other groups. Christian and Scruggs had nothing against affirmative action programs for blacks, Hispanics, women, Eskimos, and others, but there were now some thirty-three separate ethnic and social categories that received preference. It was bad enough that the veteran was forced to compete with all these other groups on an equal basis, but now the President wanted to abolish veterans' preference altogether. They complained to Roland Mora, the nation's highest-ranking Native American and Secretary of Veterans' Employment, and Roland Mora complained to Jimmy Carter.

In the summer of 1978 Christian was sent to Oklahoma to appear as an administrative endorser of Governor David Boren, who was under political attack. After his speech, he was asked by a newsman what he thought of Carter's proposal to abolish veterans' preference. He replied simply and honestly, ''If it becomes a reality, it will make my job tougher.''

Newspaper headlines the next day highlighted a "feud" between Christian and the President. When Christian returned to Washington, three Labor Department officials took him for a ride. Parked in a limousine next to a quiet lake, they advised him to say only good things about the government. "You take care of us and we'll take care of you," one of them promised.

From that day on, he knew that his days with the Carter administration were numbered.

After a year of such frustration, he could see little progress. Even as he stumped the country to speak encouraging words about the veterans HIRE program, the federal effort languished. Out of a $140 million annual budget, only $10 million was actually spent.

Other vaunted programs fell by the wayside. A year earlier, the President received good press when he announced a $33 million program to train 2,000 Vietnam veterans as job counselors; they, in turn, would help find jobs for 40,000 disabled Vietnam veterans. Now, no one in the Labor Department knew what had happened to the program. It seemed to be nonexistent.

The President, in a grand gesture, had promised that Vietnam veterans would receive 35 percent of the available jobs under the Comprehensive Employment Training Act (CETA), but about 75 percent of all Vietnam veterans were ineligible because of various CETA restrictions.

One of the most asinine moves, in Christian's view, was the government's arbitrary decision to redefine who was and who was not a Vietnam veteran. Under the new CETA definition, you had to apply for a federal job within four years of your discharge from the military to be classified as a Vietnam veteran and receive whatever preference you could. By 1978 that automatically wiped out nearly all Vietnam veterans. And what if it took you more than four years to finish your education and prepare yourself to work? What if it took you more than four years to overcome an array of physical and/or emotional problems? The redefinition was a form of government Newspeak. By its parameters, Christian himself could no longer be considered a Vietnam veteran.

Christian thought it was symptomatic of President Carter's lack of regard for veterans' issues that he became the first President in memory to turn down a request to speak at the annual VFW convention.

In the meantime, the jobless rate for Vietnam veterans doubled, rising above 14 percent. One-third of all Vietnam veterans still earned less than $9,000 per year.

He concluded once more: it's all bullshit. Anyone who looks can see

that the king has no clothes on, but we all keep applauding and saying,
"Isn't this a wonderful parade?"

51

Arlington, Virginia
November 11, 1978

"All we want you to do is lead the pledge of allegiance," an official said.

At the age of 28, Christian had been elected 1978–1979 national commander of the Legion of Valor, the youngest man ever to hold the post. This honor increased his public relations value to the Labor Department, and the politicos liked this, but they also wanted him to keep his mouth shut. Following his candid comment to the press concerning veterans' preference, Christian found himself gradually limited to ceremonial appearances like this one.

It was Veterans' Day once more, at Arlington National Cemetery. Christian was scheduled to appear on the platform of the main pavilion along with President Carter and the joint chiefs of staff. The President was going to dedicate a plaque to the Vietnam vets—as a weak substitute for the burial of an unknown soldier to lie alongside the unknowns from the two World Wars and Korea.

Christian mused: Twice a year, on Veterans' Day and Memorial Day, people remember veterans. They don't realize that there are veterans with problems 365 days a year. You shouldn't just parade us out for show-and-tell on special occasions.

One small accomplishment of the year was reflected in his mode of dress. Once more, his medals were affixed to the lapel of his coat jacket, but this year it was legal. The general who had protested the practice the previous year had lodged an official complaint against Christian, but the Pentagon responded favorably, issuing a directive allowing medals to be worn on civilian attire for appropriate ceremonial occasions. McGowan referred to the new order as "the Dave Christian Regulation."

But it was only window dressing. There was so much more to do for veterans, and the real issues lay heavily on Christian's mind. Challenging the inequities of the system just seemed to be the American way. Wasn't this one of the rights the Butchers had fought to preserve?

When the moment came to deliver the pledge of allegiance, Christian strode up to the microphone with a glimmer in his eye. Behind him, the President of the United States placed his hand over his heart and the joint chiefs of staff stood at rigid attention. Warning himself not to start with the word "I" or the audience would intone "pledge allegiance," he began, "Let me tell you about the plight of American veterans, from my mother, who served with MacArthur in the South Pacific, to my brothers, who served in Vietnam."

He spoke for three minutes and forty-nine seconds, outlining the woes of the Vietnam vet. As he spoke, the eyes of the joint chiefs of staff glowered in anger. A perplexed expression crossed the face of the President as his right hand quivered. Secret Service men moved in close, but no one seemed to know how to respond to the maverick speechifier. "We need more than a plaque," Christian concluded. Only then did he ask the audience to "join our President in saluting the greatest flag of the greatest nation in the world."

Those three minutes and forty-nine seconds were expunged from the official transcript of the ceremony, as was President Carter's comment when Christian sat down. But Mary McCrory, reporting for the *Washington Star*, overheard the President say, "Son, you are going somewhere."

It was a prophecy.

52

New York, New York
January 25–26, 1979

On the "NBC Nightly News," reporter Jessica Savitch declared: "David Christian has been told by the Labor Department that time has run out on his year-long term as Veterans' Consultant and he will have to move out of his office. . . . Among the things he will pack—the Distinguished Service Cross, seven Purple Hearts, and two Silver Stars. David Christian is one of the most decorated veterans of the Vietnam War and, since taking the Labor Department job, he has become a persistent spokesman for other Vietnam veterans. It is that outspokenness, he says, that cost him his job."

All three major networks reported the story, and Tom Brokaw prophesied, "we haven't heard the last of David Christian."

The next morning, Christian appeared on both the "Today" show and "Good Morning America." He explained that Labor Department officials had waited until January 23 to inform him on four days' notice that his one-year contract would not be renewed. When he asked for an explanation, he was told that he was "too visible."

He related the litany of his hassles with the Carter administration and pointed out, "If they do this to *me*, if the Department of Labor Veterans Employment Service can't find me a job, what are they doing to the guys who have trouble filling out the forms? The government," he said, "is the peoples' business. We shouldn't be afraid of being *too visible* in talking business." He characterized the administration's record on veterans' issues as "pathetic."

53

Washington, D.C.
January 27, 1979

As he cleaned out his office at the Labor Department, Christian wondered what to do with the approximately 50 CoffeeMate jars filled with tobacco juice that had collected in his file cabinet. He toted over a huge metal trash can lined with plastic and dumped the contents of the CoffeeMate jars into it. The liquid slime, some of it sporting aged bacterial growth, fell out in rancid globules. The task seemed like a fitting activity for his last day on the job.

When he was finished, he picked up the overflowing portable cesspool and headed for the elevator. The dumpster was five floors below.

Alone in the elevator, he realized how vile the concoction was, and it appeared even worse to passengers who boarded at another floor. The smell was unbelievably fetid and the appearance worse, reminiscent of his first impression of the shit-burners.

"What is that stuff?" someone asked in disgust.

Christian answered honestly. He told them that it was a year's worth of tobacco spittle, and added, "It belongs to Mr. Christian."

Peering into the gamy sludge, the passenger commented, "He must be a real asshole."

With a grin, Christian acknowledged, "Yeah."

54

Washington Crossing, Pennsylvania
February 1979

A half dozen concerned veterans rose to their feet. They stood in the living room of Christian's home and saluted the flag. Then Joseph Kennedy, president of AmVets Post #1492, called for a moment of silence in memory of the dead and missing. A burly man who still suffered headaches from his World War II wounds, Kennedy had a heart that ached doubly. His son Joey was a paraplegic, crippled, ironically, in an accident following his return from South Vietnam.

As host of this AmVets meeting, sitting in the comfortable living room of his split-level suburban home, Christian heard an all-too-familiar recitation of woes:

"I keep running into closed doors."

"We're now on food stamps."

"Sure, there are CETA jobs around, but, man, I don't want to be a dishwasher or cook. How can I support three kids on three dollars an hour?"

"It sickens me. The guys who went to Canada and jail, those guys are the heroes. We're nothing."

"Dave, I got a job picking up dead cats and dogs from the highway. Jesus, that does terrific things to a man's ego, you know?"

Most of these guys still can't figure out what happened, Christian thought. They've been on a ten-year guilt trip. They feel as if they participated in something wrong. They feel scolded. While they were in Asia, their peers moved ahead of them. They came back and high school kids jeered at them. Some of these guys had the lives of men in their hands, had awesome responsibilities, dealt with millions of dollars in machinery. They wanted to keep that momentum going. They came back and people said, "Forget it. Block out Vietnam. What you guys did was worthless."

Everything was so confusing. Only five days after he was fired by

President Carter, Christian received a certificate of appreciation, signed by V.A. Director Max Clelland, thanking him for participating in the Veterans' Day ceremonies—the very action that had cost him his job.

That night, after the AmVets meeting, Christian reviewed the pile of letters that had poured in from total strangers, responding to his television appearances.

A middle-aged widow wrote: ". . . nobody really is interested in anything or anyone else unless it affects them personally. If Vietnam had been closer to our shores, and had been an all-out war, our people would have paid attention."

From Traverse City, Michigan: "Thank you, Viet Nam veteran, for caring enough about freedom to put your lives, your Fortune and your Sacred Honor on the line."

From Forest Hills, New York: "Perhaps ten years had to go by before we could all face this dark chapter in our country's life. We are not used to defeat, but we are maturing. An election is approaching, as you know, and I sincerely hope you and all other Vietnam veteran groups make some substantial headway in the political scene. Give the politicians hell, Mr. Christian."

The more he thought about it, the more Christian realized that this was a pretty good idea.

After all these years, it finally dawned on him: this was still war!

55

Fairless Hills, Pennsylvania
April 3, 1980

Hugh Carcella Hall, home of the local steelworkers' union in Fairless Hills, Pennsylvania, was packed to capacity with 300 cheering well-wishers, most of them proudly displaying their union buttons. A heavy contingent of reporters was in attendance, as well as the usual cadre of stern-faced Secret Service men. The audience was a carefully chosen friendly forum of solid Democrats.

Unbeknownst to the politicos who had orchestrated the event, a platoon of about twenty infiltrators dispersed themselves at various points throughout the room, indistinguishable from the union membership. The point man was Al Reef, senior vice commander of VFW District 9. Reef was, indeed, a former steelworker and a member of the union, but the mustached, bespectacled, genteel-appearing veteran had come dressed in his full VFW uniform and was armed with a plan. John Crocker, a veteran of the 173d Airborne Brigade whose insides were being eaten away by the residual effects of Agent Orange, wore an inexpensive suit with the steelworkers' union button pinned fraudulently to his lapel. Charlie Capella's lumbering, 300-pound body was attired in work clothes; in his hand he carried a small American flag. Christian was dressed in denim and exhibited the union button on the side of his "jeff" cap.

Promptly at 8 P.M. the Harrowgate String Band struck up the tune "Happy Days Are Here Again" to announce the arrival of the redoubtable "Miss Lillian," the feisty, 81-year-old mother of President Carter. She was stumping the hinterlands, campaigning for her son's reelection. This was her final stop on a very busy day.

As Mrs. Carter entered the hall, the steelworkers exploded with wild applause, but she quieted them quickly with the words, "If you are as tired as I am, you'll want to sit. My fingers are just dripping to fall off and I won't let them."

She then offered a simple homily, extolling the labor movement. The audience listened politely and interrupted with applause at the appropriate moments, such as when she said, "I feel very sure of Pennsylvania this time. Now that I'm here they can't refuse."

After her speech, Mrs. Carter was not disposed to take questions but, as she turned to leave, Christian flashed a surreptitious signal to Reef to activate the prearranged battle plan. Reef jumped up, calling out in a kindly voice, "Miss Lillian! Miss Lillian!"

Mrs. Carter hesitated for a moment, then bestowed a sanguine, Southern smile on the kindly looking man in the VFW uniform. She allowed, "Surely a sweet old lady can take a question from a sweet old veteran."

To her consternation, Reef launched into a rambling tirade, raising numerous veterans' concerns. The floodgates were open, and the spitfire mother of the President—no slouch when it came to verbal infighting— stiffened her back in an effort to staunch the assault.

Another veteran jumped up to complain that V.A. hospitals had 29,000 empty beds. He wanted to know why these beds were not filled, since disabled vets were fighting to be admitted.

"I do not take care of that situation," Mrs. Carter replied, demurring, "I'm an old lady."

Other questions came rapid-fire from various points in the room.

Mrs. Carter moaned, "I don't know the answers to these issues. Go to your congressman. That's what you elected him for." At one point she added, "Jimmy can't do everything for everybody."

But Crocker was on his feet now, and he delivered a litany on the subject of Agent Orange. He pointed out that U.S. troops had found it to be a highly effective defoliant; therefore, it was reasonable to assume that it might also adversely affect its handlers.

Miss Lillian inquired innocently where she might be able to purchase some of this Agent Orange, so that she could use it to get rid of weeds in her garden.

This brought a vociferous response from Capella, who lifted his rotund body from his chair, aimed his small American flag directly at the President's mother, and shouted, "You better know what you're talking about! Your son doesn't know what he's talking about!"

Secret Service agents accosted Capella and warned that he would be charged with conspiracy to incite a riot if he did not back off. Suddenly afraid, Capella sat down.

But other veterans were on their feet, shouting more questions. Christian led a chant: "Enough's enough! Enough's enough!"

As Secret Service men escorted Miss Lillian out of the hall, she turned to scream, "I'm nev-ah coming back to Bucks County again!"

A knowledgeable newsman approached and shouted over the din, "Aren't you Dave Christian?"

"Not tonight," Christian replied with a grin. Tonight he was Victor 6.

56

Levittown, Pennsylvania
1980

After the media flap following Christian's firing, Labor Department officials agreed to rehire him in order to counter the adverse publicity, with the understanding that he would work outside of Washington, from a less visible base in Pennsylvania. He was ultimately sequestered in a cubbyhole at the state Employment Services Office on Levittown Parkway in Levittown.

From there he launched a double-pronged attack, cooperating officially with federal, state, and local governments to improve the lot of the veteran even as he worked unofficially with a cadre of other concerned citizens to publicize the veteran's myriad problems.

A decade had passed before the nation could even begin to accept the Vietnam veteran, and then only because the seeds of a new social revolution sprouted locally, regionally, and nationally. Concerned men and women sought simple justice. Leaders emerged. Four of the most visible and vocal were Bobby Muller, Jan Scruggs, Dave Christian, and John Kerry. These four men increasingly crossed one another's path. Coming from diverse corners of the political spectrum, they nevertheless banded together to fight an entrenched army of stateside enemies that seemed more elusive than the VC or the NVA.

Muller was a leftist-leaning paraplegic, confined to a wheelchair and bestowed with such a surgically effective tongue that Christian nicknamed him "Rolling Thunder." In the early 1970s, as the war dragged toward a close, Muller was a moving force in Vietnam Veterans Against the War, perhaps the stickiest thorn in the establishment's side. After the war Muller organized the Council of Vietnam Veterans in an attempt to fill the void left by the unsympathetic national leadership of the VFW, American Legion, and AmVets. This group evolved into Vietnam Veterans of America (VVA).

Kerry tried to work within the system for changes.

Scruggs quit his job as a public relations man at the U.S. Department of Labor to devote his energies to the creation of a lasting memorial to Vietnam veterans.

Christian found himself involved with these men as well as scores of others, addressing a wide variety of issues. Suddenly, awareness of Vietnam Veterans' needs seemed to spread like a napalm fire.

Working from his Levittown-based Labor Department office, Christian persuaded Pennyslvania Governor Richard Thornburgh to establish a series of Governor's Outreach Centers—the first such statewide network in the nation—targeting five localities for programs to provide full-range counseling in compliance with federal regulations. Despite their troubles, Vietnam veterans were skeptical of submitting themselves to government bureaucracy; they had seen enough of it already. As a result, the majority spurned even the few programs that were available. It was the center's task to combat that reluctance.

Funded by $5 million in federal and state grants, the centers were designed to show veterans how to take advantage of whatever the government offered. The first outreach center was dedicated on August 1, 1980, in Levittown Shopping Center in Tullytown, staffed primarily by disabled Vietnam vets. Others followed in Wilkes-Barre, Harrisburg, Erie County, and Westmoreland County.

The Carter firing, Christian came to realize, was one of the best things that had ever happened to him. He was now a national spokesman for veterans, in demand throughout the country for speeches and media appearances.

"I turned a lemon into lemonade," he said to Peggy.

57

Washington, D.C.
February 1981

Christian's friend Stanley Swain picked him up at the train station in his gray Chevy Malibu and dropped him off at a White House security gate. As a guard checked his ID, Christian stared at the imposing building. After the guard passed him through, he took a deep breath and moved forward, wondering what the outcome of all this would be. As he walked up toward the door, he debated whether he should remove his floppy gray hat and garish rings. He decided to wear them. You've got to be yourself, he thought. You don't change in one day.

He stepped inside and compromised by removing his hat.

An old friend was there to greet him. It was Bill Hotz, the former marine weightlifting enthusiast who had marshaled a cadre of guards to prevent protest back at Villanova, when Christian had invited the South Vietnamese ambassador to speak. Now Hotz was a Secret Service agent, assigned to protect the president.

Hotz asked, "You gonna take the job?"

"Don't know," Christian replied. "They haven't offered it yet."

After Miss Lillian's son lost his reelection bid, V.A. Director Max Clelland, seeing the handwriting of a new administration on the wall, gave his farewell speech on Veterans' Day, 1980. Since that time, Christian had found himself courted by the incoming Republicans. Drew Lewis, deputy chairman of the Republican National Committee, and Pennsylvania Senator John Heinz recommended him to President Ronald Reagan as a likely candidate to succeed Clelland as director of an agency with 225,000 employees and a $26 billion annual budget.

Considerable correspondence had passed between Christian and the Office of Presidential Personnel. Newspapers reported that he was a prime candidate. If it came to pass, 31-year-old Christian would be the youngest V.A. director ever. Finally he had been called in for an interview.

He met first with presidential personnel adviser John Herrington, who pushed Christian to accept. He explained that here was a chance to serve his nation once again, and promote the cause of veterans' rights in the process. There was one obstacle, Herrington said, and his name was E. Pendleton James, director of White House personnel. James was a political animal who was leery of Christian's status as a registered independent and his record of service to the Carter regime. They needed a high-profile veteran who would be good for the new administration's image, but James preferred a bona fide Republican.

Herrington led Christian into James's office for the key interview. Both men waited for a moment, as James finished reviewing Christian's file.

When James finally began to spell out the terms of the deal, Christian found himself squirming in his seat. Appearances on the network news shows were already prearranged for the President's nominee for V.A. director, and the purpose was to defuse the two most volatile veterans' issues, Agent Orange poisoning and delayed stress syndrome. James informed Christian that the new director was to go on national television and say, in effect, "Look at me. I'm a Vietnam veteran. I have no problems. Agent Orange, it has been discovered, only causes teenage acne, and the people who are supposedly suffering from stress are malingerers."

It was a sellout, no bones about it, yet Christian did not refuse the deal outright. He pondered; here was a chance to infiltrate. If he followed the prearranged scenario, it would be like donning the enemy's uniform in order to gain access to his big guns. Christian believed that he could do much good from the inside, as head of the V.A. Was the compromise worth it?

Seeing the indecision, Herrington suggested, "Before you decide, why don't you take a few minutes to think about it? Would you like to sit quietly for a while—in the President's chair?"

The question required no answer.

President Reagan was away on a trip, so the Oval Office was vacant. Hotz led Christian inside, and left him alone.

Christian nestled into the President's chair, behind the President's desk, his mind overcome by awe. He glanced up at the pattern of the ornate molding. His eyes blurred and he had a misty vision of his teenage years in Levittown, when the family was on welfare. He remembered how embarrassed he was to wear the gray trousers with a pink stripe down the side of each leg, and the awful red shoes—clothing his mother had received from Catholic charities. Mom, he thought, was the greatest soldier I've ever known. She'd really be proud to see her son sitting here.

Instantly he realized that he could not take the job—not under these conditions. His mother, Dorothy, would have been horrified.

After a time, he walked slowly back to James and Herrington and declared, "I don't think I can take the job. It's not right."

Herrington seemed to understand; James was close to rage.

Christian left, feeling empty.

58

Washington Crossing, Pennsylvania
April 17, 1981

Staring at a draft of his letter, Christian crossed out a sentence and added another. The words had to be just right. He let out a deep sigh.

The selection process for a new V.A. director had dragged on for months. The press knew nothing about his private conversation with Harrington and James, and still considered him to be a leading candidate. Thus far, he had done nothing to halt their speculation. But now, Budget Director David Stockman had announced plans to slash $300 million from the V.A. budget, close ninety-one readjustment counseling centers, eliminate Agent Orange health studies, and reduce education and employment assistance.

As Christian rolled a fresh sheet of paper into his typewriter, he muttered, "I'd have to be a male whore to take the job now."

His fingers punched the keys angrily as he composed an open letter to the President, officially withdrawing his name from consideration. Noting that 64 percent of the nation's Vietnam veterans had voted to elect Mr. Reagan, he declared, "The proposed cutting of the Vietnam veterans' programs is politically and socially wrong."

When he delivered copies of the letter to the press, he commented that he hoped his withdrawal "brings to the attention of the President that what's going on is wrong. I hope that whoever gets the post has a viable budget to work with.''

The *Philadelphia Bulletin* and *Philadelphia Journal* headlined: CHRISTIAN TO PREZ: STICK YOUR VA JOB.

59

Washington, D.C.
April 1981

Robert Nimmo, a friend of Christian's, accepted the post of V.A. director.

Almost immediately he appeared on ''Good Morning America'' and the ''Today Show,'' declaring that Agent Orange was relatively harmless and that the delayed stress syndrome was little more than a psychological cover story used by malingerers.

60

Philadelphia, Pennsylvania
June 1981

Jan Scruggs eyed the hundreds of people who massed inside the auditorium, and he knew that this press conference could turn ugly, fast. The hall was packed with men decked out in veterans' paraphernalia, grumbling pointedly that they did not need a monument that would simply collect ''pigeon shit.'' Hecklers whipped them into a nasty mood.

Scruggs was the driving force behind a grand plan to create a Vietnam Veterans Memorial on a two-acre site between the Washington Monument and the Lincoln Memorial. When he had first announced the formation of Vietnam Veterans Memorial Fund, Inc. (VVMF), to the press on May 29, 1979—the tenth anniversary of the day he lay bleeding in the South Vietnamese jungle, reciting the Lord's Prayer—he had declared, "The only thing we're worried about is raising too much money."

The early prediction was naive, to say the least. It had taken Scruggs two years to reach the point where he could present a visual representation of what VVMF had in mind; only then could serious fund-raising begin. He had used a $160,000 seed grant from Texas millionaire H. Ross Perot (who had lost one of his closest friends in a helicopter crash in South Vietnam) to finance a national design competition, and the results were highly controversial.

Out of 1,421 entries, the winning plan was submitted by a 21-year-old Chinese-American, Maya Ying Lin, an architecture student from Yale. She originally sketched her concept of the memorial for a class on funerary architecture, and her instructor had given the plan a B+.

The proposed design consisted of two polished black granite walls, each more than 200 feet long, joining to form an open V. Installed in the ground on the northwest corner of Washington's Mall area, one leg would point toward the Lincoln Memorial and the other across the reflecting pool to the Washington Monument. At the ends, the walls would be even with the ground, but they would slope downward, taking the visitor on a solemn walk into a gentle abyss. The walls would be inscribed with the names of more than 50,000 dead and 2,500 missing, listed in chronological, rather than alphabetical, order. The design did not include a flag, not any statement about the war, nor even the word "Vietnam."

It was unlike any other war memorial ever built in the United States, and it evoked strong feelings. One former VVMF volunteer who had resigned in order to enter the competition had denounced the winning design as a "black gash of shame and sorrow." He contended that the United States was involved in two wars during the years in question, a military war in Vietnam and a political war at home, and he argued that the proposed design was a memorial merely to the political war, the dark side of the controversy.

The *National Review* characterized the design as "Orwellian glop."

But the issue that polarized most Vietnam veterans seemed to be money. VVMF needed to raise $7 million to construct the memorial, and many vocal veterans were concerned that this would eat into their chances for achieving other goals.

Scruggs was desperate to fulfill a promise to Perot that the veterans themselves would approve the design, and this Philadelphia press conference was the first public test of how well the controversial project would be received by other Vietnam veterans. Scruggs had asked Christian to be one of the speakers and, sensing the mood of confrontation, decided to alter the program sequence. He called upon Christian to speak first, trusting in the strength of his image as a committed spokesman for veterans.

As Christian approached the podium, a few well-timed catcalls rang out, followed by laughter. There were people here who thought they had him in a bind. If he supported the memorial, he would go against the disgruntled majority of the audience, who clearly preferred social programs. If he failed to support the memorial, he would betray his friend Scruggs.

Victor 6 charged the enemy, screaming into the microphone: "Should we erect a monument when we have such a strong demand for social programs?"

The crowd roared in answer to the rhetorical question, "No! No! No!"

"Should we erect a monument for pigeon shit when we have high unemployment and Agent Orange problems that could use these memorial monies?"

"No! No! No!" The crowd was on its feet now, applauding, and Scruggs' face registered shock.

Christian let the ovation continue for a few moments; then he gestured for silence. He held the collective ear now, and he spoke softly: "In a country as rich as the United States, can we not have good social programs for our veterans *and also a memorial*? Don't allow the politicians to have us fighting among ourselves. We need both a memorial *and* social programs, and I am today going on record endorsing both goals. We took care of our own in that crazy Asian war and we must take care of our own back here in the world."

Few in the crowd had thought of the matter in this way, and they now roared their approval. They could have both. They *should* have both!

After the press conference, Christian was surprised by the vehement reaction of an old friend, reporter Carlton Sherwood. Over the course of a decade, the two men had crossed paths many times. Sherwood had waged a successful newspaper war to call Rutgers University to task for its cavalier treatment of Christian in particular and veterans in general. He also supported Christian in print after his firing by the Carter administration and his reluctance to be considered as President Reagan's V.A. director. Each considered the other man to be a good friend.

Christian listened to Sherwood, now a Washington television reporter, argue against the design of the proposed memorial, and simply agreed to disagree with him, thinking that there was an end to the matter.

61

Austin, Texas
June 1981

Dan Jordan was an American Indian from Austin, Texas, who had served with the First Air Cavalry in South Vietnam. He was wounded twice in war, but in the ensuing years he was plagued by inexplicable maladies that had nothing to do with his combat injuries. He battled neuromuscular difficulties, blood disorders, liver problems, and a lingering depression. His two children were born with birth defects of their arms, hands, and wrists.

He went to the V.A. for help, but was rebuffed. A V.A. doctor suggested that the birth defects might be due to drugs that Donna Jordan took during pregnancy. He had no explanation for the other physical manifestations. As far as counseling for Jordan's depression, the physician said that only those veterans committing violent crimes qualified for counseling at this time.

The Jordans suspected a link between Dan's problems and their children's disabilities, and Donna Jordan, who was working on a degree in genetic anthropology at the University of Texas, began to collect research. They learned much about what Vietnam veterans were beginning to realize was a time-delayed booby trap set for them in South Vietnam, not by the VC or the NVA, but by their own government.

During the early years of the 1960s, the U.S. military experimented with several types of defoliants, named for the color code emblazoned on the 55-gallon drums that contained them. Agents Green, Pink, and Purple were discarded in favor of Agents White, Blue, and Orange. Agent Orange was determined to be the most toxic synthetic chemical in existence. Between 1962 and 1971 some 18 million gallons of it were dropped onto the terrain of South Vietnam. The spray was so effective that jungle growth was stopped within days, and entire areas were completely barren of all growth within two months, eliminating the triple-canopy jungle cover so critical to enemy operations.

The chemical component in Agent Orange that caused the greatest concern to veterans was a form of TCDD, better known as dioxin. Even before Agent Orange was used in South Vietnam, it was known that dioxin caused malignant tumors in animals and birth defects in their young, but this did not deter American military planners from ordering its deployment in the war zone. Ironically, dioxin was not even an active defoliant agent; it was simply a by-product of the Agent Orange manufacturing process, deemed too expensive to remove. In South Vietnam, dioxin exposure came through the ingestion of contaminated food and water, direct contact to the skin, and inhaled fumes.

By 1969 the South Vietnamese and U.S. governments were aware of an increasing incidence of birth defects among people exposed to Agent Orange. As a precaution, the U.S. Department of Defense decreed that henceforth Agent Orange would be sprayed only on "less populated" areas; these happened to be the areas in which U.S. combat troops saw the greatest action.

Two years later the evidence of Agent Orange's health effects was so overwhelming that the U.S. government banned its use altogether. Following this directive, the U.S. Air Force dumped existing stockpiles into the high seas.

But the damage had been done. By the early 1980s Dan and Donna Jordan, and countless other veterans, believed that there was enough evidence to prove beyond a doubt that Agent Orange destroyed people as well as foliage. It caused unexplained skin sores, liver damage, and disorders of the respiratory and cardiovascular systems as well as the urinary tract. It brought on neurological disorders, such as weakness in the lower extremities and a reduction in sensory perception. Furthermore, it could bring on an entire range of psychiatric problems. One veteran described the combined effects as "what a fly may feel like after being sprayed with insecticide."

The Jordans spearheaded the nation's first state-level law providing for a study of the effects of Agent Orange, and Christian flew to Texas to present his own testimony to the Texas State Legislature. He told the lawmakers how, one day, he had noticed that his older brother Doug resembled someone who might be his father, not his brother. Doug had spent nine years in the army as a chemical warfare specialist, four of them in various areas of South Vietnam. In South Vietnam his job was to mix the Agent Orange and now, Christian realized, he was suffering the legacy. His body was covered with open sores.

Three of Dot Christian's sons became disabled veterans as a result of the Vietnam War. Younger brother Daniel was injured in training accidents at Fort Leonard Wood, Missouri, and again at Fort Hood, Texas, and never made it to South Vietnam. But he had recovered. It was Doug who was experiencing the most severe problems.

Christian had taken him to numerous doctors for treatment. Several tumors were excised, but Doug continued to lose weight. "My brother receives 10 percent disability for a wound to his leg," Christian testified. "But he doesn't receive any aid for the illness caused by Agent Orange."

Thanks to the Jordans' efforts, aided by Christian's testimony, the Texas bill passed.

Finally someone had begun to address the problem. Christian said goodbye to his new friends, the Jordans, and flew back home, vowing to put the subject of Agent Orange on the national agenda.

62

Levittown, Pennsylvania
July 7, 1981

Staring at the broken lock on his desk drawer, Christian growled, "I'd like to fry the bastards who did this." He wanted to cry; he had come so close.

He had persuaded Democratic State Representative John Cordisco to sponsor Agent Orange legislation in Pennsylvania. Drawing on his law school background, he had authored the Agent Orange Victims Act, then helped Cordisco push it through in record time.

Following that, he was surprised by the volume of correspondence that poured into his office. Most explosive was the 240-page file, sent to him anonymously, containing medical testimony and White House and Defense Department reports on the effects of Agent Orange. Much of the material was dated from the 1960s, meaning that certain businesses and government offices knew a great deal about Agent Orange *before* it was used in South Vietnam.

Christian had decided to sit on the material over the July 4th weekend as he pondered how to use it; he locked the files into his desk in the state Employment Services Office on Levittown Parkway.

On July 2, he had traveled to a federal courtroom in Philadelphia to testify before a special session of the U.S. Senate Veterans' Affairs Committee. There, he disclosed the existence of the volatile files and agreed to forward them to the committee.

He was in Washington over the weekend, and happened to mention the existence of the documents to a group of veterans. He hinted that he had some "really hot" information locked away in his office.

But when he had returned to his office on this Tuesday morning, he discovered evidence of a burglary.

According to State Police Detective James McAndrew, the intruders jimmied open an outside door that led them into the building's boiler room. From there, they drilled and chipped their way through a half-inch concrete ceiling, cut through its supporting wire mesh, and hoisted themselves between narrow iron structure rods into a two-foot-high attic space. McAndrew conjectured that the burglars then crawled along an eight-inch-wide steel girder above the false ceiling—in order to avoid detection through the front windows— and dropped down onto Christian's desk. Then they broke into the desk and stole the Agent Orange documents, but nothing else.

63

Washington, D.C.
February 4, 1982

Christian held a press conference to announce the formal establishment of the United Vietnam Veterans Organization (UVVO). In the past, he had attempted to work with Bobby Muller's Vietnam Veterans of America, but this now proved impossible.

Prior to Christmas 1981, Muller and three other VVA officials, Michael Harbert, Thomas Bird, and John Terzano, made a six-day trip to the now-unified Republic of Vietnam, paid for by *Penthouse* magazine. In Hanoi, Muller placed a commemorative wreath at the tomb of Ho Chi Minh. Upon his return to the United States, Muller announced that he had received a pledge from Vietnam's foreign minister, Nguyen Co Thach, that the Vietnamese government would undertake "renewed efforts" to account for some 2,500 U.S. soldiers still listed as missing in action. He also reported that the Asian nation had promised to allow visits by U.S. scientists to study the effects of Agent Orange.

Christian could not stomach the image of Muller laying a wreath at the tomb of Ho Chi Minh when there were so many Americans back home lying in graves that no one bothered to visit. He decided that it was time to make a formal break with "Rolling Thunder."

UVVO sought a new image for the Vietnam veteran as a successful contributor to society. The old image of the drug-using, social misfit, Christian declared, was part of a general trend toward negativism in American society. He proclaimed, "The whole country, not just the Vietnam veteran, needs a good shot in the arm and a good kick in the butt. It's about time we all stopped waiting for someone else to magically solve our problems. Our problems can be solved, but we are the magicians."

The new organization had a unique twist. It would open its membership rolls not only to veterans, but to their family members as well, on the theory that the lingering effects of the war were just as painful to them.

Christian resurrected old tactics. Wear the enemy's uniform so that you blend in; in most cases, this meant a three-piece suit, and it also meant that he would have to get rid of the chaw of tobacco in his jaw. Walk the enemy's trails—the halls of Congress and the fifty statehouses. If you find yourself caught in an ambush, rush the enemy. And don't forget the war whoops.

Dan Jordan, Christian's Agent Orange ally from Texas, was installed as acting national commander. He declared, "The biggest obstacle in the veterans' issues has often been the veteran himself, his lack of involvement. We can't sit back . . . and expect someone else to carry the ball for us."

Christian sent Muller a cordial letter wishing him the best, and Muller responded in kind. But the race was on for national recognition and, more importantly, funding. V.A. Director Robert Nimmo quickly certified UVVO as the second national organization authorized to fully represent the Vietnam veteran. This allowed UVVO access to the V.A.'s master computer tapes containing the names and addresses of veterans. But the real plum was to receive certification by the Combined Federal Campaign (CFC), and thereby become a national charitable payroll deduction. The campaign's strict rules required any applicant organization to overcome numerous federal paperwork obstacles. Clearly, whichever of the two Vietnam veterans groups was certified by CFC would win this latest war.

On this Washington trip, Christian also visited with Carlton Sherwood, his friend the television reporter, and once more was amazed with the man's opposition to the Vietnam Veterans Memorial.

In quick succession, the basic design concept of the memorial had been approved by the National Capital Memorial Advisory Committee, the Commission of Fine Arts, and the National Capital Planning Commission. But a vocal opposition of veterans, led by a cadre of former officers, argued that design changes were needed. In particular, many wanted the memorial to be aboveground, not sunken, and white, not black.

A compromise was reached. The original design was to be augmented with a more traditional statue and, further, a flagpole would be installed to fly Old Glory.

Christian was surprised to learn that even these alterations had not mollified Sherwood. The reporter dropped a hint that the ground-breaking ceremony for the memorial would never take place. He whispered that he had inside information: there would be a "coup."

Sherwood told Christian that he was on the "wrong team" by supporting the memorial. Christian was stunned at this statement, partly because he considered Sherwood to be a friend and partly because the man was supposed to be an unbiased and uninvolved reporter. What business did he have taking sides in the design controversy? But he kept his own counsel and allowed the reporter to ramble on.

Sherwood criticized the speech Christian had made in Philadelphia, launching VVMF's public fund-raising campaign. He seemed to assume that Christian was upset by the "black gash" design and urged him to turn against Scruggs. Pointedly, he noted that he could put Christian in touch with others who would join the fight. Repeating a racial theme that was becoming more apparent in the private statements of some of the design opponents, he asked Christian how he could support a memorial created by a "fucking gook."

64

Washington Crossing, Pennsylvania
1982–1983

In 1982, a colorful former colonel from Los Angeles named James J. "Bo" Gritz attempted an improbable mission with a private army. After training at Clint Eastwood's ranch, the group of commandos flew out of Mexico, then stopped in Thailand and Cambodia; from there they attempted to infiltrate South Vietnam. They were determined to rescue American POWs still held there. But they found Vietnamese troops waiting for them at the border. A firefight erupted, during which a few of the commandos were killed. Gritz and the others escaped.

Back home, Gritz was hauled before a congressional committee, where an angry legislator demanded, "Who gave you the authority to carry on a private war?"

Gritz replied serenely, "God and David Christian."

The remark brought Christian unwelcome scrutiny from congressional investigators. He tried to explain:

Two years earlier, in Buffalo, New York, Jim Donahue and Pat Kelly had organized a group of disabled former Green Berets to run in the Skylon International Marathon. The group included Donahue himself, Christian, Scott J. Whitting, and Gritz. The four men pushed their scarred bodies forward for the full marathon distance of 26 miles plus 365 yards, carrying the American flag over the same "Peace Bridge" formerly traversed by a protesting army of draft dodgers, to highlight the positive accomplishments of disabled Vietnam veterans. They were greeted by the combined cheers of Canadians and Americans. Mayor Jimmie Griffin presented them all with keys to the city of Buffalo. New York Governor Hugh Carey awarded them the Conspicuous Service Cross (the state's highest peacetime award to a soldier or veteran).

After the marathon, Gritz solicited Christian's opinion of his plan to invade Vietnam. Christian listened to the fanciful scenario and replied in a cavalier manner, "Go for it."

It was an offhand remark, but now he was linked to the raid by Gritz's congressional testimony, and UVVO was linked by association. Christian had no choice but to decertify Gritz's local UVVO chapter in Los Angeles.

The congressional inquiry signaled the beginning of pressure from all sides. As Christian's Outreach Centers in Pennsylvania amassed larger budgets, leaders of the traditional veterans' organizations attempted to snatch them away. Their own members were gradually dying off, and they realized that they needed the Vietnam vets in order to survive. Representatives of the VFW and the American Legion met privately with Governor Thornburgh to discuss the issue.

Shortly thereafter, in a private conversation, Thornburgh aide Paul Critchlow told Christian that if he did not "make peace" with the traditional veterans organizations, "we're going to have to get rid of you."

On a hunch, Christian bought a simple electronic gadget that monitored the amount of current drawn off by the telephone. He tested it on his office phone and then his home phone and announced to Peggy, "We're being tapped."

Angrily, he reported the information to the telephone company and was told that the taps were legal. A company management official declared that he could not reveal the identity of the individual or individuals who were monitoring his conversations.

In January 1983, the War Veterans Council, an independent advisory group to the governor, held hearings and without receiving testimony from Christian, concluded that the Levittown Outreach Center was mismanaged. It also asserted that UVVO was not a nationally accredited war veterans organization and therefore was not eligible for government funding. The latter statement hurt UVVO's recruiting efforts, and the former triggered a series of investigations into Christian's private life and his financial dealings with the Governor's Outreach Centers.

One of the allegations was that Christian was a "double-dipper," supervising the day-to-day operations of the Governor's Outreach Centers while he was supposed to be working for the Labor Department; Christian reassured Peggy that this was a "bullshit" charge, and was confident that he had the paperwork to back it up.

The most bothersome allegation—because it signaled a change in his heretofore harmonious relationship with the governor—was a charge of impropriety in the rental of the new UVVO headquarters building. It was a matter of public record: the Levittown building that housed the first Governor's Outreach Center was sold to a Canadian firm, which served thirty days' notice for the tenants to clear out. Bill Gallager, Christian's uncle, wanted to help, so he had purchased a dilapidated building at 10th and Diamond Streets in Philadelphia for $10,000 and resold it to UVVO for a single dollar. The site was just off the campus of Temple University, in the toughest part of the ghetto. The plan was for UVVO to renovate the building for $50,000 and lease it to the Governor's Outreach Center for $1,500 per month. The plan was preapproved by Thornburgh.

But after the fact, state investigators, applying their own formula, declared that the $1,500 monthly rental fee was ten times the appropriate amount. Even though the governor had approved the deal beforehand, and even though the cost per square foot was less than the state previously paid for the Levittown property, investigators charged that the rental contract was an instance of price gouging.

Christian assumed a defensive posture. He hand delivered a memo to the governor's office announcing that UVVO would allow the Outreach

Center to operate rent-free until such time as a fair-market fee was determined by an outside source. Thornburgh turned down the offer and state investigators moved forward on the case.

In response, Christian telephoned the state attorney general and asked him to investigate the governor. He declared to the press, "I'm willing to hang out my underwear if the governor is willing to hang out his. I'm sure the governor has skid marks to show."

The governor kept his pants on, and the feds jumped into the act. The State Department still sought to clarify Christian's role in the Bo Gritz affair. The Labor Department probed the allegations of double-dipping. The IRS wanted the minutiae of his financial life.

In tears one day, Peggy, pregnant with their fourth child, told her husband that she had been humiliated when she went to the bank and found that investigators had been there to examine their private accounts.

"This," Christian cried, "is a bloody nightmare."

Bitter comfort came from the knowledge that "Rolling Thunder" was subjected to a similar onslaught. The IRS combed Bobby Muller's financial records and leaked insinuations. A newspaper reporter questioned where Muller had gotten the money to have his driveway paved. Every attack led to more vicious, and personal, attacks. At any media appearance now, Muller, paralyzed from the chest down, could expect questions about his sex life.

Who was the mysterious enemy who appeared to have coordinated the attack? To Christian, it was reminiscent of the government's response to the civil rights movement of the 1960s, when federal agencies were marshaled against those who dared speak out against injustice. Whatever parties were aiming the guns knew the targets well, for they had singled out the most vocal spokesmen.

Christian entered the Philadelphia V.A. hospital for a hernia operation. While he was there, Peggy delivered a daughter officially named Kathleen, but dubbed K.C. by the proud papa.

At home convalescing, grumbling to himself that his body did not rebound from physical punishment as quickly as it used to, Christian took a call from Governor Thornburgh, who coolly informed him that he was eliminating state grant money for the UVVO Outreach Center.

It occurred to Christian that he was fighting an enemy that utilized the hit-and-run tactics of the VC. They did not have the honor of the NVA, to stand up and fight. They were more like gnats. It was the gutless approach, waylaying the trail with pungi sticks and booby traps, baiting you into losing your temper.

He could deal with physical pain more easily than he could handle emotional torment. A bullet wound heals rather quickly, but an emotional injury festers, and that is the goal of guerrilla warfare.

He tried to respond appropriately, applying the lessons of combat. He had to remind himself: it's all bullshit.

On Friday, May 13, 1983, Christian and fellow UVVO officers Frank (Doc) DeSumma, George Schaffner, and Dave Hill sat around a conference table and watched George Mezalis read the sheet of paper Christian had slid in front of him. It declared:

"I, George Mezalis, misappropriated funds and misused my position with the United Vietnam Veterans Organization . . . to establish personal businesses on company time and to purchase and use supplies for said businesses. . . . I misrepresented myself to my superiors and my fellow corporate officers and I fully understand and hereby confess that I have committed the crimes of misrepresentation, fraud and embezzlement. . . ."

Short and bearded, Mezalis had reminded Christian of Kris Kringle when he came in a year earlier pleading for a job. He was going to lose his apartment if he did not come up with the rent. UVVO initially hired him as an $8,000-a-year clerk, but Mezalis quickly proved to be a fund-raising genius. As a result of his work, contributions had poured in. Within seven months, Mezalis and his wife Lynn brought a new level of competence to UVVO's offices, and the grateful, understaffed organization was paying them a combined salary amounting to about $47,000 a year.

By 1983 UVVO had chapters in all fifty states and was on target to become certified by the CFC, a reality that would vault it into the lead as the spokesman for Vietnam veterans. Then had come the state and federal inquiries into its activities. And now, the officers had discovered incredible sums of money missing from the bank accounts.

Speaking slowly, attempting to keep obvious venom from his voice, Christian said, "George, we know you stole at least $200,000. Our accountants have established that you used a very tricky system of inflated invoices and dual receipts, that you rigged our computers to transfer money into your own unauthorized bank accounts. George, you are a crook. We all befriended you, and you stabbed us in the heart."

Wordless, Mezalis signed the confession and slid it across the table.

As Christian reached for it, Mezalis pulled a gun out of his suit jacket, leaned forward, and pointed the barrel at Christian's face. The other men at the table froze. A couple of them were gun nuts, packing heat, but no one dared move. Mezalis had the drop on them. There was a silent standoff for a moment before Mezalis said quietly, "Here, I bought this with your money." He laid the gun on the table, slid his chair back, rose, and walked out of the room.

"We ought to kill him," one of the men at the table grumbled.

"No," Christian said, "just let the system take care of him." He turned Mezalis's confession over to the Philadelphia DA's office, which declared that it was reticent to prosecute white-collar crimes, and let the matter drop.

Shortly thereafter, Bobby Muller's Vietnam Veterans of America received accreditation from the CFC. It was a death warrant for UVVO.

65

Washington, D.C.
September 6, 1983

Jan Scruggs met WDVM-TV reporter Carlton Sherwood at the Gaslight Club in an attempt to clear the air.

Scruggs's public and personal lives had been subjected to the same intense scrutiny as had Christian's and Muller's, and he was growing weary of it. The worst day had occurred nearly a year earlier. VVMF had planned a five-day National Salute to Vietnam Veterans, keyed to Veterans Day 1982. The wall and its names were now in place, and although final ceremonies could not take place until 1984, when the compromise statue and flagpole were ready, the Salute would serve as an unofficial dedication of the memorial. It was to be the biggest event of Scruggs's life.

On November 8, the day before the beginning of the Salute, an IRS agent appeared at the VVMF offices with a summons in his hand, announcing a government audit of the books. Scruggs complied, believing that he would be cleared subsequently of all indications of impropriety, but he was bitter about the timing. His enemies had succeeded in taking the joy out of the occasion.

After the IRS audit, VVMF opened its books to an independent auditing agency. Those two audits cleared the organization, and Scruggs thought the troubles were over.

Now there was Sherwood. He was working on an investigative report for his TV station, and Scruggs took the direct approach, called Sherwood, and set a date for lunch, so they could talk out the issues.

Scruggs's first impression was that Sherwood had an open mind, and he explained what he thought was the heart of the matter. Some people simply did not like the design of the memorial, he said, and they were determined to stop it. They had tried to stop the groundbreaking. They had tried to stop the National Salute. Unknown accusers had already reported allegations to the IRS, but subsequent investigation had exonerated VVMF. And now, obviously, they were whispering accusations to the press because they had failed to achieve their goals through official channels. Sherwood feigned a sympathetic ear, and Scruggs left the meeting convinced that he had made his points, unaware that Sherwood, some time earlier, had allied himself with the opposition.

Soon, disturbing reports began to come in from people Sherwood had questioned. They claimed that he was defamatory, biased, and prejudiced in his questions about VVMF and the people associated with it.

Through his own investigation, Scruggs learned that Christian and Sherwood had known each other for a decade. Scruggs phoned Christian and asked him to "feel out" the reporter's intentions. It was a Recon mission, and Christian did not wish to undertake it. But he agreed reluctantly.

In mid-August, Christian had reached Sherwood by telephone and asked a few leading questions. It was easy to loosen the reporter's tongue on the subject of the memorial. Sherwood complained that the memorial was a "left-wing statement" and vowed that he was going to expose it as such. He contended that the VVMF was going to come under further federal scrutiny for financial impropriety, and that some of the leaders of the organization were going to go to jail. He said he was going to "nail" Jack Wheeler, VVMF chairman. He charged that VVMF had paid $5,000 to Congressman Don Bailey to stifle his criticism of the memorial, and he said that VVMF had paid $50,000 to designer Maya Lin to quiet her own misgivings about the proposed additions to her original concept.

Christian reported the preposterous allegations to Scruggs. Both men knew that Sherwood's biased campaign, his secret alliance with the memorial's opposition, could place him in serious jeopardy with his employers, but they decided not to take direct action yet.

Instead, Scruggs arranged a second face-to-face meeting at the Gaslight Club. The two men were joined for dinner by a "surprise" guest, Christian, who "happened to be in town."

Over dinner Sherwood, convinced that Christian was on his side, was bold enough to threaten Scruggs, saying, "I hope there is room on the memorial wall, because I am going to put your name up there."

Christian was caught squarely in the middle of the battle between two of his longtime friends. With great reluctance, he decided that the memorial was more important than the maintenance of his friendly relationship with a reporter. He told Sherwood that he had agreed to Scruggs's request that he testify to the reporter's duplicity.

Sherwood knew that he had lost any chance to claim a reporter's objectivity. Over the years he had said too much to Christian. His story was dead. Beyond that, his job was in jeopardy. Speaking privately to Christian, he offered a compromise plan that only compounded his problems. He wanted Christian to persuade Scruggs to have an off-the-record meeting with WDVM-TV's management, wherein Scruggs would admit that some mistakes had been made, including misspent money and poor judgment, but he would affirm that there were no instances of crime or fraud. Sherwood would back this up and then, he contended, his bosses would probably direct him to drop the story. Thus, he would be allowed to save face, not to mention his job.

If Christian promoted this plan, Sherwood promised, he would use his influence with media personnel to ensure that he, Christian, received some favorable publicity.

Here was a reporter creating the details of his own story. Christian sighed heavily, concluded that Sherwood's word was now about as reliable as the body counts in Vietnam, and refused.

Three months later, WDVM-TV accepted Sherwood's resignation due to a "disagreement with management."

By then, the Vietnam Veterans Memorial was already being visited by as many as 10,000 people every day. It was second only to the Smithsonian's Air and Space Museum as a Washington, D.C., tourist attraction.

66

Washington Crossing, Pennsylvania
1983

When an incumbent President is running for reelection, local party pundits are coerced into finding candidates for all races. It is an embarrassment not to field a candidate for a local congressional district, even if the cause is perceived as lost from the start.

Pennsylvania's Eighth Congressional District was just such a location as the 1984 elections approached. The Democratic Incumbent, Representative Peter H. Kostmayer, was popular, and considered to be unbeatable. No one among the local Republican politicos dared to take him on, and the party was forced to seek a fresh face. It settled on Christian, although he was registered as an independent, although he had served in Washington for a year under a Democratic President and had declined a job in a Republican administration, and although press reports contended that he was currently under investigation by at least three federal agencies and the state of Pennsylvania.

It *is* all bullshit, Christian said to himself when Harry Fawkes, the local Republican Party chairman, phoned and asked him to run for Congress. The two men were friends, and Christian knew Fawkes to be a man of honor. He accepted.

Here was a concept straight from the writings of Chairman Mao—to beat the system, you have to get inside it. Christian had been attacking politicians for fourteen years; suddenly he saw the opportunity to war on the government from within. As a congressman, he could put the V.A. budget under close scrutiny. From the inside, he could demand accountability. Who was responsible for all these nebulous investigations on men who had served their country back in South Vietnam and were still trying to do so?

Only later did Christian realize that he, and perhaps Fawkes also, had been suckered. He had been solicited as a sacrificial lamb. At an executive meeting shortly after he had decided to run, one of the local political pundits, with a few drinks under his belt, laughed in Christian's face and predicted, "You're gonna have your ass handed to you."

Christian smiled as he whispered, "Fuck you."

On the issues, Christian was more Republican than Democratic, but he took them one by one. Although he remained a critic of the administration's veterans' policies, he supported President Reagan's concept of a strong defense as a deterrent against war.

He viewed the V.A. as a boondoggle staffed by too many nonveterans. Sometimes he mused: The V.A.'s annual budget is close to $30 billion now. There are 30 million veterans. Maybe we'd be better off if we took the $30 billion, divided it up among the veterans, and wished everybody good luck. "If I *do* get into power," he mumbled, "they better look out."

When Kostmayer, the incumbent, realized that Christian had no intention of assuming the role of sacrificial lamb, he opened old wounds. Some years earlier, at a Memorial Day ceremony, he had noted: ". . . our feelings about Vietnam are full of ambiguity. When I was a student at Columbia, I took part in marches against the war, but here I am at a Memorial Day service for veterans. There were no heroes in Vietnam." Now he reiterated that theme in his speeches.

The comments angered one of Kostmayer's Democratic Party workers who, unbeknownst to the congressman, was a Vietnam veteran himself. The man quietly set about to investigate his own candidate, and shared his information with the Christian camp.

This surreptitious investigator, Rich Montgomery, used the provisions of the Freedom of Information Act to gain access to Kostmayer's Selective Service record. What he learned was that Kostmayer as a young man was a virtual fugitive from the Selective Service for a period of seven years during the time of the Vietnam War. On several occasions he had been ordered to report for his preinduction physical, but had failed to show up. By law, he was a draft dodger, and he could have been prosecuted as such if President Carter had not extended amnesty.

Despite this information, the VFW endorsed a slate of incumbents that included Kostmayer. In addition to Christian, the VFW snubbed West Virginia congressional candidate Robert Altman, a West Point graduate and holder of the Silver Star—another recognized hero of the Vietnam War.

67

Washington, D.C.
1984

Dave and Peggy Christian sat around a table in a meeting room at the
Georgetown Inn. They, along with other congressional candidates and their
spouses, were confronted by the chairmen of several Political Action Committees (PACs). These were men and women with gargantuan egos who
controlled enormous amounts of campaign contributions. One of them sat
at the far end of the table and asked each candidate to identify himself or
herself and provide a brief verbal resumé.

When his turn came, Christian spoke softly. "I was the youngest military officer in Vietnam," he said. "I was hailed as one of the most decorated
soldiers in that war. After the war, I served as a special assistant to the
Labor Department under President Carter. President Reagan considered me
for the post of V.A. director, but I turned it down. I'm the founder of the
United Vietnam Veterans Organization."

Around the table, Peggy saw eyes bulging in amazement. Her cheeks
reddened as she heard quiet chuckles. It was all true. In fact, it was somewhat understated, but it always sounded impossible.

After the other candidates had finished identifying themselves, the lob-
byist at the head of the table, whom Christian had already dubbed PAC
Man, pointed a finger directly at Christian and said, "I want to tell all of
you something. You better not be lying, about education, about things like
military service or being war heroes. We'll find out if you're lying. The
youngest officer in Vietnam. Turning down a presidential appointment.
Things like that can be checked. Don't say it unless it's the truth!"

Peggy felt the rage ready to burst out of her husband. She quickly placed
her hand on his leg, trying to hold back the torrent that she knew was
coming, but she was unsuccessful.

"Sir!" Christian asked, "are you calling me a liar? You call me a liar,
I'll rip your heart out. No one calls me a liar!"

It was even worse than Peggy had feared. I'll rip your heart out—had
he actually said that?

PAC Man's face paled. His voice quavered as he replied, "I carry a
gun."

"I don't care," Christian snapped. He felt Peggy's grip tighten under the table, and he said no more.

The remainder of the morning sessions were tense. For his part, Christian could not wait until PAC Man returned to his office and ordered someone to check out his background.

He also anticipated with relish the next scheduled activity.

"You can't talk to the President," the advisor said. "Just hustle in, sit down, smile for the camera, and move out."

Wait a minute, Christian thought, as he entered the formal White House sitting room, this is my life. The President is heavy artillery for any election, and I need him.

He sat next to President Reagan, so close, at the photographer's insistence, that their knees almost touched. Then, instead of smiling benignly for the camera, he stared directly into the President's eye and said, "Mr. President, nice meeting you. I know we can smile real quick for these pictures, but I have to cut right to the point. I need you in my district. I need you to help me get media attention."

Mr. Reagan smiled warmly and replied, "David . . . it is David . . . ?"

"Yes, David Christian. An easy name to remember."

"Yes, uh, David, I'll do everything I can to help you win the election."

"Will you come to my district? I'm serving my country. I also need my country to serve me."

"I'll do everything I can, David," the President vowed.

68

New Britain Township, Pennsylvania
August 1984

The Secret Service man's countenance was stern as he decreed that Christian had to surrender his package. "We have to take that from you," he declared.

"Why?"

"Cause you can't have anything in your hands when you meet the President."

Christian tried to explain that he was one of the two reasons the President was coming here to the Shrine of Our Lady of Czestochowa. Mr. Reagan was here to endorse the congressional candidacies of Eloise DuPont, the Republican from the neighboring state of Delaware, and himself, the Eighth District candidate. "I'm running for Congress," he complained. "You gotta be kidding me—I can't give a gift to the President?"

"No, we're going to take it. It could be a weapon."

"It's a t-shirt! I'm going to choke the President with a t-shirt in front of 80,000 people? I'm running for Congress. I need to use this opportunity."

"You can't have it."

"Fuck you," Christian snapped. "I'm giving this to the President of the United States. So shoot me, okay?"

The Secret Service man ran off to report this exchange to his superiors.

Christian was allowed to keep his package as he struggled for a seat on the platform close to the President. Mr. Reagan's speech was essentially nonpolitical, but everyone knew its punchline. After talking for several minutes, the President declared, "We need people in Congress like Elise Du Pont . . . and David, uh . . . David, uh. . . ."

Christian whispered to himself, "It's an easy name to remember."

Several hundred people in the audience shouted, "Christian!"

"Christian," the President recalled.

"Christian! Christian!" the crowd roared.

The candidate saw his chance. He leaped from his seat and thrust the t-shirt into the President's hands, as Secret Service men gulped. Mr. Reagan grinned and held up the gift for all to see. It proclaimed: "Run, Christian, run."

69

Washington Crossing, Pennsylvania
November 8, 1984

Daniel Christian called his older brother. He was crying as he reported the news. Daniel had been dating a woman on Representative Kostmayer's staff, and she had reported inside information: Dave was to be indicted on federal charges. Tomorrow.

"For what?" Christian asked.

"I don't know," Dan said. But it's tomorrow."

As it had been with Jan Scruggs, the timing was incredible. Christian looked back to yesterday and ahead to tomorrow. Both were supposed to be days of great celebration.

During the height of his congressional campaign, yet another investigation began. As the result of an anonymous complaint lodged with the House Government Operations Committee, the V.A. was examining charges that UVVO had supplied a list of veterans—obtained from the V.A.—to the Union Fidelity Life Insurance Company. If true, the action violated federal provisions against the unauthorized disclosure of confidential information. The unnamed tipster charged that Union Fidelity had used the data to peddle insurance and, in turn, provided financial support to UVVO.

UVVO National Commander Joe Buscher, a former Spec 4 who still suffered headaches from the NVA bullet that had entered his skull and nearly taken his life, had responded with a vehement denial of any impropriety, and noted pointedly to the V.A.'s general counsel, "UVVO national officers would like to know who made charges against our fine organization."

This information was not supplied. Buscher could only speculate.

Despite this latest hassle, Christian had managed to close an originally wide gap in the polls. Throughout the endless round of campaign debates and speeches, his considerable charisma took over. Reporters said he looked like Robert Redford and exuded a sense of calm control. His friends teased him about becoming a power broker. They dubbed him with the nickname "The Kingfish." He liked it.

Only two weeks before the election, *Roll Call*, the newspaper of Capitol Hill, reported that Christian had forged a slight lead in Pennsylvania's Eighth District.

Suddenly, the Kingfish was subjected to more "incoming," a barrage of enemy artillery.

Kostmayer had called a special press conference on October 30 and raised the issue of Christian's financial propriety with regard to the building that UVVO had rented to the Outreach Center. It was an old charge that was never proven, yet never officially dropped. ". . . this man's integrity has already been questioned and now he is under federal investigation," Kostmayer alleged. "Do you want this man to be your congressman? I don't think you do."

Reporters inquired of various federal and state agencies whether they were investigating Christian. When officials replied that they could neither confirm nor deny that the candidate was under scrutiny, the incumbent quickly charged that Christian's integrity was the "central issue" of the campaign.

By election eve, polls showed that the draft dodger and the Vietnam veteran were running neck and neck, and the Kingfish envisioned a double coup. Two days after winning the election, he would be one of the featured speakers at the unveiling ceremony of the Frederick Hart statue at the Vietnam Veterans Memorial in Washington.

But he lost the election by 0.8 percent of the vote. A swing of 1,500 votes would have brought him victory.

And now his brother's phone call announced his pending arrest. For what? Was it on one of the old charges, or the newer allegation about selling the V.A. lists to an insurance company?

There was no sleep in the Christian household this night. "I don't know what's going on," Christian said to Peggy. "I did nothing wrong, that's all I can tell you. If a federal marshal shows up here with papers, tell him I'm in Washington giving a speech, and I'll be back."

He considered a difficult question: quite apart from the issues of right and wrong, did the nebulous powers-that-be really have the ability to convict him of a violation of law? Yes, he decided. Victor 6 may have been naive, but the Kingfish is not. "If I have to go to jail, I'll go to jail," he said to Peggy. "But I did nothing wrong."

"Why do you have to help the world?" Peggy implored. "Why don't you just help David Christian for a change?"

Nearly a year would pass before he could provide the answer.

70

Washington, D.C.
November 9, 1984

The moment Christian stepped up to the speakers' podium at the Vietnam Veterans Memorial, he felt ostracized. The word was out; none of the attendant politicians or bureaucratic dignitaries wanted to stand or sit near him, to be captured on news film as he was served with a federal indictment.

Will they arrest me before or after the speech? he wondered.

He stared out at the memorial, with its controversial design. Its 140 rectangular slabs of polished black granite, imported from Bangalore, India, etched with the names of 57,939 dead and missing soldiers, reflected a shaded image of the observer, forcing him toward introspection.

By the time he rose to speak, he discovered that his personal problems had faded for the moment. "Medals come with a price," he proclaimed softly, sadly, "a terrible, terrible price.

"I came out of the war with a respect for life. I don't have guns in my house, and I hope never to go out with a rifle again. But I'm still extremely patriotic and I still love this country. If they asked me to die tomorrow so nobody in this country would ever have to see the atrocities of war, would never have to see people blown away, I would give my life and I would give it gladly."

He waved his arm toward the names engraved on the solemn memorial, and continued, "Their pain and suffering were the same as in any other war. Their loneliness was the same as the loneliness felt by the Revolutionary soldiers at Valley Forge. The valor they displayed was the same valor displayed in the trenches of World War I. They shed the same honorable blood that was shed at Normandy on D-Day and at Inchon, Korea. Why are they not, today, being treated with the dignity befitting fallen warriors?"

He answered his own question, warning, "America should never again commit its troops to a war unless its heart is committed. Otherwise, it will never be committed to those troops *after* the war. People should tell elected officials, 'My son will go second if your son goes first.' "

He finished the speech and sat down, waiting for someone to appear with handcuffs or papers of indictment.

But nothing happened. He was not arrested, and no one told him why, or why not. *It was all bullshit!*

An entire day of festivities was planned, but he was too morose to join in the celebrations. During the drive back home, his mood was solemn. He did not speak to his driver and former campaign aide, Rick Weis.

After a time, a national news report came over the radio, and Christian heard excerpts from his own speech. He broke into a smile and shouted, "Hot damn!"

71

Detroit, Michigan
1985

"I may not agree with your political philosophics," Christian told his old friend and enemy, Bobby Muller, "but you've been good for veterans. We should put principles before personalities."

During his congressional campaign, Christian had turned the reins of UVVO over to Dan Jordan, Stan Swain, and Joe Buscher. Amidst the onslaught of investigations, the trio had managed to keep a shoestring operation going through 1984, but the rival VVA was clearly more vital, and it had money coming in from CFC contributions.

So Christian and Buscher journeyed here to the 1985 VVA convention, intent upon making peace. Christian said that if Muller would agree to dissociate VVA from international political questions, he and Buscher would pledge, on the convention floor, to encourage their membership to merge. "We've got to focus on our brothers," he declared. "If we do that, we can be very effective."

"Rolling Thunder" looked up from his wheelchair and smiled in agreement.

UVVO merged into VVA, and now Vietnam veterans had achieved a single voice.

It was a sensible move, but Christian had always viewed himself as a winner. He was growing weary of losing.

72

Bucks County, Pennsylvania
May 30–31, 1985

On May 30, 1985, at 2:35 P.M., Christian was driving on Newbold Road in Fallsington, Pennsylvania, with his friend and business associate Larry Silvi.

The business world was keeping him busy these days. Since losing the election, he had decided to heed Peggy's advice, to take care of himself and his family for awhile and try to leave the problems of the world to others. He knew that his four children—Coleen, David, Maureen, and K.C.—deserved a full-time father.

By now he had rejuvenated DAC Consulting and purchased a controlling interest in Financial Network, an insurance firm in Pennsylvania. In addition, he helped out at Peggy's Garden Center, also a thriving business, and at her new venture, a nail salon. He joined a group of investors who purchased the national rights to a soft drink and bottled water company and, in the process of researching the business, discovered a long-lost uncle in the personage of Foots Clements, chairman of the board of Dr Pepper. Life was comfortable and relatively easy.

On quiet nights, Christian sometimes lay back and glowed in the memories of those old glory days with the Butchers. Holy shit! he thought. Some of the things we did were really crazy. But if we had not acted, sounded, looked, and even smelled crazy, we probably wouldn't be alive today.

There had been equal amounts of craziness, he realized, in his years of work for veterans' rights.

Was all that past him now? he wondered. Would he spend the rest of his life as a creature of the business world?

Answers to those questions began to formulate as Christian's car rounded a sharp curve. A small foreign car, traveling directly toward them, suddenly swerved out of control for no apparent reason. It hurtled across in front of Christian and Silvi's field of vision, narrowly missing them, and crashed into a gully, flipping over on one side. Christian jammed on the brakes. His own car squealed to a stop. He and his passenger jumped out and looked back, realizing immediately that the driver and a young boy were trapped inside. Gas lines ruptured and burst into flames.

"Stand back," someone yelled. "It's going to blow!"

For a moment Christian found himself paralyzed. Let someone else help them, he thought. The sight of the fire made the nerve cells of his scarred skin crawl with agonizing memories.

But the screams of the child pierced his eardrums. As his mind objected, Christian's body raced forward into the gully. Through the open sun roof he could see that the boy was trapped by his shoulder harness. He had given in to panic and his small hands flailed uselessly at the strap that held him inside the fiery wreck. Christian wedged his shoulders in through the sun roof and reached toward the harness latch. He had to push away the boy's frantic clutches; the driver, too, grabbed at him.

The belt would not give way. Christian swatted at the flames with his bare hands, wondering how much time he had.

Suddenly he realized that Silvi was at his side, throwing dirt on the engine fire. Christian backed out of the sun roof and joined him. With handfuls of loose dirt, they squelched the flames.

With the danger of explosion minimized, they worked more deliberately, finally loosening the boy's safety harness. The lad was whimpering but apparently unharmed as they pulled him through the sun roof to safety. Then they turned their attention to the driver. He was wedged against the latch of his own shoulder harness. Silvi held up the man's weight as Christian's hands labored with the clasp. Finally they were able to free the man and drag him out to safety.

That night, when he recounted the story to his family, Christian was met with comments such as "Oh, sure," and, "Really, Dad." The sarcasm in his children's voices reminded him of PAC Man and made him wonder how much they believed about his old war stories. For that matter, how much did anyone believe?

In the morning, the story of the rescue was on the front page of the *Trenton Times*, and Christian saw a new look of respect in the eyes of his children.

The following evening, he was home alone. Peggy and the kids were out shopping. A single light in the kitchen illuminated the quiet house. He warmed a plate of leftovers on the stove, then sat at the kitchen table to eat and read the newspaper. He rose to open the kitchen door, seeking a summer breeze.

Just then, the front doorbell rang.

"Christ, always when I'm ready to eat," he muttered.

He trudged toward the front of the house and opened the door to find a muscular black man and his seven-year-old son standing outside. He recognized them immediately.

"Won't you come in?" Christian asked.

"No, I just wanted to bring my boy here to thank you for saving our lives." The father looked down and commanded, "Son, thank Mr. Christian."

The boy extended his hand. "Thank you, sir," he said politely.

As Christian grasped the small, warm hand, he knew the answer to Peggy's question. He knew what he had to do. And he knew that he had to keep doing it.

73

Bensalem, Pennsylvania
July 29, 1986

They assembled in a hotel north of Philadelphia, here for the purpose of helping Victor 6 win election to the U.S. Congress.

Was the Kingfish, as he proclaimed to Marinelli when they first met so many lifetimes ago, "the toughest son of a bitch you'll ever meet?" He had a chance to prove it, as he again challenged Kostmayer for Congress. The moment the campaign got underway, all the old war wounds oozed fresh blood. This time Kostmayer characterized Christian as a hawk who "never met a missile he didn't like" and openly questioned the validity of Christian's neon billboardlike display of medals.

The Kingfish thought about that. It was, he had to admit, a most improbable story. How could he prove that those medals were real and meaningful?

He had grinned with satisfaction when the idea hit him. There was one simple way to attest to the validity of the exploits of ChrisTian's Butchers.

And so they had gathered.

Ape Pawlata traveled the shortest distance, from nearby Pottstown, yet it was he who had changed the most. After refusing the offer of a beer, he explained to the others what had happened. He was married briefly, but that escapade ended in divorce in 1978. After that, he had slithered more deeply into a barroom lifestyle. He was vaguely aware that he was running with the wrong crowd, and that if he kept to his current track, he might well end up in the slammer for some crime that he committed during a blackout. But life held no hope for him. His job at the auto parts plant was a dead end; if he stuck it out until retirement, he could look forward to a miserly $300 per month pension.

It had all changed on Sunday evening, February 11, 1979, when Pawlata's friend and coworker Jimmy Goetz dragged him to the Exeter Bible Church outside of Pottstown. With a somewhat self conscious but ingratiating grin, Pawlata admitted that he was not an altogether unwilling worshipper, for he was aware of the deep void in his life.

But as he listened to the fundamentalist preacher on this Sunday evening, he grew increasingly angry with Goetz. That rat, he thought. He came down here ahead of time and briefed the preacher about me. The sermon was a harangue against the sinful life of booze and failed marriages, of pleasure-seeking and aimless indulgence. The more the preacher ranted, the more Pawlata cringed—knowing that he was the topic of the discourse.

Near the end of the service, the preacher issued an altar call, encouraging sinners in the audience to repent, come forward, and be born again. Pawlata sat still, red-faced, unwilling to acknowledge that *he* was the reason for this entire meeting.

Afterward, the preacher took up a post in the rear of the church, at the one and only exit. Pawlata did not want to file past and shake the man's hand, but he had no choice. He followed Goetz to the door, determined to vent his wrath on his friend at the earliest opportunity.

"It was nice being here," he mumbled as he pumped the preacher's surprisingly strong grip and avoided his gaze.

The preacher asked sharply, "Are you saved?"

Pawlata did not know what to say. "Probably not the same way you are," he admitted sheepishly.

"Do you want to go back and talk about it?"

I don't want to be impolite to this guy, Pawlata thought. I'll just go back with him to satisfy him, listen to what he has to say, and then leave. Then I'll have it out with Jimmy.

He followed the preacher back into the church. Moments later he was on his knees, asking God to forgive a life of sin.

Now he was sober and straight, stoned on a Jesus high, pointedly waving away the cigarette smoke of the others. His wife Maria was with him, along with their three boys, Gary Allen, Joseph Thaddeus, and Micah Aaron. He had plans to take his GED test and then the state civil service examination, with an eye toward landing a job as a corrections officer at Graterford

Penitentiary, a maximum security prison housing more than 3,300 inmates, the largest in the state.

The thought of the Ape man as a prison guard made the others want to laugh, but they stifled their chuckles as they saw the resolve in Pawlata's eyes. The Ape was gone; Gunnar Pawlata had taken his place.

Sam Janney had also experienced a dramatic turnaround. Ten years after the war, he woke up one morning in a detoxification facility. As he sobered up, he ruminated upon the fact that he had pretty much blown the entire decade. He had finished college and then, after his mother became incapacitated, had taken over management of the family's affairs. The estate was large enough to preclude any real need for him to work. He tried his hand as a free-lance photographer and dabbled in other businesses, skippering a charter yacht, opening a restaurant. But looking back, he reflected that his major activity had been to party. Drinking was his big problem, but he had also experimented with illegal highs.

The cornea in his useless right eye suffered a steady deterioration, causing him periodic and intense pain. Doctors treated this with alcohol injections.

In the detox center he realized that three days of his life were lost from his memory, and doctors told him he had tried to commit suicide. He questioned that, but he did not doubt the deep roots of his substance abuse problem. He was still in the hospital when his wife filed for divorce. He sold his restaurant business in order to distance himself from its ever-present alcohol temptation, and he went back to school to learn the computer business.

His job with Integrated Systems Analysts sent him on business trips throughout the Pacific, and carried a secret security clearance, which he was able to maintain only by staying dry. "Eight years now without a drink," Janney declared with a combination of pride and determination.

Dennis Going, decked out in a trim beard and a tailored suit, no longer answering to the nickname "Dong," was a draftsman with National Semiconductor in West Jordan, Utah. "I've put a lot of the war out of my mind," he explained to the others. "I don't even look at my pictures anymore. I think it was a good idea, good therapy." But this, he said, waving his hand and smiling at the Butchers, was like a seventeen-year reunion with your long-lost brothers.

Jim Lowe, half-owner of Lowe Excavation Company in Grand Junction, Colorado, still indulged in "libation" at every opportunity. Sporting a fierce-looking caveman beard and the rough-hewn facade of a successful contractor, he beamed a broad smile. He explained how he had considered himself to be a civilian the moment he set foot back on American soil, and that strategy had worked well for him.

Max Marinelli brought his wife Sandy and their children, Sammy, Rosemary, and Matthew. He wore a suit, as befitted his position as owner of a retail store and a hair-dryer maintenance company, and he showed off pictures of their comfortable suburban home in Stratford, New Jersey, only about an hour's drive away.

They recalled the good times, the outrageous adventures of the Butchers as they decimated enemy units in Cambodia, jumped into an air force swimming pool in their filthy uniforms, or dueled with beer cans. "Don't shoot the fuckin' rubber trees," someone reminded them.

No one spoke of the Chinese soldier they had used as an experiment of war. No one spoke of Scotty, or of Pete Andrews. Christian could not help but bring up October 29, 1968, and the Butchers' final four-hour firefight. It had been the culmination of their adventures and was, Christian thought, a natural topic of conversation.

To his surprise, only Pawlata picked up the theme. The others moved on to different subjects.

Janney told of a recent experience that occurred on a business trip, while he was riding in a car from Manila to Subic Bay in the Philippines. "It's no mystery to me why movies about Vietnam are filmed there," he said. "It looks like it, tastes like it, feels like it." So much so, he added, that he had almost gone into a trance. With a start, he realized that he had been scanning the tree line alongside the road, looking for signs of an ambush.

This brought knowing chuckles. When they subsided, Christian once more broached the subject of the October 29 battle. Pawlata's eyes shone with memory, but it occasioned only brief comments from the others. Marinelli quickly grabbed for another can of beer.

In the early evening, they gathered in a banquet room at King's Caterers for a Stars and Stripes Rally attended by 500 well-wishers and a heavy press contingent. Then they proceeded to a formal dinner at the Trevose Hilton. It was an event staged to counter Kostmayer's skepticism concerning Christian's war record, but Lowe dubbed it "The Night of the Generals."

Special guests of honor included Jan Scruggs as well as two men who had made many of the high-level decisions that sent ChrisTian's Butchers into battle: General Alexander Haig and General William C. Westmoreland. Both men had cooperated with Christian on numerous veterans' issues over the years, and were eager to endorse him for Congress.

But the heroes of the evening were a handful of otherwise ordinary

American men who, long ago, had been plucked from their mundane lives and ordered to fight for their country. Historically this was a common phenomenon. Had they been Latin legionnaires, they would have returned to a triumphant welcome in Rome. Had they worn either the blue of the North or the gray of the South, they would still be venerated. Had they liberated France, they would have been covered with ticker tape. Why, they *all* wondered, was their lot so different?

The Butchers marched into the hall single file, led by a navy color guard. The attention scared Going and brought tears to Pawlata's eyes; finally, he thought, here is our reward.

During dinner, Lowe showed off his collection of photographs, and some of the more gruesome shots panicked Christian's campaign advisers.

Christian responded, "What do you think we were doing over there, playing patty-cake? It was war."

Janney leaned toward Christian and said, "I think you're nuts to go into politics."

After dinner, the dignitaries spoke first. Both generals applauded Christian's stance in support of a strong national defense. Said Haig: "I think Dave embodies a complete understanding that this nation is living in a dangerous time."

Westmoreland added: "I think the country would be far better off if there were more Vietnam veterans in Congress." After he sat down, he whispered a question at Christian: "Are you still under investigation?"

"No, I think that stuff's all been cleared up, it was all bullshit," Christian responded.

Scruggs declared to the audience, "We might not have a Vietnam Veterans Memorial in Washington if it wasn't for Dave."

Then it was the Butchers' turn. Each man spoke briefly. Some were obviously nervous, but all were genuine in their reverence for the memory of ChrisTian's Butchers.

"Dave taught us how to take care of ourselves," said Marinelli.

"I served under a number of officers in Vietnam," Janney said. "Most of them were poorly trained and made a lot of mistakes. Dave was the exception. He took a group of individuals and spun us into a team. He had a sixth sense when it came to making decisions. At times, we would think his decisions were crazy, but they would turn out to be right. You people in Bucks County have the opportunity to elect a very special person. It is rare that someone like Dave chooses to go into politics."

Going said simply, "I have a lot of respect for Dave. He made me a better man."

"I am proud to have served with Dave in Vietnam," Pawlata said, and he added, "If you don't vote for Dave, you're a fool."

It was Lowe who spoke with particular eloquence: "Dave was equipped to personify some of the things lacking in the American system. We don't carry on our traditions. Honor and glory aren't on the top of the list. But Dave had the stamina and charisma to do it. Dave illuminated us, took our own unique characteristics and made us feel good about them."

Finally Victor 6 spoke. "Today, still, few Americans can tell you about the whys and why nots of Vietnam," he said. "No one knows who was on first.

"I was there as a young soldier, not knowing what communism was or how to spell ideology. I was there because my government said it was time for me to serve, and I still believe it is the best government in the world. I didn't want to be a war hero, I didn't want to be in Vietnam. I'd have been perfectly happy if they had sent me to Tahiti.

"I left my youth in Vietnam. There, I experienced the most significant events that ever happened—or will happen—to me. It was the ultimate hunt. I have no animosity toward the Vietnamese. I respect them. We have a common denominator; we fought each other.

"I have this to say to all Vietnam veterans: Ours was honor. We should forever carry our heads high."

74

Washington Crossing, Pennsylvania
January 1987

Once more, Christian lost the election by a slim percentage. It hurt, but at the same time it brought a strange sense of peace.

For five years he and his family had lived in legal limbo. Since 1982 his business and personal life had been under scrutiny by the Pennsylvania State Department of Labor and Industry, Internal Audit Division, and a Special State Investigative Unit. On a federal level, his affairs were probed by the Justice Department, the Inspector General's Office, the V.A., and the Labor Department, as well as by officials of the State Department and agents of the Internal Revenue Service, and by the Government Operations

Committee of the U.S. House of Representatives. Despite Christian's state-ment to General Westmoreland, it was only after his second campaign loss that he managed to clear the air completely.

He had to hire an attorney and invoke the provisions of the Freedom of Information Act to do so. It was January 1987 before he finally received notice of formal clearance of the last of the investigations.

Included with that dossier was a memorandum written on January 14, 1985 (*two years earlier*), from Raymond J. Carroll, regional inspector general for investigations, to William J. Haltigan, the U.S. Department of Labor's regional administrator of the Employment and Training Adminis-tration, declaring: "Our investigation concluded that Subject's involvement in talks with CETA grant recipient (Commonwealth of Pennsylvania) and the United Vietnam Veterans Organization were not incompatible with his duties as a U.S. Department of Labor, Veterans Employment Represen-tative; that Subject held no official, or paid position in the UVVO; and that more evidence exists that Subject did not misrepresent the cost of the building previously donated to the UVVO by his uncle, than to the contrary.

"Based on the above, this case is being closed by our office and you need take no further action."

Thus Christian was cleared of all charges—but the government did not bother to make that fact public. Scruggs and Muller were also completely in the clear.

The Kingfish was left with the conclusion that their "crime" was their collective determination to fight for the rights of veterans and their families.

He wondered if it was finally over.

75

Grand Junction, Colorado
June 1989

"You have to go home," said the face.

Jim Lowe's house in Grand Junction, Colorado, was quiet this morning. Lowe was off to tend to his excavating business; Max Marinelli, who had flown out for a visit, was in the kitchen, sipping a cup of coffee. He was alone, or so he thought, until the face intruded.

"I'm gonna make sure you get home today," the face prophesied.

"It's impossible," Marinelli said to the face. "I can't do this."

"Yes you can. Go upstairs."

Marinelli followed the face's commands. He packed his luggage and straightened up the guest room.

"You gotta call the airport."

"Yes."

He scrambled out to the airport and caught a plane for the four-and-a-half-hour trip to Philadelphia. During most of the flight, he stared at the soldiers who stood outside on the wings, unaffected by the jet-stream winds at 35,000 feet; on occasion the soldiers made their way into the passenger cabin and asked unanswerable questions, such as "Why did you make it?" and "How come you survived?"

"Don't listen to these things," the face counseled.

76

Washington Crossing, Pennsylvania
June 1989

Christian was sad as he spoke with Sandy Marinelli on the phone.

She poured out her story: Following the Butchers' reunion, Max had grown increasingly moody, and he took to drinking heavily. One night she found him alone in the den, tears flowing from his eyes.

"Why are you crying?" she asked.

Through the years of their marriage, Marinelli had often shared stories of the war, but they were always upbeat, often humorous. Now, for the first time, he told her about the mission he had missed, the battle of October 29, 1968, when Scotty was killed and Victor 6 was badly wounded. If he had been there, he sobbed, maybe he could have saved Scotty. He told her about his angry but idle threat to kill the Lone Ranger, and how it resulted in his transfer from Recon. If the Butchers had remained together, he conjectured, maybe Tiny would not have died.

Sandy listened sympathetically, but didn't know how to respond. This was old baggage, two decades old. Max was a highly decorated war hero. He had nothing to be ashamed about. Even after he announced that he was going to move the entire family out to Colorado, to make a fresh start, Sandy had thought: He's a good man. For all these years he took care of us. He always came through, no matter how bad things were. Now we have to take care of him. Maybe moving to Colorado would help.

They put the business and the house up for sale. To their surprise, the business sold quickly, and they were forced to speed up their plans. Max had rushed off to Colorado, but the face had sent him back home, lifeless, aimless.

Christian promised that he would try to help. The moment Sandy hung up, he phoned Lowe to ask about Marinelli's visit.

"It was hell," Lowe reported. "Max didn't want to talk about anything but Vietnam. If anyone didn't want to talk about Vietnam, he got mad."

Dennis Going had come over from Utah for a weekend of fishing, and he, too, angered Max with his disinterest in old war stories. "It's therapy to put it out of your mind," Going declared.

Marinelli had sworn at him.

This was a spectre that haunted them all.

The psychiatric community calls it posttraumatic stress disorder (PTSD), and considers it to be a normal human response to a highly stressful situation like war. Suffering from PTSD does not mean that a person is mentally ill; the condition merely mimics many of the biological, psychological, and emotional symptoms of true mental illness. It is characterized by the guilt of surviving when others did not, the guilt of having killed for what may later appear to be no justifiable reason, the feeling that one has been treated as a scapegoat by society, rage over a whole realm of real and imagined slights, and an alienation resulting in an inability to love or even show positive emotion. The great danger is that, left untreated, it can lead to clinical depression and other complications.

Christian was convinced that the long-lost Pete Andrews was a victim of PTSD, and had long held a disquieting fear that others would succumb. PTSD is a time bomb, a lingering booby-trap legacy that can fester within a man for decades. No one quite knows what activates the trip wire, but the best psychiatric evidence indicates that PTSD can strike just about any veteran at just about any time.

77

Franklin Township, New Jersey
July–August 1989

After a few false starts, Christian persuaded Marinelli to sign himself into the psychiatric ward of the Philadelphia V.A. Hospital. He remained there for twenty-one days, after which he declared himself to be cured. He was placed on a regimen of tranquilizers and antidepressants, instructed not to drink, and released.

He moved to a trailer in the Cedar Lake area of Franklin Township, New Jersey, taking his twelve-year-old son Matthew with him, demanding that Sandy and the other kids come to see him as often as possible. He grew a full beard.

For several weeks his mood showed improvement, but then Sandy began to worry about the drinking. Max was not supposed to ingest alcohol along with his medication, but he broke that rule constantly.

One weekend night, Sandy and Max sat in the trailer. As usual, he was telling war stories. Suddenly he leaned forward and said in a matter-of-fact voice, "Do you know that I could kill you with just one whack? I know just where to hit you."

In a shaky voice Sandy acknowledged, "Well, I guess you could. But why would you want to do that?"

"I'm just saying that I could."

Sandy thought: what if he wakes up in the middle of the night and thinks that the kids and I are gooks?

"When we get there," Christian said to his friend Roger Berner, "you take the kids. Drive them around for awhile. Just get them away from Max."

Once more Sandy Marinelli had appealed to Christian for help. She grieved for Max, but she also worried about her younger son Matthew. The immediate need was to get him away from his father. She implored Christian to go to the campsite to bring Matthew home. Her older son Sammy would drive down, showing the way to the isolated campsite.

Christian enlisted Berner's aid. He was a Vietnam-era veteran and a construction contractor who had migrated from Texas to do some renovation work on the Christian home. As they drove into Jersey through the sweltering heat of a summer's day, Christian explained that Berner's task was to watch the kids; he would try to handle Max.

Sammy Marinelli, driving an aging Chevy Impala ahead of Christian's Mercedes, led the way to a ramshackle trailer on the outskirts of a campsite that was frequented by religious revivalists. Christian found Max and Matthew Marinelli living in darkness and filth. Matthew had amassed a collection of black snakes, a dozen or more, which he kept in large plastic buckets scattered around the trailer.

Berner took Sammy and Matthew off for a drive, and Christian launched into a lecture. He warned Marinelli that he should not be drinking. Marinelli scoffed at the advice, claiming that his stint on the psychiatric ward and his medication had him on the road to recovery. But he agreed that it was time for Matthew to go home.

When he returned to the trailer, Matthew scurried about, tossing his favorite snakes into a large plastic bucket so that he could show them off to his friends.

In an attempt to lighten the day for Sammy, Christian asked, "You want to drive Roger back in my car?"

Sammy jumped at the chance to drive the Mercedes. Christian and Matthew piled into Sammy's jalopy, and they drove off. Only as they baked in the near 100-degree heat of the day did Christian realize that the Impala's air conditioning system was broken. He was glad he was wearing shorts.

On the Atlantic City Expressway, they ran into a traffic jam. Stuck behind a long line of cars moving forward only by inches, they found the heat intolerable. "Matthew," Christian suddenly suggested, "why don't you bring the bucket of snakes up here and take the cover off. They're gonna need some air. This heat is going to kill them."

Matthew reached into the back seat for the bucket. As he swung it into the front seat, the car lurched and the top of the bucket fell off. Black snakes spilled across the front seat and onto Christian's bare legs. One of them slithered into a vent of the broken air conditioner, and Christian yanked on its tail.

By the time the traffic jam cleared up, Matthew's favorite pet had nearly succumbed to heat stroke. As the boy held the four-foot-long black snake out the window into the headwind, he turned to ask Christian a tough question: "What's wrong with my father?"

Christian spoke slowly, raising his voice to carry above the noise of the traffic. "Well, in war, people get injured," he said. "I was injured,

and you can see my injuries.'' He gestured toward the scars on his arms
and legs and mused, ''Maybe I'm fortunate that my injuries are on the
surface. People can see them and allow for them. Your father's also injured.
If you can understand that your father has an injury from the war, you'll
understand what's going on. They call it delayed stress and it happens years
after the war. Your father was in some of the heaviest combat in Vietnam,
and it finally came to the front of his mind.''

Matthew continued to hold the snake out the window, but he said
nothing.

Marinelli woke up on a Sunday morning in August and thought he was
crippled. His body was covered with bruises and scratches. His feet were
burned painfully, not on the soles, but higher up, toward the ankles.

''What happened?'' he muttered aloud. Try as he might, he could not
remember. He theorized that thieves had broken into the trailer, beaten
him, and left him for dead.

A long day passed. He sat in a stupor, trying to remember, and the
more he mused, the more confused he became. As evening neared, he knew
that his enemies had surrounded the trailer and were waiting for the cover
of darkness before they came in to finish him off.

''Well, this is it,'' he declared.

He was dressed only in shorts. He laced his tennis shoes on over his
burnt feet. He grabbed his long hunting knife and tucked it into the waistband
of his shorts. He turned off all the lights in the camper, so that the enemy
could not see him. Moving stealthily, he sneaked across the length of the
trailer and found a shirt.

He moved out into the darkness, wary of snakes and scorpions, his ear
tuned for telltale sounds of danger. Wait-a-minute vines hampered his
progress, but he persevered.

Slowly, he made his way through the campground, pounding on the
doors of other trailers. Nearly seventy campers had gathered this weekend
for a religious retreat. They were aroused from their evening lethargy by
a wild-appearing man with a hunting knife, who simply growled, ''Let's
go!'' Figuring it was some sort of game, the campers complied. Within a
few minutes, Marinelli had gathered sixty-eight of them, and he ordered,
''Follow me.''

Marinelli padded off down the main trail, toward the front gate of the
campground, and the campers followed dutifully, wondering what was
supposed to happen next.

At the pay phone outside the main gate, Marinelli dialed the operator and asked quickly for the police. When an officer's voice sounded on the other end of the line, Marinelli called out, "I'm surrounded. I need help!"

"We'll be there," the officer assured him. "Where are you?"

Marinelli told them the name of the campground, and he added, "I'll be hiding behind the bushes when you get here."

The campers had dispersed in confusion by the time a Franklin Township police cruiser arrived. An officer jumped out, but at first he saw nothing. Suddenly Marinelli ran out from the bush, his knife in his hand.

"Okay!" he yelled, "let's go get them."

The officer drew his gun, aimed it at Marinelli's belly, and commanded, "Put the knife down."

Marinelli stopped in his tracks. "Wait a minute," he said, slapping his forehead in amazement and confusion. "I called you. I just captured sixty-eight gooks and you gotta do something with them."

"Put the knife down!"

This time Christian brought along Don Faughnan, one of his insurance associates, for added security. He did not know what to expect from Max.

Torrential rains reminiscent of the monsoon season pelted down on the Mercedes as it approached the trailer park. Christian left Faughnan in the car and slogged through the mud toward the trailer. Dressed only in his undershorts, Marinelli was waiting for him at the door. Christian walked into the dank, smelly trailer and accepted a seat on the sofa, hunching his shoulders forward because a large black snake lay on the window sill behind him.

Marinelli sat across from him in a chair and said, "Let me tell you what happened. The gooks were everywhere last night. Everywhere. I captured them, but the police were going to shoot *me*."

"Look at your feet," Christian commanded.

Marinelli glanced down at the burns on his feet.

"Look at your body. You're all scratched up."

Marinelli grinned, as if to slough off minor injuries. "I fought hard," he declared. "You'd be proud of me."

78

Washington Crossing, Pennsylvania
1989

It was not until months later, when Marinelli was off the bottle and into V.A.–provided therapy that the pieces of the puzzle began to fit together.

The 1986 reunion provided vital clues. That was the start of Max's problems. Christian played it over in his mind. What bothered him was the reluctance of the Butchers, with the notable exception of Pawlata, to discuss the October 29 battle. This was somehow significant, but he could not figure out why.

He thought of the five old soldiers who had shared the spotlight during the "Night of the Generals." What was the common bond? He had lost touch with most of the Butchers, but how had he been able to maintain contact with these five men?

Pawlata was a special case. He lived only an hour away, in Pottstown. As Recon's point man, he had shared a unique relationship with Christian, and they had maintained it, off and on, over the years. Much the same was true of Marinelli. He lived nearby, and he had been one of the emotional leaders of the warriors' band; he had created that awful nickname, ChrisTian's Butchers.

But where did Janney, Lowe, and Going fit in? Why them, and not Jesse Lascano or Wild Bill Divoblitz or Milam or Gooney?

The surface answer was easy. It was Marinelli who had remained in touch with Janney, Lowe, and Going. Christian was able to contact them through Max. Was it mere coincidence? Perhaps. Or was there some sort of hidden connection?

Only as he thought back over two decades, only as he pieced together his memories of the Butchers, did he realize that Marinelli was held out of the battle on October 29, 1968, in order to hassle with the supply sergeant; Janney was at the aid station being treated for leg wounds; Going was suffering from malaria; Lowe was on R&R. *All four had missed the grand finale.* Was that why, perhaps even without knowing it, these four had remained close afterward? For them, there was never an ending to the story. Perhaps Janney, Going, and Lowe had worked out the frustration, but Marinelli was still dealing with unfinished business.

If that was true, how in the world could it *ever* end?

One day Christian said to Peggy, "I'd like to go back and find my airborne pinkie ring, the one that slipped off in the fire."

Peggy laughed and asked, "How in the world would you ever find it?"

"Well, I would go to the hill. I could find the hill. And I would take a metal detector. I know it's a long shot, but it was the last thing I wore before my whole life changed, and I'd like to have it back."

Peggy grew solemn as she realized that her husband was serious.

79

Newtown, Pennsylvania
1989

Past and future leaders of Cambodia sat in Christian's office, their eyes growing wide as they viewed photographs of their host posing with such notables as Henry Kissinger and Presidents Jimmy Carter, Ronald Reagan, and George Bush. They leaped to the natural conclusion that Christian was a force in the American governmental structure.

Christian saw no reason to tell this group that the Kingfish had no clothes on. I'll just roll with it, he thought. But he asked himself: what could they possibly want from me?

They had first made overtures to Professor Al Blaustein of Rutgers Law School, an expert on Third World constitutions. They wanted him to help prepare a constitution for their new democratic government, set to take over when the Vietnamese army pulled out of the country late this year. As he spoke with the Cambodians, Blaustein remembered his old friend and ally, and suggested that David Christian might be a good man to consult with on various issues of creating and securing a new government. They had called immediately.

Now, in halting English, one of the politicos asked, "Would you like to come to Cambodia to witness the transfer of power?"

Christian pondered. No, he replied, he would not come during the change of governments, but he would be happy to visit at a later date. He knew that the situation with the rebel Khmer Rouge and their murderous leader, Pol Pot, might be very explosive at the moment that power changed hands. But if the new democratic government survived its initial trauma, he would be happy to act as a consultant on economic issues.

As best he could through the limitations of the language barrier, he explained his philosophy. The way to squelch the threat posed by the Khmer Rouge is to win the hearts and minds of the people. Guerrillas are like fish who need water to survive, and the people are the water.

"Now, how do you win the people?" he asked rhetorically. "The common thread throughout the world is economics. The only thing that's going to make them satisfied is being able to put food on the table for their families. Everything else is bullshit."

He could see that the Cambodians were struggling with his vocabulary.

Weeks later, one of the politicians called from overseas to declare, "Cambodia is yours."

"I don't want Cambodia," Christian replied. "I want you to have Cambodia. I can show you how to take advantage of business opportunities to build up your economy. One of the things I can do is create jobs." It will be unofficial, he thought, but then, most of my life has been unofficial.

"I'm not going to make a cent on it," he explained to Peggy. "But it will help me resolve some issues. I can complete the circle."

80

Vietnam
January 2–3, 1990

Joe Jingoli felt as if he had been here before. The first thing he saw from the window of the descending airplane was the Saigon river, twisting with the landscape. The outlying areas appeared to be modernized suburbs, but what he could see of the city itself appeared stark, almost mystic. That feeling was compounded by the apprehensive silence of his companions, Charles "Doc" Simone, M.D., business consultant Pat Deon, and Christian.

Simone's mind dwelt on the bizarre scene back at Christian's office, at

5 A.M. on New Year's Eve, the day of their departure. At that ungodly hour, while Coleen Christian was busy making Xerox copies of the photos from the wall, her father had forced them to sign up for fourteen-day, $500,000 life insurance policies. Simone was one of the world's leading authorities on cancer and nutrition and considered himself to be a lifesaver, not someone who risks life.

Jingoli, a construction engineer and contractor from New Jersey, wondered what in the world he was doing here. He had just rebuilt the infrastructure of Trenton's water and sewer system, and was awaiting a similar contract for Camden. Why was he wasting his time here? What could he do to help in Southeast Asia? Jingoli spotted old bunkers below, the remnants of war, and he felt sadness encompass him. He asked himself what all the other men felt like when they came here and there was a war going on.

Deon was president of the largest retail beverage distribution company in Pennsylvania. He owned seven shopping centers. He had interests in cable TV companies. Of this group, he was the only one who had accompanied Christian before, on similar junkets to other countries, and he was more comfortable with the rules of survival: stay close to Dave, do what he does, eat what he eats, drink what he drinks.

Inside the airport, all the Vietnamese seemed to be dressed in green uniforms and wore red stars. It was immediately apparent that there was a problem with their papers. This was supposed to be merely an intermediate stop en route to Phnom Penh, Cambodia. A Cambodian official named Chhang Song was scheduled to meet them with the necessary visas, but he was nowhere to be found—someone hinted that he had run off with a woman—so the Vietnamese police confiscated their passports. Now what?

The police seemed to single out Simone, tall and slim, the least intimidating in appearance. A soldier poked his rifle into the American doctor's belly.

"Oh gods, oh gods," Simone moaned.

The Kingfish swung into action. He gathered some of the Vietnamese officers around him and displayed sheets of Xerox paper. He pointed toward his own image and then to himself. "Me," he said. Then he pointed to the other man in the photo and declared, "Jimmy Carter." A guard grunted and fingered his rifle nervously.

"Oh gods, oh gods," Simone said.

Christian moved on to the next picture. "Kissinger," he said.

This brought grins of recognition.

"Bush."

The soldiers laughed, and Christian laughed with them. But Jingoli thought: I'm scared shitless. I think we are in trouble.

Christian tapped his finger on the final photo and said, "Reagan."

The soldiers grunted, "Ahhh" in a reverent tone.

Nevertheless, the four Americans were informed that they were under arrest. They were lodged in the Tan Binh Hotel and ordered not to leave.

As soon as the soldiers departed, Christian bribed the desk clerk into silence and led the others out the door, in search of the Cambodian embassy. On the street, Jingoli found the people bright, lively, exciting. They looked curiously at the Americans, as if they were interlopers in Paradise. Bicycles and Mopeds filled the crowded streets. Vendors hawked all manner of goods—stamps, drugs, bullets, and their ubiquitous "sisters." Capitalism was thriving.

There were ghosts here, personified by old Esso signs. The Americans had been here, there was a war, and then they disappeared, leaving empty army bases and a population that now generally spoke Russian as a second language. American consumer goods had been replaced by shoddy, Russian-made merchandise. Curiously, although this was now officially Ho Chi Minh City, the locals still called it Saigon.

By the time they reached the Cambodian embassy, Jingoli had outlined in his mind four alternatives: (a) we get treated like royalty and go to Cambodia; (b) they throw us out and we're fucked; (c) we talk our way out of the country and go to Bangkok; (d) we stay here.

No one at the embassy professed to know the mysterious Chhang Song who had failed to show at the airport and no one understood their attempts to explain their plight in English. Officials opted for Jingoli's plan b and simply kicked them out. "We're getting the bum's shuffle," said Deon. But as they left the building, they spotted a black, Russian-made limousine backing into the drive. Christian approached the passenger and asked, "Excuse me, do you speak English?"

"Yes." The answer was noncommittal.

Christian displayed the photos of himself with Kissinger, Bush, and Reagan; he kept Carter's picture discreetly out of view. "We have been invited to visit Cambodia," he said. "We want to invest money in your country."

The man smiled broadly.

He was Deputy Prime Minister Cham Prasidh, the closest advisor to Hun Sen, President of Cambodia. He declared that he would send his people to the airport to retrieve the Americans' passports. In the morning, he would load them and their luggage into a car and send them off on an eight-hour drive to Phnom Penh. The cost was only $100 apiece, American.

"I can't believe it," Jingoli muttered. "He pulled off plan (A)."

The Kingfish said to the others, "Don't worry, be happy. We'll go back to our hotel and we'll sneak out again tonight to see Saigon."

The next morning, they left Saigon/Ho Chi Minh City in a two-car caravan, Christian riding in the black limo with Mr. Cham and his wife, Bo Tep Pol, the others jammed into a Toyota.

As he bounced along the dusty roads, Jingoli decided to keep a journal. He wrote: "One thing you learn quick is that anytime you stop, you drink whatever liquid you can, preferably Coca Cola, and eat whatever you can, because you don't know where your next meal is coming from or where you are going. You are going into the unknown and we are all very excited. It is like another time and another place.

"I am afraid as I am writing. I have to write everything so that if this gets taken away from me, the person who finds it will be able to read it."

They drove north on Highway 1, right through the Parrot's Beak/Fish Hook section of Vietnam, and Christian decided it was much nicer riding than tramping along trails. His eyes searched the landscape, looking for traces of fire bases Rita, Dot, and Jane. It was right here where his greatest, most glorious battles took place. But all he saw were thatch-roofed peasant huts, water buffalo, and rice paddy dikes. The dense growth of the tropical jungles had healed the geographical wounds of war long ago. The only remnants were the shreds of memory in his American mind.

Mr. Cham offered him a banana and a warm bottle of Coca-Cola.

When they reached the border, Vietnamese soldiers demanded to search them. Jingoli whispered, "For God's sake, Dave, don't tell them that you volunteered to kill Ho Chi Minh."

Once more Christian pulled out his photo collection. He compared scars with some of the troops and said, "The only reason I didn't kill you was so that you could stay here and help us get across the border."

The soldiers laughed and let the strange party through.

81

Cambodia
January 3–8, 1990

As soon as they crossed the border, Christian detected a difference. Here and there were bomb craters, signs of fire, and bits of discarded heavy matériel. This was not evidence of an old war, he realized. These were fresh signs.

Now they were in the realm of more troubling memories. This was where Pawlata took the machine gun slug in his buttocks. This was where Scotty died.

For a time, Christian grew silent.

Cham announced that he and his wife would treat the group to lunch, and ordered the driver to halt at a restaurant.

They were served some sort of shredded gray meat. Jingoli asked, "Is this the same as calamari?" Squid was a delicacy to Jingoli, Simone, and Deon—all of them Italian-Americans.

"Yes," Cham answered.

Christian elbowed Deon and pointed to a wooden rack near the kitchen. Scores of small, flattened *somethings* were displayed on it.

"What's that?"

"Bats," Christian said. "That's what you're eating. It's not calimari." He grinned and added, "You have to eat it, or you will offend the deputy prime minister."

Deon turned green and forgot his vow about eating whatever Christian ate. He waited until Cham's attention was diverted, and then slipped the bat meat off his plate and held it beneath the table, offering it to a mongrel who sat there begging.

The dog licked the bat meat but refused it.

Christian had to labor to hide his laughter. "Pat, you gotta eat it," he said.

"But the dog licked it!"

"You gotta. Here. Put some of this on it." Christian pulled a small vial out of his pocket. "I bought this sauce in Saigon," he said. He dabbed a bit onto Deon's bat meat.

Deon took one whiff and nearly fainted. "What the hell is that?" he whispered.

"*Nookmom*. It's great."

*   *   *

On the night they arrived in Phnom Penh, the capital city of Cambodia, the four Americans were told by a Frenchman that there were only two clubs to go to. The Monorom was relatively safe and a short walk from their hotel. The Militia was rougher; patrons brought their guns inside, and sometimes used them to settle their arguments. The Americans decided to go to the Monorom.

The next day, Christian was up at 5:30 A.M., standing alone on the balcony of the hotel room he shared with Jingoli. He listened to the soft chimes of the Buddhists, but he could also see, hear, and smell war, and the sensation was at once repulsive and compelling. Even this early in the day, the air was oppressive. The heat, he thought, has not changed.

He took a shower and found the water ice cold. For breakfast, he had a Coca Cola. Just like the war, he thought. Through the thin walls of the room he heard Simone shriek when he jumped into an icy shower.

Jingoli wrote in his journal: "The poverty is overwhelming. The smoke from the cooking fires burns your eyes and in front of you the children beg. I miss Saigon. We are supposed to meet with the Prime Minister today. Why doesn't our government help over here?

"Last night the Militia came out and David was playing with their AK-47s. They are like little boys armed with machine guns. Doc seems confused, Pat is realistic and David loves this stuff. You feel safe with David, especially when the shit hits the fan, but when it is all quiet it is like he is looking to stir up some more trouble."

The Cambodians insisted on referring to the four men as "the American delegation," ignoring their lack of ties with the U.S. government. They assigned an interpreter and guide, a woman named Chan Tah. She took them for visits to the Ministry of Health, the Ministry of Industry, the Committee for the City, the Committee on Tourism, and the Vice Consulate. Every facet of this four-month-old government needed assistance, and speed was essential. The new, non-Communist, officially neutral government that had replaced the retreating Vietnamese army had to make the people happy—quickly—to prevent Pol Pot and his Khmer Rouge troops from regaining power.

Chan Tah had difficulty translating the American names. In Cambodia, the first name is the last name, so Christian became "Mr. David." Jingoli was simply "Jo." Chan Tah looked at the somewhat hefty Pat Deon and dubbed him "Mr. Fat." Doc Simone, to his horror, was named after his most prominent feature. "She called me, 'Doctor Nose,' " he complained.

"I go through years of medical school. Twenty years of practice and research. I come here to help these people and they insult me. Oh gods, oh gods."

"Dr. Nose" was the star at the Ministry of Health. Through the interpreter, he asked about the country's problems. The minister explained that when Pol Pot and his Khmer Rouge came into power in 1975, they were determined to kill off the nation's intelligentsia and thereby stifle dissent. Before Pol Pot's regime, there were 300 doctors in Cambodia; now there were 30. These were augmented by a force of 9,000 nurses, as well as midwives and technicians. Tuberculosis and dysentery were severe problems. One-third of the population suffered from malaria.

The minister of commerce, Dr. Yit Kim Seng, treated the visiting Americans to miniature bananas, which, he declared, were fit for kings. He discussed his country's dire needs: water plants, power plants, textile plants, centering his attention on Jingoli, the construction expert. The local water was high in iron and needed proper treatment. Some of the machinery was in good shape, but manufacturing processes required better management. Labor was plentiful, with the average wage translating to about $30 a month. Jingoli pondered where to start, and advised that the first priority should be adequate electrical power; everything else could come from that.

Pat Deon scribbled the notes of a basic business analysis. Because of the heat and the country's poor supply of potable water, beer and soft drinks were extremely popular. There was some Heineken, San Miguel, and *bom-de-bom* available, but the demand was far greater than the supply. The one brewery in Cambodia had been damaged and closed during the Khmer Rouge regime. Pol Pot had nationalized the Coca Cola plant, and this now produced Pepsi-Cola, Orange Crush, and a few local flavors. Coke was bootlegged in from Thailand and Malaysia. European brands of bottled water sold for $1.39 per liter. Deon saw profitable business opportunities in importing beer and soft drinks through the Port of Kom Pong. From there, the wares could be trucked throughout the country to a thirsty market. Beyond that, once the Cambodians got their water treatment facilities working properly, local bottling plants could be refurbished.

Deon also suggested glassmaking as a good industry for Cambodia. The port area contained good quality sand and there was dolomite in the north. A modern glass manufacturing plant could provide Cambodia with an exportable product.

The textile industry held promise. Much of it was currently conducted on a Mom and Pop basis, and it needed to be systematized.

The country's greatest asset, Deon told the minister, was its people.

He was amazed at the optimism and industrious nature of the people after the horrors they had suffered. "With labor costs rising in other Pacific time zone countries, Cambodia can keep its neutral position and stabilize its government," he predicted. "It would be a prime area for many economic developments."

After the meeting, the minister took them to a Buddhist temple to pray for success amidst the exotic smell of incense and the distraction of chattering monkeys.

A news flash came in. The Khmer Rouge had blown up three bridges on Highway 4.

On the following day the Americans met with Deputy Prime Minister Cham Prasidh, the man who had brought them into the country. The Kingfish, with a grin, invited him to America to meet President Bush. Once more the discussion settled on the nation's immediate needs of water, electrical power, and sewage treatment.

They visited an orphanage, where the children staged a dance exhibition.

Then they went to view the Museum of Degenasi, where the atrocities of Pol Pot's "Killing Fields" were documented. Jingoli wrote: "It is horrible. The son of a bitch took a fucking school, you can't believe it, the tortures that they used on these people. They took the swing sets and little gym sets and used them to hang people and torture them, drown them. We have all the pictures to go with this. It is really disgusting. You get a feeling of guilt and when they mention the date '75 or '76, I can't help but remember what I was doing when all this happened. Pol Pot killed 3 million people. I am really angry."

Pol Pot had bristled at any hint that the great god Buddha was omnipotent. He dynamited one temple and proclaimed the deed as proof that Buddha was not almighty, or he would have saved his temple. He turned some temples into actual pigsties, and used others as execution chambers.

The walls of the museum were plastered with small black-and-white photos. Their interpreter, Chan Tah, explained that Pol Pot demanded documentation. He had ordered that each of his more than 3 million victims be photographed before they were executed. She marched over to one photo, high on the wall, and said, "This is my husband."

She shared her story. She remembered when Pol Pot marched into Phnom Penh in 1975, cheered as the victorious commander who had liberated the country from the government of Lon Nol. One of his first actions was to invite all the "intellectuals," especially the doctors and military officers, to come to Phnom Penh from all over the country. There, from a base in the capital, they would set out on the task of rebuilding the country. Chan Tah's husband, as a pilot, qualified, and they journeyed together to join in the great venture. That summer, she gave birth to a son.

Two months after Pol Pot came to power, Chan Tah's family was arrested and confined to a temple that had been converted to a prison. As a pilot, her husband might some day decide to fly against the Khmer Rouge; therefore, he was an enemy. Chan Tah's husband was shackled and, during the first ten days, the family subsisted on a single bowl of rice and one can of beer.

The interpreter showed them the list of the Khmer Rouge's ten "security regulations," translated into imperfect English and prominently displayed: "1. You must answer accordingly to my questions. Don't turn them away. 2. Don't try to hide the facts by making pretexts this and that. You are strictly prohibited to contest me." The Americans read silently. Regulation 6 ordered, "While getting lashes or electrification you must not cry at all."

Chan Tah remained at her husband's side for two months. She was assigned the task of watering vegetables, and one day as she labored, her husband's face appeared at the window, begging for water. She took a cup to him, but was stopped by a 14-year-old Khmer Rouge soldier, who poured the water onto the ground.

The last time she saw her husband, he was a link in a human chain, bound hand to hand, ready to be marched off to the killing fields. He asked to see his son. Permission was granted, but he was instructed to show no emotion. Chan Tah brought the baby and held him up. The father could not touch, for his hands were chained to the others. Tears flowed from his eyes and dripped onto the infant. Seeing this, Khmer Rouge troops pushed aside the mother and child. One soldier plunged a knife into the belly of the crying man and ripped it open. Then the chain of men was marched off, dragging Chan Tah's husband in their midst.

On the streets of Phnom Penh, Christian was approached by an English-speaking Vietnamese refugee, a woman named Yvette, who asked if he was interested in seeing some American POWs. Christian perked up his ears and went with her for a short distance. But when she headed into a maze of dark alleyways, heavy with the odor of incense and marijuana, his mind screamed: It's an ambush! and he ducked back into the main streets.

Yvette ran off and Christian screamed at her, "Number ten!"

*   *   *

January 7 was Independence Day, the eleventh anniversary of the day the Vietnamese Army "liberated" the country from the rule of Pol Pot, and the Cambodians wished to take the "American delegation" to view one of the wonders of the world, the Buddhist palace-like temple at Angkor Wat. There was an air of foreboding, concern that the Khmer Rouge might stage some military action to disrupt the holiday.

The Cambodians told them they would be the first American delegation to visit Angkor Wat in years. At the airport, waiting for their brief flight, they watched MI-8 and MI-11 Russian-made helicopters practice "touch and goes"—quick landings and takeoffs. A Swiss man talked about a bomb that went off the night before. He informed them that it had been fashioned of some sort of plastique, but he said there were no nails embedded in it, so it was relatively safe.

Angkor Wat was a complex of interconnected sandstone structures a full five miles wide and fifteen miles long, impressive not only for its size, but also for its serene atmosphere. The carvings of Buddhas and dancing girls dated back to the thirteenth century. It *felt* holy and remote from the terrible history of this country.

"You could each take a piece of the sandstone back with you as a souvenir," Chan Tah said.

Doc Simone bent to grab a piece that had crumbled away from a wall.

". . . but you might get shot," the interpreter added.

"Oh gods, oh gods," Simone yelped, dropping the stone.

As they reached the sculpture of a mammoth Buddha, Chan Tah said, "This Buddha is so large, no one has ever been able to embrace him, to put their arms around his arms all the way."

Jingoli, a gargantuan man, accepted the challenge. Straining with effort, he encircled the Buddha's arm and touched the tops of his fingers together. Chan Tah was delighted.

Christian was sitting in the Buddha's lap posing for a picture when gunshots sounded, not very far away. A guide mumbled, "They are shooting at birds, but we had better get back to our plane."

The Americans looked at each other and Christian acknowledged their fears. "There's a firefight near," he said knowingly. For Christian knew that in a country that counts its bullets, the soldiers do not shoot birds. "Let's follow the guide quickly back to the plane before we meet the Khmer Rouge," he suggested.

*   *   *

On the evening of January 8 the four Americans dined at the home of Vice President Kong Som Ol along with six cabinet members. The entrée consisted of whole chickens, baked and sliced into thin cross sections. "Mine has a beak on it," Jingoli whispered.

"Mine's got guts in it," Deon complained.

"Want some *nookmom*?" Christian asked.

"No!"

After dinner, Christian, wearing a white suit with its lapel laden with miniature replicas of his military medals, said in a cavalier fashion that he would try to keep a seat open in the United Nations for the new Cambodian government. The foreign affairs officer seemed to appreciate this.

The conversation was disrupted by a series of explosions, close by. Even the Cambodians, familiar with war, paled.

"Dinner is over," the vice president announced in a shaky voice.

Some rose to leave, but Christian caught the vice president's eye. Something in the American's expression made Kong Som Ol pay attention. Christian was, suddenly, removed from the scene. Time had turned back, nearly twenty-two years. He was not in the vice president's home in Phnom Penh; he was with "the general" and his CIA cronies in Saigon.

Slowly, through clenched teeth, Christian said, "Mister Vice President, do you want me to kill Pol Pot for you?"

"David, no!" Jingoli hissed.

Deon was speechless.

"Oh gods, oh gods," Simone said.

Christian repeated. "You want me to kill Pol Pot for you?"

Almost imperceptibly, the vice president nodded.

"Tell you what," Christian said, conjuring a figure out of thin air, "you give me $6 million, and I'll kill Pol Pot for you."

No one spoke.

Candlelight reflections shimmered off Christian's array of war medals.

Would I really do it? the Kingfish asked himself. Is my big mouth getting me into serious trouble here?

Deon finally found his tongue. "David," he said, "tell them you're kidding."

Christian thought: Well, I'd make damn sure the check cleared the bank before I did anything. Aloud, he said, "Mr. Vice President, I speak to you with the voice of experience. I am a guerilla fighter. I tell you, the way to kill the Khmer Rouge is with butter, not guns."

The vice president did not understand.

"You find the right people to help you pour money into this country and Pol Pot will die," Christian continued. "Maybe his own people will kill him. What you need is jobs. Give a man a job, let him bring home decent pay, and he'll be too satisfied—and too tired—to fight you. People don't care about ideology. It's all bullshit.''

From outside came the sounds of sirens, from fire trucks rushing to the scene of the latest bombings.

Vice President Kong Som Ol declared, "I agree. But when is somebody going to listen? For too many years armies have walked across our country. The Siamese, many years ago. The Chinese. The French. You Americans. The Khmer Rouge. The Vietnamese. Now the Khmer Rouge again. Where is the end to war?''

Victor 6 answered: "I don't know.''

David Christian is a member of the following organizations:

American Concrete Institute
American Legion
Builders Association of Bucks and Montgomery Counties
Commonwealth Licensed Beverage Association
Disabled American Veterans (Life Member)
Eighty-Second Airborne Association
First of the Twenty-Sixth Infantry Association
Honorary Eleventh Armor Cavalry Regiment
International Phoenix Society of Burn Survivors (Member,
    Board of Directors)
Kiwanis International
Knights of Columbus
Legion of Valor of the United States (Past National
    Commander and Past National Adjutant)
Massachusetts Mutual Life Insurance (Career Agent)
National Association of Display Interiors
National Association of Industrial Office Parks
National Association of Life Underwriters
National Rifle Association
Officers of First Infantry Division
Pi Sigma Alpha National Political Science Honor Society
Professional Grounds Maintenance Society, Lawns and Gardens
Retired Officers Association
Sons of the Confederacy
The Big I, Independent Insurance Agents Association
U.S.A.A. (20-Year Member, San Antonio, Texas)
Veterans of Foreign Wars (Life Member)
Vietnam Veterans of America (Life Member)
Villanova University Alumni Association
Villa Victoria Fathers Club

INDEX

Affirmative action, 180
Agent Orange, 55, 82, 93, 187, 188, 195; documents, theft of, 198–199; effects, issue of, 191, 196–198, 199; health studies, elimination of, 192; Robert Nimmo on, 193
Agent Orange Victims Act, proposed, 198
Air Medal, 158, 168
AK-47 rifles, 13, 56, 102, 240
Allied Veterans of New Jersey, 173
Alpha Company (Alice Company), 66–67, 69, 72, 73, 134; at Parrot's Beak, 82; reassignment of Pawlata to, 133; transfer of Gooney to, 117
Altman, Robert, 210
American Legion, 156, 173, 189, 202
Amnesty, for draft dodgers, 179, 210
AmVets, 156, 185, 186, 189
Andrews, Pete, 46, 47–48 112, 223, 228; adjustment problems of, in America, 157, 158–160; in Cambodia, 91, 95, 100; enemy blood consumed by, 95–96; hospitalization of, with malaria, 132; letter to Christian from, 117–118; at Parrot's Beak, 86, 98–100; and plan to assassinate Ho Chi Minh, 88, 98; Recon patrols of, 55–62 passim, 69
Angkor Wat (Cambodia), Buddhist temple at, 244
An Loch base camp (South Vietnam), 19, 23, 31

Antiwar protests, 96, 123, 156, 164–166, 169–170
Arlington National Cemetery, 176, 182
Armed Forces Network, 89
Army of the Republic of South Vietnam (ARVN), indentified, 9
Assassination squads, 118

Bailey, Don, 207
Baker, Rusty, 44, 51, 76, 79, 87; in Cambodia, 91, 95, 101, 105; Recon patrols of, 55 62 passim, 70–71
Battalion-plus troop movement, defined, 19
Bent, Peter, 172
Berner, Roger, 229–230
B-52 strikes, 58–59, 60, 62, 70–71, 72; in Cambodia, 81, 82, 90
Bien Hoa (South Vietnam), 77–80, 154
Bird, Thomas, 199
Black choppers, 88
Blaustein, Al, 234
Bom-de-bom, 46, 126, 241
Booby traps, 85, 90, 92, 204
Boren, David, 180
Bo Tep Pol, 238
Bravo Company, 59–60, 61–63, 65, 133–134
Brokaw, Tom, 184
Bronze Star, 53, 157, 158, 159, 168
Brooke Army General Hospital (San Antonio), 142
Brzezinski, Zbigniew, 178

Buddha, 242, 244
Buddhists, 126, 240, 242, 244
Buis, Dale R., 154, 155
Burt (patient), 122, 141; reconstruction of, 111–112
Buscher, Joe, 214, 217
Bush, George, 234, 237, 242
Butchers, ChrisTian's, 84. *See also* Reconnaissance platoon
Byrne, Brendan, 174, 179

Calley, William, 158
Cambodia, 19, 35–36, 145, 223, 234–237; ambush at border between South Vietnam and, 85–86; B-52 strikes in, 81, 82, 90; Christian's visit to, 239–246; Ho Chi Minh trail in, 36, 80; North Vietnamese regiments in, 80–81; Reconnaissance platoon in, 90–97, 100–108; U.S. invasion of, 172
Camp Zama (Japan), 122, 124–125, 129, 141, 149, 151; Christian's convalescence at, 111–114; letters to Christian at, 117–119
Cam Rahn Bay (South Vietnam), 111
Capella, Charlie, 187, 188
Carey, Hugh, 202
Carnavelli, "Doc," 53
Carroll, Raymond J., 226
Carter, Jimmy, 183, 191, 211, 234, 236, 237; his amnesty for draft dodgers, 179, 210; cabinet of, 178; campaigning by Miss Lillian for, 187–188; firing of Christian by, 184, 185–186, 190, 195; reelection lost by, 190; and veterans' issues, 179, 180–181, 182
Carter, Lillian, 187–188, 190
Central Intelligence Agency (CIA), 18, 27, 83, 120, 123, 245; and Pete Andrews, 160; and black choppers, 88; Christian's desire to work for, 30–31, 33–35, 126, 136; and Parrot's Beak, 80; and plan to assassinate Ho Chi Minh, 34–35, 88, 98

Chamberlain, Wilt, 125
Cham Prasidh, 237, 238, 239, 242
Chhang Song, 236, 237
Chan Tah, 240, 242–243, 244
Charlie Company, 67, 117
Christian, Coleen Ann, 176, 218, 236
Christian, Daniel, 7, 197, 213–214
Christian, David, Jr., 176–177, 218
Christian, Dorothea, 7
Christian, Dorothy, 6, 7, 8, 192, 197
Christian, Doug, 7, 32, 34, 197–198
Christian, Kathleen (K.C.), 204, 218
Christian, Maureen, 177, 218
Christian, M. J., 5, 6, 149–150
Christian, Peggy, 27–29, 32, 126, 145, 154, 203; her advice to Christian, 215, 218; business ventures of, 218; children of, 176–177, 204, 218; and Christian's failure to graduate from law school, 175; and Christian's injuries, 110, 119, 151; and Christian's return to Vietnam, 234; her frustration with Christian, 168; her husband's celebrity status, 190; her husband's congressional candidacy, 211–212; letters between Christian and, 118–119, 146, 149; Pawlata's letter to, 110; pregnancy of, 112, 119, 121–122; visit to Tokyo of, 121–125
Civil Service, 180
Claymore mines, 23–25, 44, 51–52, 60, 69, 141; ambush of, 85, 91; Christian's injuries from, 92, 93; destruction of Vietnamese, 72–73; enemy, 92, 143
Clelland, Max, 178, 186, 190–191
Clements, Foots, 218
Colorado State University, 44
Columbia University, 210
Combat Infantryman's Badge, 168
Combined Federal Campaign (CFC), 200, 205, 206, 217
Commission of Fine Arts, 200–201
Comprehensive Employment Training Act (CETA), 181, 185, 226
C-130 military transport, 142

Congressional Armed Services
Committee, 7
Congressional campaigns, Christian's,
209–215, 217, 220, 225, 226
Congressional Medal of Honor, 100,
108, 113, 126–127; Christian's,
167, 168, 178
Conspicuous Service Cross, 202
Cordisco, John, 198
Council of Vietnam Veterans, 189
Crawford, Tom, 138
Critchlow, Paul, 202
Crocker, John, 187, 188
Cross of Gallantry, 168
Cuisine, jungle, 49

DAC Consulting, 176, 218
"Dave Christian Regulation," 182
Davis, Ernest P., 20–21, 31, 32
Debriding process, 140
Deeny, Frank, 149
Defense, U.S. Department of, 197, 198
Delayed stress syndrome, 191, 193. *See
also* Posttraumatic stress disorder
Delta Company, 99, 101, 105–107
Democratic Party, 209, 210
Deon, Pat, 235, 236, 237; visit to
Cambodia of, 239–246 *passim*
DeSumma, Frank (Doc), 205
Dioxin, 196–197
Distinguished Service Cross (DSC),
168, 178, 183
Divoblitz, Wild Bill (Gabby Hayes),
55, 72, 73, 116, 233; in
Cambodia, 94, 96; Recon patrol
of, 55, 57; and visit of Christian to
Recon, 132, 133
Donahue, Jim, 202
Dong, *see* Going, Dennis
Draft dodgers, 155; amnesty for, 179,
210
Drug use, 39, 45, 69–71
Du Pont, Eloise, 213

Eastwood, Clint, 201
Eighteenth MP unit, 130, 142
Eleventh Armored Cavalry Division, 38

Employment Services Office
(Levittown, PA), 188–189, 198
Enlisted Men's Club, 67, 132, 133, 138

Fairbanks, Russell, 171–172, 175
Faughnan, Don, 232
Fawkes, Harry, 209
Financial Network, 218
First Air Cavalry Division, 81, 196
First Battalion (Twenty-sixth Infantry
Division), 37, 38
First Infantry Division ("Bloody Red
One"), 9, 13, 14, 33, 81, 148;
Intelligence Battalion of, 76
Fish Hook, *see* Parrot's Beak
Ford, Gerald R., 155
Freedom of Information Act, 210, 226
"Free kill" zone, 68–69, 70
French Foreign Legion, 66
Friendly fire, 55; woundings and deaths
of U.S. soldiers in South Vietnam
attributable to, 142

Gallager, Bill, 203
Garcia, Staff Sergeant, 31
Geneva Convention, 85
GI Bill, 6
Gimpperling, William, 166
Goetz, Jimmy, 221
Going, Dennis (Dong), 38–39, 43, 50,
114, 228; in Cambodia, 90, 94;
malaria attack of, 100, 233; at
Parrot's Beak, 83, 98; postwar life
of, 157, 159, 222; Recon patrols
of, 62, 70; and Recon reunion,
224; transfer of, 117
Gonzalez, Adam, 102, 118, 133, 136
"Good Morning America," 184, 193
Gooney, *see* Koenig, Gooney
Graterford Penitenitiary, 221–222
Green Berets, 202
"Green breads," 73
Griffin, Jimmie, 202
Gritz, James J. "Bo," 201–202, 204
G-2 (Intelligence), 9, 17, 26, 35
Guest, James, 53–54, 97
Guiterez, Linda, 151

Gulf of Tonkin resolution, 155
Gwertz, Ken, 179

Hager, George, 175, 176
Haig, Alexander, 223, 224
Haltigan, William J., 226
Hanoi Hannah, 98
Hanson, James M., 54, 84, 89, 114
Harbert, Michael, 199
Harrison, Captain, 134–135
Hart, Frederick, 215
Hazardous duty pay, 14, 68
Headquarters Company, 117, 133
Heinz, John, 190
Herrington, John, 191, 192
Hill, Dave, 205
HIRE program, 181
Ho Chi Minh, 36, 61, 70, 102, 136; his
    belief in victory, 18–19; City, see
    Saigon; plan to assassinate, 34–35,
    88, 98, 112, 238; sandals, 56, 57,
    93, 100; tomb of, 199; trail, 36,
    80, 93
Hotz, Bill, 170, 190, 191
House Government Operations
    Committee, 214, 225–226

Idaho State University, 157
Inspector General's Office, 225
Integrated Systems Analysts, 222
Internal Revenue Service (IRS), 204,
    206, 207, 225

James, E. Pendleton, 191, 192
Janney, Sam, 41, 44, 60, 73, 74;
    injuries to, 100, 108, 116, 117,
    233; and new commander for
    Recon, 115–116; and North
    Vietnamese regiments in
    Cambodia, 81; origins of, 112; at
    Parrot's Beak, 99; postwar life of,
    158, 159, 222; and Recon reunion,
    223, 224
JFK Special Warfare Center (Fort
    Bragg, NC), 5, 7
Jingoli, Joe, 235–238; visit to
    Cambodia of, 239–246 passim

Jordan, Dan, 196, 197, 198, 200, 217
Jordan, Donna, 196, 197, 198
Justice Department, 225

Kanamycin, 148
Kelly, Pat, 202
Keloid scar tissue, 171
Kennedy, Joey, 185
Kennedy, Joseph, 185
Kerry, John, 189
Khmer Rouge, 234–235, 240–246
    passim
"Kill zone," 47
Kissinger, Henry, 234, 236, 237
Koenig, Gooney, 55, 57, 116, 117,
    136, 233
Kong Som Ol, 245, 246
Korean War, 14, 96, 157, 182, 216;
    veterans of, 155, 156
Kostmayer, Peter H., 209, 210, 213,
    214, 220, 223

Labor, U.S. Department of, 189, 203,
    204, 225, 226; Christian's position
    as special assistant to, 179–182,
    211; firing of Christian from, 183–
    184; OUTREACH program of,
    179; rehiring of Christian by, 188
Lai Khe base camp (South Vietnam), 9,
    10, 13–19, 30–32, 35–37, 66–68,
    74, 114–117, 132–137
Lang, Mr. (physical therapist), 147–148
Laos, 36
Lascano, Jesse, 41–42, 46–47, 51–52,
    87, 233; in Bien Hoa, 78; in
    Cambodia, 92, 104; family waiting
    for, 112; letter to Christian from,
    118; made NCO, 132; marijuana
    burned by, 71; and new
    commander for Recon, 115; and
    nickname for Recon, 84; Recon
    patrols of, 55, 57, 65, 66, 69; and
    secret mission, 76–77
LAWs (Light Anti-tank Weapons), 40,
    99, 103
Law School Admissions Test (LSAT),
    171–172

Law School Veterans' Association, 174;
Military Law Program of, 174
Leeches, insect repellent for, 10–11
Legion of Valor, 178, 182
Lewis, Drew, 190
Lone Ranger, 114–117, 132, 137, 227
Long Binh (South Vietnam), 53, 109–
111, 117, 127, 128–131
Long-range reconnaissance patrols
(LRRP, "Lurps"), 9, 11, 35, 38,
88; and CIA, 18, 30–31;
dangerous role of, 13; missions of,
42; NVA soldiers killed by, 15,
26; pay for, 13–14
Lon Nol, 242
Lowe, Barry, 158
Lowe, Jim, 44–45, 51, 52, 68, 223; in
Cambodia, 94; and Marinelli, 74,
75, 115, 226, 228; and new
commander for Recon, 115; at
Parrot's Beak, 83; postwar life of,
158, 159, 222–223; his R&R in
Hong Kong, 83, 100, 233; Recon
patrols of, 55–66 passim, 71; and
Recon reunion, 224, 225
Lowe Excavation Company, 222

McAndrew, James, 199
MacArthur, Douglas, 6, 183
McCrory, Mary, 183
McGowan, Art, 178, 182
Mao Tse-tung, 209
Marijuana, 39, 69–71
Marinelli, Matthew, 223, 229, 230–231
Marinelli, Max, 39–40, 45, 85, 112,
156, 220; and death of Scotty,
108; and Lowe, 74, 75, 115, 226,
228; and new commander for
Recon, 114–117; and nickname for
Recon, 84; at Parrot's Beak, 83,
89, 99, 100; and plan to
assassinate Ho Chi Minh, 88, 98;
posttraumatic stress disorder
suffered by, 226–233; postwar life
of, 157, 158–160, 223; and Recon
reunion, 223, 224; return of, to
Recon, 74–75; transfer of, 117;

Marinelli, Max (Cont.):
and visit of Christian to Recon,
132–137 passim
Marinelli, Rosemary, 223
Marinelli, Sammy, 223, 229, 230
Marinelli, Sandy, 159, 223, 227–228,
229
Marshall, Ray, 178–179
May, Ernie, 50, 74
Mayaguez, U.S.S., 155
Maya Ying Lin, 194, 207
Melioidosis, 148, 154
Memorial Day, 182, 210
Mezalis, George, 205–206
Mezalis, Lynn, 205
Milam, Spec 4, 55, 57, 132–133, 136,
233; in Cambodia, 100, 103
Missing in action, U.S. soldiers listed
as, 199
Montgomery, Rich, 210
Mora, Roland, 178, 179, 180
M-16s, 11, 24, 68, 69, 87; tendency to
jam of, 48, 116
Muller, Bobby ("Rolling Thunder"),
189, 199–200, 204, 206, 217, 226
Murphy, Audie, 127, 142
Murray (patient), 141–142
Mutilation, of enemy, 54
Mutt and Jeff (morgue crew), 149, 150,
153
My Lai massacre, 158

Namath, Joe, 147
Napalm, 138–139, 142, 171
Nash, Dick, 125
National Capital Memorial Advisory
Committee, 200
National Capital Planning Commission,
201
National Review, 194
National Salute to Vietnam Veterans,
206, 207
National Semiconductor, 222
Nau, Tony, 6
Navy Cross, 178
"NBC Nightly News," 183
New York Times, 175

Ngo Dinh Diem, 131
Nguyen Cao-Ky, 27, 29–30
Nguyen Cao-Ky, Mrs. 29–30
Nguyen Co Thach, 199
Nice, Captain, 148, 150
Night defense perimeter (NDP), 20, 24,
    52, 55, 65, 66; Nui ba Cam,
    37, 74
Nimmo, Robert, 193, 200
Ninetieth Replacement Company, 128
Nixon, Richard, 168
Nookmom, 49, 239, 245
North Vietnamese army (NVA),
    identified, 9
Nui ba Cam (South Vietnam), 37–41,
    53–54, 74–75

Office of Presidential Personnel, 191
Officers' Candidate School (OCS),
    7, 13
Optical Scanning Corporation, 6
Outreach Centers, Governor's, 189–
    190, 202, 203–204, 214

Palmer, Larry I., 175
Paris Peace Accord (1973), 155, 173
Parrot's Beak (or Fish Hook, South
    Vietnam), 77, 80–84, 86–90, 98–
    100, 114, 238
Patton, George S., Jr., 38
Pawlata, Gary Allen, 221
Pawlata, Gunnar (Ace, Ape, Bluto),
    66–68, 69, 71, 79; in Cambodia,
    91, 95, 96, 100–108; drunken
    misconduct of, 133–135; injury to,
    102, 104, 106, 107, 157, 239; his
    letter to Christian, 118; his letter to
    Peggy Christian, 110; and new
    commander for Recon, 116–117;
    at Parrot's Beak, 98–100; partying
    by, in Japan, 112–113; and plan to
    assassinate Ho Chi Minh, 88, 98;
    postwar life of, 158, 220–222; and
    Recon reunion, 220, 223, 224,
    225, 233; recuperation of, 109–
    110, 111; transfers of, 117, 133;
    and visit of Christian to Recon, 134

Pawlata, Joseph Thaddeus, 221
Pawlata, Maria, 221
Pawlata, Micah Aaron, 221
Pennsylvania's Eighth Congressional
    District, Christian's candidacy for,
    209–215, 217, 220, 225, 226
Penthouse magazine, 199
Perot, H. Ross, 194
Peters, Michael, 34
Philadelphia Bulletin, 193
Philadelphia Journal, 193
Philadelphia Naval Hospital, 171, 174
Philadelphia Navy Yard, 174
Physical Evaluation Board, 167
Political Action Committees (PACs),
    211, 212
Pol Pot, 235, 240–246
Posttraumatic stress disorder (PTSD),
    228–233. *See also* Delayed stress
    syndrome
POWs, American, 201–202, 243
Princeton University, 164–166
Provincial Reconnaissance Units
    (PRUs), 118
Public Defenders' Office (NJ), 175
Pungi sticks, 10, 204
Purple Hearts, 42, 52, 93, 130, 158; for
    Christian, 168, 183

Quan Loi base camp (South Vietnam),
    77, 88, 108
Quarles, Francis, *Epigram,* 161
Qui Nhon base camp (South Vietnam),
    130, 138–142

Rangers, South Vietnamese, 20, 22, 23,
    24, 26
Reagan, Ronald, 210, 212–213, 234,
    237; and consideration of Christian
    for post of V.A. director, 190–
    191, 192–193, 195, 211
Reconnaissance platoon (Recon), 37–
    38, 156; ambush by, at South
    Vietnam/Cambodia border, 85–86;
    in Cambodia, 90–97, 100–108;
    Christian's visit to, 132–137;
    layover of, at Bien Hoa, 77–80;

Reconnaissance platoon (Recon)(*Cont.*):
men of, 38–42, 53–54, 66–68;
missions of, 55–66, 68–73; new
commander for, 114–117;
nickname for, 84; at Parrot's Beak,
77, 80–84, 86–90, 98–100;
postwar adjustment problems of
men of, 157–160; reputation of,
74, 117; reunion of, 220–225,
227, 233; secret mission of, 76–
77; training missions of, 42–53
Red Cross, 146, 149, 150
Redford, Robert, 172, 214
Reds (patient), 146–147
Reef, Al, 187
Republican National Committee, 190
Republican Party, 209
Rice, Grantland, *Two Sides of War,* 1
"Roam plough," 55, 56
Roll Call, 214
"Rolling Thunder," *see* Muller, Bobby
Rosenbaum, Gerry, 166, 168
RPGs (rocket-propelled grenade
launchers), 56, 57, 58, 72
"Rusty," Colonel, 120–121, 123–124,
125, 126–127, 131
Rutgers University at Camden, 171–
172, 174–175, 195, 234;
Scholastic Standing Committee at,
174, 175

Saigon, South Vietnam, 33–35, 126–
127, 237, 238
Savitch, Jessica, 183
Schaffner, George, 205
Scott, James (Scotty), 53, 71, 100,
105, 223; in Bien Hoa, 79; in
Cambodia, 94, 95, 96, 102, 104;
death of, 104, 107, 108, 157, 227,
239; enemy blood consumed by,
95–96
Scruggs, Jan, 180, 189, 214, 223, 226;
and Carlton Sherwood, 206–208;
and Vietnam Veterans Memorial,
193–195, 201–224
Search-and-destroy missions, 14
Selective Service, 44, 210

Senate Veterans' Affairs Committee, 198
17th Parallel, 36
Sherwood, Carlton, 195, 200, 201,
206–208
Sihanouk, Prince, 36
Silver Star, 158, 159, 168, 183, 210
Silvi, Larry, 218, 219
Simone, Charles, "Doc," 235–236,
visit to Cambodia of, 239–246
passim
Skip waves, 44
Skylon International Marathon, 202
Smithsonian's Air and Space Museum,
208
Social Security, 167
Social Security Administration, 169
Spanish-American War, 157
Special Forces, 7, 20, 35, 38, 48–49,
164
Stars and Stripes Rally, 223–225
State, U.S. Department of, 204, 225
Stockman, David, 192
Stryker frame, 140, 141, 144
Swain, Stanley, 190, 217

Temple University, 170, 203
Terrence, Lieutenant Colonel, 113–114,
120, 121, 122, 129–130
Terzano, John, 199
Tet offensive, 18
"Tex," Pfc, 138–139
Texas, University of, 196
Thailand, 58
Thiery, Pfc, 85, 91, 94
Third Marine Division, 179
Thornburgh, Richard, 189, 202, 203–
204
Tiny, 114, 116, 137, 159, 227
"Today" show, 184, 193
Tokyo, Peggy Christian's visit to, 121–
125
Trenton Times, 219
Triage, 109, 139
Trinkwell, Pfc, 148–149
Turner, Father Jack, 152–154
Twenty-fifth Infantry Division, 81
Twenty-sixth Infantry Division, 37, 38

Uniform Code of Military Justice, 7
Union Fidelity Life Insurance
    Company, 214
United Farm Workers' Movement, 179
United Nations, 245
United Vietnam Veterans Organization
    (UVVO), 200, 202, 211, 214, 226;
    charge of impropriety against, 203
    –204; establishment of, 199;
    merger of, with VVA, 217;
    misappropriation of funds at, 205–
    206
Unknown soldier, 182

Valley Forge (PA) General Hospital,
    163–164, 165, 166, 176
Vandegeer, Richard, 155
Verano, Tony, 122–123
Veterans, Vietnam, 155–156; Carter's
    efforts on behalf of, 179, 181,
    182; Christian's counseling center
    for, 167, 168–169; Christian's
    work of behalf of, 188–190;
    educational benefits for, 166;
    employment for, 179–181;
    fraternity for, 169–170;
    government's reaching out to, 177;
    new image for, 200; programs,
    Reagan's cutting of, 192; suicide
    of, 160; unjust treatment of, 156,
    166–167, 174, 182–183
Veterans Administration (V.A.), 166–
    167, 169, 178, 191, 196, 211;
    budget of, 192, 209, 210;
    Christian's view of, 210; director,
    selection process for, 192–193,
    195; hospitals, empty beds at, 187;
    investigation of Christian by, 225;
    and Max Marinelli, 229, 233; and
    UVVO, 200, 214
Veterans' Day, 176, 178, 182, 186,
    190, 206
Veterans of Foreign Wars (VFW), 158,
    173, 181, 187, 189, 202; and
    elections of 1984, 210; and World
    War II veterans, 156
Vietcong (VC), identified, 9–10
Vietnam Veterans Against the War, 189

Vietnam Veterans Memorial
    (Washington, D.C.), 154–155,
    206–207, 208, 215, 224;
    Christian's speech at, 215–216;
    creation of, 193–194; design of,
    194–195; opposition to, 195, 200–
    201
Vietnam Veterans Memorial Fund, Inc.
    (VVMF), 193–194, 201, 206–207
Vietnam Veterans of America (VVA),
    189, 199, 206; merger of, with
    UVVO, 217
Villanova University, 171, 174, 190;
    Alpha Sigma Mu at, 169–170

Wait-a-minute vines, 11–12, 42, 60,105
War Veterans Council, 203
War Zone C (South Vietnam), 9, 14,
    19–27, 41–52, 55–66, 68–73, 74,
    76–77
War Zone D (South Vietnam), 8–
    13, 14
Washington, Sergeant, 88–89
Washington Star, 183
Wayne, John, 48
WDVM-TV, 206–207, 208
Wecker, Joe, 122
Weis, Rick, 216
Western State University, 158
Westmoreland, William C., 167, 223,
    224, 226
West Point, 210
Wheeler, Jack, 207
Whitting, Scott J., 202
Willie Peters, 37, 63, 69, 71, 103,,
    116; ambush of, 85, 91; defined,
    24–25
Woodruff, Staff Sergeant, 11–26
    passim, 30, 32
World War I, 81, 156, 182, 216
World War II, 127, 148, 182, 185,
    216; clear-cut nature of, 157;
    veterans, 155, 156

Yale University, 194
Yit Kim Seng, 241
Yokohama, 106th General Hospital in,
    142, 144–154